BANKRUPT

Lowell L. Bryan

BANKRUPT

**Restoring the Health and Profitability
of Our Banking System**

HarperBusiness

A Division of HarperCollins*Publishers*

International Standard Book Number: 0-88730-511-3

Library of Congress Catalog Card Number 91-9045

Printed in the United States of America

Library of Congress Cataloging-in-Publication Data

Bryan, Lowell L.
    Bankrupt: restoring the health and profitability of our banking
system / Lowell L. Bryan.
        p.   cm.
    Includes bibliographical references and index.
    ISBN 0-88730-511-3
    1. Banks and banking—United States.   2. Banking law—United
States. I. Title.
HG2491.B77   1991
332.1'0973—dc20   91-9045
                                                CIP

91 92 93 94 PS/HC 9 8 7 6 5 4 3 2 1

*This book is dedicated
to Debbie, Russell, Amanda, and Than*

Contents

Acknowledgments

═══

I would like to acknowledge the broad institutional support I received from McKinsey & Company. In particular, I would like to thank two fellow directors: Don Waite (head of the New York office) and Fred Gluck (Managing Director of our firm). Don and Fred gave me the encouragement and support I needed to undertake this effort.

Much of the book is drawn from the results of a self-funded project launched by McKinsey & Company under my direction in late 1986 that has continued ever since. The primary purpose of the project was to improve McKinsey's ability to serve its extensive client base of financial institutions, including money center banks, regional banks, securities firms, financial subsidiaries of industrial companies, and insurance companies. A second purpose was to contribute constructively to the public dialogue on what changes in laws and regulation are required to ensure an efficient, effective, and safe financial system. Consultants at McKinsey & Company who worked with me on this project include Karen Butler, Gordon Cliff, Tom Copeland, Larry DiCapua, Jean Driscoll, Stuart Flack, Kirsten Hund, Ian Lowitt, Christine Nounou, Mimi James, Scott Sims, Jim Rosenthal, Ken Westlund, and Greg Wilson.

Over the intervening years we have worked with literally hundreds of individuals, including bankers, investment bankers, lawyers, and accountants, in addition to members of McKinsey & Company. We have also had numerous meetings with the Treasury, the Federal Reserve, the FDIC, the Office of the Comptroller of the Currency, the Office of Management and Budget, the General Accounting Office, White House staff, and the Senate and House Banking Committees. In these discussions, there has been a free flow of ideas. In the process, we have contributed to the thinking of others and have drawn on the thinking of others. The opinions expressed in this book, however, are my own.

I would particularly like to thank Greg Wilson, who has collaborated with me on both the project and on the book. Greg is a consultant in our financial institutions practice based in our Washington, D.C. office. Greg was formerly a Deputy Assistant Secretary of the Treasury and is as knowledgeable about banking regulation and law as anyone in the country. Greg is a truly remarkable person who combines professionalism, outstanding judgment, and good humor. Moreover, he is a friend.

I would also like to thank Stuart Flack, who worked closely with me in the writing and rewriting of this book. Stuart improved not only my writing but my thinking as well. Special thanks go also to my good friend Bill Matassoni, Director of Communications for McKinsey, who played a critical role in encouraging me to write this book.

My administrative assistant, Lore McKenna, was instrumental in keeping the entire effort under control. I particularly want to thank her for her energy and her patience. I am very lucky to be working with such a talented and enthusiastic associate.

I would also like to thank my good friend Simon Clark, who suggested the title for this book. Simon was also the coauthor of my first book, *Unbundling Full Service Banking*, published in 1973, which was based on a research project we undertook together at the Harvard Business School.

Finally, I would like to thank my wife, Debbie, and my children, Russell, Amanda, and Nathaniel, to whom this book is dedicated. Much of the time I took to write this book came out of time I would have otherwise spent with them.

BANKRUPT

PART ONE

THE BANKRUPT
SOCIAL CONTRACT

===

1

Rethinking the
Social Contract

Our current approach to regulating commercial banks is bankrupt. We have mixed a witches' brew of market forces and obsolete regulation that is destroying not only our banks but our economy. After years of benign neglect, we are now engaged in debate over the future of the banking system at a time when our banking system is, along with our economy, fundamentally weaker than at any time since the Depression.

The recession we entered in 1990 caught many economists by surprise because they were watching the wrong indicators. Since World War II, recessions have been preceded by an unexpected buildup in manufacturers' inventories due to cyclical factors and/or by deliberately tightened monetary policy that led to a credit crunch. This time the Federal Reserve has not deliberately tightened monetary policy. Indeed, the very economists who missed foreseeing the current recession lack sufficient knowledge of economic history to understand the root cause of this recession.

This recession was triggered by the oil shock brought on by the Iraqi-Kuwaiti crisis, but it is founded on a domestic economy overburdened by uneconomic debt—and a banking industry that is becoming increasingly hesitant to lend.

In fact, a credit crunch is underway. Owing to their own fears, and under growing pressure from concerned regulators, banks are cutting back on credit extensions. In particular, many troubled banks are doing so to shrink their balance sheets to meet capital guidelines. Credit began to tighten noticeably in the second quarter of 1990 and since then has tightened further. This has led to a significant cutback of economic activity as certain sectors of the economy—small businesses, mid-sized companies, and particularly real estate—in certain geographic regions, having been unable to find further credit, cut back on their expenditures. As 1990 progressed, the credit tightening spread to more customers, to more categories of loans, and to an ever increasing number of cities and states.

The greatest danger facing the national economy now is that a continued cutback of credit will turn this recession into one that, in Federal Reserve Chairman Alan Greenspan's words, "feeds upon itself." As the economy weakens, the cash flows supporting the debt payments of all sectors of the economy erode. As defaults mount, bankers curtail credit further. Borrowers curtail their expenditures further. Economic activity falls. Cash flows fall. Credit flows are curtailed further, and the cycle continues. Given the heavy debt burden of many sectors of the economy and the weakness of the banking system, a downward spiral, once started, could continue for quite a while.

How close are we to this kind of development? Such a downward spiral may well have already started. Perhaps as much as 25 percent of the banking system, representing well over $750 billion in assets, has begun to post such massive loan losses that it has no choice but to focus on credit collection, rather than credit extension. Once problem loans develop, they become all-consuming for bank managers. It takes far more effort to work out a bad loan than to make a good one. Moreover, the banks without credit problems naturally get more cautious as well.

The challenge from a national policy perspective is how to stop this downward spiral while there is still time. It is clear that the traditional "cure" for recession—an injection of liquidity by the Federal Reserve—will have less impact than normal because no one can force a terrified lender to extend credit. Remember that in the Depression there was plenty of liquidity. The prime rate remained at 1.5 percent for years during the 1930s because no creditworthy borrower wanted to borrow and no bank wanted to lend to any but the strongest credits.

Even if we are lucky, and are able to arrest the downward spiral, the recovery is likely to be anemic.

Today, the banking system is like a long-neglected bridge. The nation has not been paying attention to it; its functions are taken for granted. It is now beginning to show signs of rapid deterioration. Unless a major effort is undertaken to shore it up, it is likely to collapse.

Fortunately, President Bush, the Treasury department, the Federal Reserve, the Federal Deposit Insurance Corporation, and many members of Congress are well aware that the problems in the banking industry need to be addressed now, and that a new answer is needed. Indeed, in early 1991, there appeared to be a concerted effort by the government to improve the profitability of the banking system. In particular, the Federal Reserve was engaged in a program to lower interest rates. Although these short-term efforts are helpful, and may forestall a devastating recession, the real answers require structural reform.

As this book was being completed, in February 1991, the Treasury proposed a set of structural reforms that are headed in the right direction. These proposals provide a good first step. Relative to past efforts at reforming bank regulation, these proposals are bold and courageous and test the limits of what conventional wisdom believes to be politically possible. Unfortunately, relative to the magnitude of the crisis we face, the Treasury proposals do not go far enough in reforming the fundamental economic problems caused by a flawed deposit insurance system.

What we need to do, as a nation, is to use the Treasury proposals as a starting point. We must go further, because without economic reform of the deposit insurance system, we will be unable to restore the long-term health and profitability of the banking system. Only by restoring health and profitability will we be able to restore the nation's confidence in its banks and bankers' confidence in themselves. Bankers need confidence in their own institutions and in the banking system as a whole, if we are to expect them to have enough courage to finance an economic recovery and the long-term growth of the nation.

This is the central issue we face. We need to restructure the industry and reform regulation so that it becomes possible for banks to make money again. Without profitability, bankers will be unable to attract new capital to the industry. And without new capital, we will be unable to restore either the nation's confidence in its banks or its bankers' confidence in themselves. Because of national memory, many people associate banking troubles with the Depression, and the more often bank troubles are on the front pages of newspapers, the less confident the nation becomes in its entire economy. And people have reason to worry. Lack of confidence in banks and a lack of confidence of bankers in themselves and in borrowers is leading us to a reduction in spending in all sectors of the economy. We are headed down a path we do not want to take.

To reverse the downward spiral of the economy, we must therefore recapitalize the banking industry. Unfortunately, given the currently depressed stock prices of the banking industry, the nation has a much greater stake in the profitability of the banking system than do the current shareholders of bank stocks. We need to enact a fundamentally sound bank reform and bank recapitalization program, as quickly as possible. Our economy is at stake.

Clearly, we are past the point of quick fixes or partial solutions. Yet as this book is being completed, in February 1991, it is not clear that the nation is ready to deal with the banking crisis we now face. The focus of the nation was on the war in the Persian Gulf, not on the domestic economy. More to the point, we are about to enter into a debate over the future of the banking industry, indeed the entire financial services industry, with inadequate knowledge of what has gone wrong or what is at stake.

The danger is that in this debate, the nation does not understand its own self-interest. Many participants in the debate lack sufficient knowledge to be able to understand what changes will make the system better or worse. Because the issues are complex, this lack of understanding makes it easy for us to gravitate to simple answers, which could have disastrous, unintended consequences.

The danger of taking the wrong action is magnified by the difficulties we are experiencing in making our government work effectively. Our difficulties in getting our political parties to work together during the budget crisis of 1990 give most observers little confidence that we will, as a nation, be able to handle the truly difficult and complex issues of reforming our financial system. In the debate, it will be easy for people to search for simple answers. One possible outcome is that the gridlock between people who believe in "markets," people who believe in "regulation," and banks and other financial institutions that try to protect their own narrow self-interest will produce patchwork legislation that leads us along the same destructive path we have already been pursuing. Such a "muddle-through" scenario would be bad enough. However, it is possible that the prospect of "another savings and loan crisis" will lead to such increased supervision that we will over-control banks to the point that they cannot play their role in the economy. If so, we will complete the destruction of our banking system and further hamstring the economy.

I believe we need to go a very different direction.

Instead of trying to muddle through, we need to fundamentally reform the system. Simple discussions over whether we should rely on "regulation" or on "markets" miss the point. Hundreds of years of history demonstrate that unregulated financial markets self-destruct. On the other hand, in today's world, market forces are too powerful to control. Our current system is bankrupt precisely because we have tried to use regulation to control market forces that are beyond our control and, in the process, have created destructive flaws in the marketplace. We need to adopt a fundamentally different approach. Rather than trying to control market forces, we need to focus our attention on making the markets work better. This will first of all mean we will need to eliminate the flaws in today's system; in particular, we need to reform our deposit insurance system. It will also mean we will need to proactively improve the operation of the financial marketplace and to liberate economic forces that can help heal the system.

Therefore, the objective of this book is to build a case through use of facts and logic for undertaking such fundamental reform. What I hope to do is to be able to convince the reader, through analysis of both banking history and the workings of economic forces, that we need to adopt a fundamentally different philosophy for how we regulate banks. I believe, indeed, that we must rethink the very social contract between banks and society if we are to restore the health and profitability of the banking system and thereby lay down a solid foundation for the economic recovery of the nation.

Let's begin.

Banks and Society

The destinies of banks and the societies they serve have long been closely intertwined. The activities of banks have always had an enormous influence on their societies. In turn, the agents of society, national governments, have long had an enormous impact on banks both as borrowers from banks and as regulators of their activities.

If you go back to the beginnings of modern banking in Europe during the Middle Ages, you can see just how enduring the interrelationship between banks and society has been. In the late 1200s the formation of banks—that is, institutions that pooled cash and working capital of business associates and families to offer credit, settle debts, and exchange currency—led to an enormous expansion of trade and economic activity throughout Europe. These early banks were big enough to provide substantial credit to borrowers—big enough, indeed, to finance kings and princes. This led to a problem that persists today. Sovereigns quickly discovered that banks could finance their ambitions without having to raise unpopular taxes. Unfortunately, sovereigns also discovered that they could simply refuse to pay when the loans came due. For example, the first spectacular cross-border default on sovereign debt occurred in 1335 when King Edward III of England defaulted on his borrowings of 1.5 million gold florins that had been provided by Florentine bankers to finance his campaigns in France. This, in turn, led to disruptions of international finance for merchants, as well as monarchs, and was a major contributing factor, along with the Black Death, to the much broader economic, human, and social crisis that befell Europe in the mid-fourteenth century.

For the next six hundred years, until the midtwentieth century, the interactions between substantially unregulated private banks and different societies and their governments led to significant economic growth periodically disrupted by credit-induced crises. Not all of these crises were defaults on sovereign debt. Bank panics were common and were often the result of private credit defaults. Nor were all of these crises confined to banks. The combination of unregulated credit extension with the development of securities markets led to periodic manias, panics, and crashes in securities markets as well. In turn, these various credit-induced banking and securities crises usually led to economic distress in the real economy. Indeed, the first six hundred years of banking history seem to show that whenever there is unsound credit extension by banks, there will eventually be significant disruption of both the real economy and the society at large.

However, the balance of power during that era of banking industry history lay with the private sector. There was no social contract between banks and society. Banks had the capital and the money. With that money and capital came power. Bankers were independent private agents with no obligations toward society. During most of the era, financiers who controlled major banks had power that rivaled the power of government leaders. In the United States during the early 1900s, J. P. Morgan was viewed by many as the most powerful man in the country except for the president.

That era effectively came to an end because of the extreme disruption of society by the worldwide financial crises of the late 1920s and 1930s, when stock market crashes and bank panics led to the Great Depression, which set the stage for World War II.

Public Sector Domination

In the aftermath of the Depression and the Second World War, the worldwide balance of power between governments and banks changed profoundly. Governments decided that they had had enough of financial crises and, in nearly every major nation of the world, created regulations designed to limit competition and to provide safety nets to prevent panics. Governments also put in place a fixed exchange-rate system, which in turn enabled them to isolate the various national financial economies from one another. The combination of fixed exchange rates and control over the banking system gave each national government effective control over its own national financial economy. The unregulated, private sector–dominated era that had characterized six hundred years of the industry's history, was replaced by a regulated, public sector–dominated era.

Banks, although they had little say in the matter, had in effect traded off their freedom in return for a relatively stable and predictable level of profitability. This implicit social contract proved to be highly profitable to banks. In fact, during the immediate postwar era, every major nation in the world established, in practice, a highly profitable, government-backed cartel, which led to a safe, stable banking industry. And in every major nation in the world, banks were more than willing to be used as instruments of national policy given the importance of their respective governments to their success. As a result, the leading banks in most countries developed close, cooperative working relationships with their governments on such issues as implementing monetary policy, financing exports, or lending to developing nations who would import their country's goods. In fact, in countries such as France and Italy, the government actually owned the leading banks outright. Banks, worldwide, came to accept their social obligations to the national societies they served.

In return, banks had the benefits of operating within a very profitable cartel. Such cartels work only if government regulation is effective in restraining competition. Otherwise, the customers who are paying excessively for the services they use would leave the system. In other words, cartels work only when some customers cross-subsidize the services of others and when some competitors are denied the opportunities to compete.

The first requirement for making such a system work is to isolate the various banking systems of the world from each other. This was accomplished worldwide through the fixing of exchange rates. Isolating the various national financial economies from one another had, as a by-product, prevented banks from competing with one another across national borders. A foreign bank could compete only if it competed as a local bank.

The second requirement for making such a system work is to contain banking competition within each nation. Different countries used different approaches to restrain competition. In the United States, the government went to elaborate lengths to restrict banking competition and force customers to use banks. Deposit regulations were of particular importance. Commercial banks were granted a checking power monopoly and were prohibited from paying interest on demand deposits. They were also limited in the interest they could pay on savings accounts. Thrifts had an interest ceiling, too, but they were permitted to pay one-quarter of a percent more, and as a result had a high share of savings deposits. To further limit competition, Congress in 1927 imposed geographic barriers to competition (such as branching restrictions or prohibitions on interstate banking). These essentially caused the industry to operate as a series of local oligopolies and caused banks' underlying character to be shaped by their geographic scope (such as money center, regional, or community). In 1933 Glass-Steagall Act barriers separated the securities and banking industries.

The final guarantor of stability and profitability was the combination of federal deposit insurance and the lender-of-last-resort function of the Federal Reserve. These safety nets also enabled the industry to operate with more assets relative to capital (that is, higher leverage) than other intermediaries (such as finance companies).

The boundaries between banking and other financial activities were strengthened further by two later legislative changes. The Bank Holding Company Act of 1956 regulated multiple-bank holding companies, limited the growth of interstate banking through holding companies, and initiated the separation of banking from commerce. The Bank Holding Company Act Amendments of 1970 regulated single-bank holding companies, allowed the Federal Reserve to define which activities were permissible for bank holding companies and completed the separation of banking from commerce. These regulations also served to prevent bank holding companies from owning commercial concerns and vice versa.

This combination of regulations gave us a sound banking system for over forty years—although much of this soundness was artificial. It was based on being able to exploit some customers by denying them the benefits of competition.

Uncontainable Market Forces

Herein lies the flaw that has led to the end of the stable banking cartels in the United States and elsewhere as well as to government control of the financial economy. Customers who are being overcharged because of regulation will move their business if given an opportunity to get the same service at a substantially lower price or to earn higher revenues. Moreover, some smart competitors, particularly participants that are not part of the cartel, are always willing to use financial innovation and new technology to evade regulation if they have the opportunity to do so.

This process has undermined regulation after regulation designed to forestall competition. Consider, for a minute, how this process undermined both the fixed exchange-rate system and the regulation of interest rates paid on deposits during the 1970s.

The fixed exchange-rate system installed after World War II was abandoned due to uncontainable market forces. Multinational companies found that they were increasingly vulnerable to large revaluations of currencies. Their response was to use such techniques as leading and lagging receivables and payables to turn expected revaluations into profits. The overseas branches of the world's banks, based in London, also found they could profit by speculating on revaluations because they were able to operate in London outside the exchange controls of individual nations. These profits were relatively easy to make because it was apparent to everyone which currencies were undervalued and which were overvalued. The truth is that the fixed exchange-rate system simply became unworkable because the various governments of the industrial world had proved themselves unwilling to maintain the financial discipline needed to keep their currencies at a relative parity in spending power. As a result, they created opportunities for smart participants to profit from speculation outside the reach of national regulators. Eventually these profit opportunities attracted more and more speculation until the system had to be abandoned in 1973.

Another example is how market and competitive forces undermined the regulation of deposit pricing in the United States. The combination of deposit regulations described earlier essentially forced all customers to keep all of their liquid funds in banks and thrifts. This deposit monopoly made the banking and thrift franchises very profitable from the postwar era through the late 1970s. Borrowers had no place else to go to borrow money and depositors had no place else to go to invest their liquidity. However, the creation of money market mutual funds by non-banks began undermining this liquidity monopoly during the 1970s. Eventually, the growth of these funds become so enormous that banks and thrifts got together, for one of the first times in their histories, to urge the elimination of interest rate ceilings on deposits. The resulting changes in law in 1982, the Garn–St Germain Depository Institutions Act, enabled banks and thrifts to compete for deposits on price. And as will be shown later, this is where we made a fatal mistake—we unleashed market forces without reforming the regulatory structure or the deposit insurance system.

Over time, this sequence has been continually repeated throughout the world as regulation after regulation has fallen victim to economic forces. The pattern is always the same. Regulation designed to forestall competition creates unexploited profit opportunities. Smart participants use financial innovation, and new technology, to capture these profit opportunities by evading the intent of the regulation. Eventually the regulation becomes unworkable and the regulation changes.

In other words, it is misleading to use deregulation as a description of why changes in banking laws and regulation have taken place. Deregulation implies there was a proactive intent to liberate market forces. A better description of what has been taking place worldwide is that changes in law and regulation are taking place in reaction to market and economic forces.

In truth, governments have been engaged in rear-guard action to insulate their national banking industries and their national financial economies from market forces. Throughout the world, regulators and legislators have tried to moderate the effects of fundamental economic forces on their national banking and financial industries through maintaining existing regulation as along as possible. When these regulations eventually become unworkable, the then inevitable rewrite of regulation causes explosive change. In country after country, this period of rapid restructuring is coming nearer and nearer. In the United States, it is already well started. It appears inevitable that there will be fundamental, continuing changes in the laws and regulations governing financial institutions in almost all nations of the world throughout the next several years.

Changes in law and regulation constitute the most important single environmental force at work in banking now simply because the heavy regulation of banks, since World War II, has been the chief determinant of industry structure throughout the world by determining where and how each participant could compete. This shaped overall industry economics and the economics of individual companies. At the industry level, any significant change in regulation, therefore, profoundly disturbs competitive equilibrium. At the participant level, any significant change in regulation directly affects the viability of the participant's business system and economics. It may even de-

fine the participant's very role and ability to remain independent. Massive changes in banking law and regulation are now occurring not just in the United States but in Europe and Japan as well.

Once explosive change gets started, it feeds upon itself. Market, economic, and competitive forces, once unleashed, build and build and build. It is hard to imagine what kind of global regulatory structure it would take to arrest the fundamental economic forces now at work or to imagine any credible scenario for how such a structure could be created. It is also hard to imagine the pace of technological innovation slowing down. Indeed, there is at least a generation's worth of fundamental change in industry structure yet to come just from the new technologies that have been introduced in the last decade.

Free the Markets

During most of the 1980s, as it became clear that market forces were being unleashed and that existing regulation was becoming unworkable, the solution for people who believe in markets was relatively straightforward. The wisdom at the time was simply to remove regulation and let market forces take over. If deposit price regulation was becoming unworkable, you simply eliminate it. Such logic proved to be very popular and, by some measures, was quite successful. Much of the expansion in the nation and the world in the 1980s was fueled by the liberation of financial markets. As will be understood, the philosophy behind the belief in markets can be traced straight back to Adam Smith. The essence of our capitalist system is the belief that allowing the natural self-interest of all participants in a marketplace to operate freely will ensure the maximum output from the economy and will therefore promote the public good. The essence of this belief was summed up by Adam Smith in his classic "invisible hand" argument. Read carefully the following passage from Adam Smith's *The Wealth of Nations* (Book IV, Chapter II).

> The produce of industry is what it adds to the subject or materials upon which it is employed. In proportion as the value of this produce is great or small, so will likewise be the profits of the employer. But it is only for the sake of profit that any man employs a capital in the support of industry; and he will always therefore, endeavor to employ it in the support of that industry of which the produce is likely to be of the greatest value, or to exchange for the greatest quantity either of money or of other goods.
>
> But the annual revenue of every society is always precisely equal to the exchangeable value of the whole annual produce of its industry, or rather is precisely the same thing with that exchangeable value. As every individual, therefore, endeavors as much as he can both to employ his capital in the support of domestic industry, and so to direct that industry that its produce may be of the greatest value; every individual necessarily labors to render the annual revenue of the society as great as he can. He generally, indeed, neither intends to promote the public interest, nor knows how much he is promoting it. By preferring the support of domestic to that of foreign industry, he intends only his own security; and by directing that industry in such a manner as its produce may be of the greatest value, he intends only his own gain, and he is in this, as in many other cases, led by an invisible hand to promote an end which was no part of his intention. Nor is it always the worse for the society that it was no part of it. By pursuing his own interest he frequently promotes that of the society more effectively than when he really intends to promote it. I have never known much good done by those who affected to trade for the public good.

Adam Smith was, of course, arguing for the removal of national barriers to trade of goods. And in the markets for goods, most restraints on trade are unnatural barriers to competition and to the operation of the invisible hand. In other words, removing regulatory barriers (tariffs, for example) to the trade of goods does build "the wealth of nations."

The objectives of "free-market" advocates are sound. If we could get the benefits of the "invisible hand" operation in financial markets, we would all be far better off. However, in the 1980s we made the mistake of assuming that by simply removing regulations we would make financial markets work better.

In fact, we found out that by removing some regulation, without fundamentally reforming the entire system, we unleashed the destructive potential of financial markets. In other words, we forgot that six hundred years of history show that unregulated financial markets self-destruct. We forgot that financial markets are different.

Financial Markets Are Different

Financial markets are quite different from the markets for goods and services. It would take another completely separate book to explore these differences thoroughly, but there are a few differences worth highlighting.

One of the major differences is the natural self-interest of the participants. In the markets for funds, there are almost always three parties: a funds provider, a funds user, and an intermediary. Unlike in the markets for goods and services, the self-interest of participants involves not only profit but risk as well. Funds providers seek the highest cash returns for the risks they are willing to take. Funds users seek the lowest cash costs for the risks they are asking funds providers to take. Financial intermediaries seek profits by serving funds providers and funds users while taking the least possible risk themselves. Historically, an intermediary has almost always been required because it is simply not efficient for cash funds providers to determine which particular funds user represents the highest risk-adjusted return—especially since many of the funds providers and funds users are individuals rather than institutions. Moreover, risk assessment is a high-skill activity that requires access and analysis of hard-to-get information and considerable judgment.

Over the centuries, financial institutions have been well paid for performing this intermediary function. In commercial banks, where the bank itself absorbs the credit risks in lending and incurs heavy expenses in providing depositors with convenient access to their deposits, the difference between the interest collected from funds users (borrowers) and the money paid out to funds providers (depositors) has been typically about 4 percent—even today.

However, as will be explored throughout this book, the financial marketplace has been becoming far more efficient through such economic forces as securitization and globalization. In fact, absent risk, modern telecommunications and information systems make possible an unbelievably efficient market. For example, in the market for trading U.S. government bonds between institutions, the intermediary earns a fee of less than three basis points (that is, 0.03 percent) for performing this function.

In a fully efficient financial market, funds from providers will flow without limit to the highest risk-adjusted return. Similarly, in an efficient market, people or companies raising money will raise the money they want at the most generous terms and conditions they can find. Intermediaries offering the most profitable terms will attract as many funds raisers as each institution's capacity to take the inherent risks allows. Finally, intermediaries who find anomalies in the market (that is, returns that are too high for the risks taken) will exploit those anomalies fully until they are exhausted.

The reason for the relative ease in making financial markets efficient is that money is as pure a commodity as can exist. All physical products, including commodities, have substantial transportation costs that impede efficiency. In contrast, financial markets are "frictionless." The financial markets equivalent of transportation costs is transaction costs, and these costs, because of technological change, are low and diminishing.

Aspects that distinguish financial instruments one from another are the specific terms and conditions and perceived risks inherent in each instrument. For example, the risks of investing in money market instruments such as U.S. Treasuries are quite different from the risks of investing in corporate bonds or equities. The risks of investing in the bonds of a very profitable company that borrows little are quite different from the risks inherent in the bonds of a company that loses money and borrows heavily. Therefore, the higher and more complex the risks, the higher the returns should be.

As the efficiency of the financial market has grown, all participants in the market have become progressively more adept in exploiting anomalies in the market. An anomaly occurs for a funds provider whenever returns, relative to other opportunities, appear too generous for the risks taken. For a funds raiser, an anomaly occurs whenever money can be raised, relative to other sources, at too low a rate or with too liberal terms and conditions, relative to the risks that the funds provider is asked to assume. Furthermore, as the efficiency of the financial markets has improved, anomalies are quickly and fully exploited by all participants as long as they exist. In normal circumstances, anomalies quickly disappear as participants arbitrage them away.

Market Flaws

And this gets to the heart of the matter. At the same time financial markets have been getting more efficient, we have endured regulation that has created enormous anomalies in the market, which have remained for years. In other words, government regulation has created and maintained enormous flaws in the financial marketplace by absorbing risk that should be borne by participants in the marketplace.

In this book we will explore many of these flaws in the financial marketplace that have been created by the combination of market forces and obsolete regulation. However, the greatest attention will be placed on the massive flaw in the market created when we simply removed the interest rate ceilings on deposits without reforming the deposit insurance system. By allowing the highest bidder to raise unlimited amounts of funds with government guarantees, we provided depositors with too high returns relative to the risks they were taking: we created a deposit anomaly. In turn, many of these institutions provided overly generous terms and conditions, relative to risks, for borrowers: thus we also created a credit anomaly. We then compounded the problem by allowing incompetent or dishonest managers of financial institutions to remain in their jobs even as their institutions approached insolvency. This created another anomaly, referred to by regulators and academics as the "moral hazard" problem, which caused managers to take more and more credit risk as they approached insolvency because they had nothing to lose from the risk-taking, but had the chance, if they took the right risks, of surviving.

Providing over-generous terms and conditions in extending credit, in turn, is the bane of all financial markets because it feeds speculative demand. In markets for goods and services, when demand rises faster than supply, prices go up, thereby reducing demand for those goods and services. However, in financial markets, when prices go up, demand sometimes actually *increases* because of speculation that prices will increase even further. This particularly happens if the instruments of value can be bought with cheap credit. The speculator convinces himself that by borrowing money, he can earn a high return if prices continue to rise, but can cover himself by selling the instrument borrowed against, if prices fall. For example, if real estate values are rising, and there is readily available credit on generous terms, more and more speculators want to own real estate and are willing to borrow to do so. When the importance of speculation begins to overwhelm fundamental demand and supply forces, you begin to get the kinds of booms and busts that have long characterized the history of financial markets. And in fact, our nation in the 1980s went through a series of booms, fed by over-generous lending terms, in such activities as real estate development and the takeover of companies. We now face the crash.

Only now are we coming to realize the full costs of these booms and the underlying deposit and credit anomalies that fed them. In addition to the $150 and $200 billion net present value cost to the taxpayer of the S&L debacle, we now have a greatly weakened banking and financial system. At stake is not only the issue of protecting taxpayers from further losses, but also the well-being of the economy, the health of our financial system, and the global competitiveness of the nation.

It is not just the deposit insurance system that needs to be reformed. The entire process of regulating our financial system must be rethought. Competitive forces have eroded the effectiveness of all the legal barriers. The Bank Holding Company Act is clearly ineffective at separating commerce from banking, as evident with General Electric, American Express, Ford, Dreyfuss, and others who offer services once thought to be the preserve of banking. The McFadden Act (which prevents banks from branching across state lines) is clearly an ineffective barrier to preventing interstate banking competition. The Glass-Steagall Act is clearly ineffective at keeping banks out of the securities business or vice-versa. But all of these laws remain on the books. In combination, these laws prevent self-healing economic forces from taking over and restructuring our present, weakened financial services industry into a powerfully effective one.

Our essential problem is that we have lost the public interest in the debate over how to reform our system. As market and competitive forces put pressure on obsolete regulation and law, it is not just a matter of wise people determining how best to change it. The economic stakes involved ensure that every participant is engaged in an effort to use law and regulation to gain competitive advantage. Participants advantaged by existing law and regulation resist change. Participants disadvantaged by existing law and regulation try to get changes that benefit their own institutions. And every participant, through political contributions and lobbying, has found supporters to defend narrow self-interests. Moreover, broad social objectives, like housing policy or community reinvestment, often get loaded on to every change in law. The result is that changes in law and regulation come far too slowly, are made in piecemeal fashion, and often create new imperfections in the marketplace.

Our capitalist system assumes that competitive and market forces are always good. However, the bitter truth is that our present policy of combining competitive and market forces with obsolete regulation is clearly leading us down a destructive path. We have created a marketplace that is efficient in the destruction of our economy. Our financial system is close to breaking down. Our regulation of our financial system, and the social contract that underlies it, is bankrupt.

Making the Market Work Better

We can head down a fundamentally different path. If we have the will, we can turn the same competitive and market forces that have been destroying the economy to healing it.

But to do so, we must first alter our philosophies. Those of us who believe in markets must realize that flaws introduced by bad regulation can turn efficient markets destructive. Those of us who want to use regulation to serve the public good must realize that regulation that creates flaws in the marketplace may well hurt the public interest far more than help it.

I believe that all of us must realize that the market, competitive, and economic forces that have been unleashed are beyond the control of regulators, or for that matter, our government. I believe we must also recognize that our government must play an essential role in making these economic forces work constructively rather than destructively. Six hundred years of economic history, prior to World War II, tell us that the social costs of unregulated banks and financial markets are profound. Therefore, it is not a question of regulation or deregulation. It is a question of what kind of regulation will be the most constructive.

Indeed, we need a new social contract between banks and society that is based neither on the unregulated model of the industry's six-hundred-year history nor the post-World War II model. I believe we must fundamentally rethink the social contract between banks, our government, and our society and then reflect that new contract in a redesigned regulatory structure.

The governing thought behind this new social contract should be that the purpose of bank regulation, indeed all financial regulation, is to improve the effectiveness of competitive, market, and economic forces as they operate in financial markets. I believe we should do our best to create what economists call a "perfect" market. A "perfect" financial marketplace would be one in which funds would flow from funds providers to funds users based on the prices, terms, and conditions that are, in their entirety, established through the informed natural self-interest of all of the participants in the marketplace.

People often confuse *efficient* markets with "perfect" markets. A market is efficient if it quickly and cost-effectively reflects, through changes in market prices, all available information. However, if the market is merely efficient in reflecting changes in speculative demand fed by governmentally created market flaws, efficient markets can be destructive. During the 1980s, the banking markets became far more efficient, but also far less perfect, because the government assumed risk that should be absorbed by participants in the marketplace. The dilemma we face is how to get the social benefits of government safety nets without the costs of creating market anomalies.

Therefore, to create such a perfect market we need to proactively redesign our regulatory structure. Specifically, we need to work hard to eliminate the flaws from government safety nets that currently exist in the market while simultaneously liberating the economic forces that can help heal the system. The potential benefits from creating such an efficient, perfect, financial marketplace are enormous.

However, to create an efficient, perfect, financial market we must first recognize that financial markets are different from the markets for other goods and services and therefore require regulation to make them effective. As we have seen, simply removing regulation can be disastrous, so we must also recognize that with the power to regulate comes the temptation to abuse that power to achieve other objectives. For example, individual participants will try to influence regulation for their own benefit, or government will use its power over institutions to achieve policy objectives it is unwilling to pay for with taxes. Under the social contract being proposed, regulation would not be used in such a manner. Such a proposal to remove banking regulation from politics may seem naive. To many of us, it seems that banking regulation and politics are hopelessly joined together. I personally believe that if we fail to separate banking regulation from politics, we will also fail to truly reform the system.

The central objective of all the proposals made in this book is to reduce the role of government in influencing risk/reward decisions that should be made by the marketplace. In particular, the government should not be absorbing risk that should be absorbed by participants in the market. I believe that if we can focus government powers on making markets work better, we can get the benefits of Adam Smith's invisible hand allocating resources in the financial markets without the destructive booms and crashes that once again plague us. That is, we will be able to gain the constructive, rather than destructive, results from the unleashing of market, competitive, and economic forces in financial markets.

To achieve such a result, let me state three principles that I believe should underlie a new social contract between the government and banks.

1. *The government's only role in regulation is to ensure that financial markets work effectively.* This means that regulation should be designed to improve financial disclosure, to ensure that accounting for assets and liabilities, income, and expenses is accurate, to prevent fraud, and so forth. Conversely, it means that banks should not be regulated either to achieve social objectives that governments are

unwilling to finance through taxation or to achieve national policy objectives. It also means that regulation
should not be used to provide an unfair competitive advantage for a particular institution or class of institutions.

2. *The government should provide essential safety nets but should
   prevent their abuse.* Markets will only work effectively if
   they are orderly. Bank panics benefit no one. Therefore,
   some safety nets are essential. Specifically, market makers
   in financial instruments need access to central bank liquidity in times of crisis, the deposits of unsophisticated
   savers should be insured against loss, and the payment
   system should be protected. However, it must be recognized that such safety nets are market anomalies (that
   is, they provide depositors with risk-free returns from
   institutions that are exposed to risks). Therefore, they
   offer significant potential for abuse. The stronger market forces become, the more market forces will cause any
   anomalies to be completely and fully exploited. Therefore, the government must also play a role in preventing the market from exploiting market anomalies created by safety nets. In particular, the government should
   not influence risk/reward decisions or absorb significant
   risk. Government also has a role in ensuring that failing financial institutions are liquidated, dismembered,
   restructured, or sold off in an orderly manner, thus min-
   imizing market disruption; ensuring that losses from clo-
   sure, liquidation, and restructuring are borne by private
   capital; and ensuring that nonproductive capacity is eliminated from the system. Under this concept, no financial
   institution should be too big to fail.

3. *Individual banks should add value to customers or perish.* The
   natural consequence of competition is to separate winners from losers. It is extremely important that the capacity of losers be eliminated from the system or else the
   system will be plagued with overcapacity and will therefore not be economically sound for the same reason that

a government-subsidized steel industry or subsidized airline industry is also economically unsound. On the other hand, institutions that add value to society should be allowed to win. Because of the unique role of banking in today's economy, care needs to be taken to ensure that our society is not disrupted by the precipitous failure of individual institutions. However, over the long term, economic forces, not regulation, should determine the role of banking in our society. If the banking system adds value, it should prosper. If it fails to do so, its functions should be replaced by more efficient non-bank providers. Regulation should be a neutral factor in determining what long-term role existing banks should play within our financial system.

Although these principles seem conceptually sensible to most people, if applied rigorously to the regulation of financial institutions, they are profound. Indeed, many of the participants in the debate conceptually agree with the principles until they begin to understand the consequences to themselves. Government regulators tend to agree with the principles until they realize that the role for regulation and the power of their own jobs will be diminished. Bankers agree with the principles until they realize the extent to which they depend on the government absorbing risk that the market would never assume. Depositors agree until they realize that they will earn lower returns if they want government insurance. Borrowers agree until they realize they will have higher costs for undertaking high-risk ventures. Indeed, the short-term costs to narrow self-interests through applying these principles are significant. However, as this book will try to demonstrate, the long-term benefits to our society of rigorously applying these principles are far greater.

Indeed, I believe the potentially fatal flaw of all the other reform proposals being made, including the Treasury's proposal, is that they rely too heavily on government supervision to make banks safe. I believe that such an approach will continue to have the government, not the market, evaluate and absorb risk.

I believe there is a better way. I believe the answer is to shrink the activities of regulated, government-insured banks to those unique low-risk, core banking functions for which banks remain as the best providers. That is, banks should stick to those activities providing economic value. Specifically, I believe the best method of limiting the credit anomaly is to restrict insured banks to lending to individuals, small businesses, and mid-size companies—categories of loans for which banks have experienced relatively little trouble. Small loans to commercial real estate projects would also be permitted under strict limits on terms and conditions. Nonqualifying loans (such as large commercial real estate loans, highly leveraged transaction loans, and developing country loans) would have to be funded outside the insured bank. This reform would essentially return the banking system to its historic low-risk customer base.

The proposed method of eliminating the deposit anomaly is simply to limit the rates that insured depositories can pay for funds to Treasury rates of similar maturity. The logic is simple. Because an insured depository should add value to the federal guarantee, then it should, if anything, pay less than the Treasury for funds. Most banks already pay rates lower than Treasuries for most of their insured deposits (checking accounts, savings accounts, money market accounts); however, troubled banks and thrifts continue to overpay for deposits. Limiting the rates paid to Treasury rates would end this practice. Yet it would permit institutions to offer rates that were competitive with equally safe investments (that is, Treasuries). By adopting a freely floating rate, we also avoid past problems of disintermediation during periods of fluctuating interest rates.

I call this approach a "core" banking model. Research work performed by my firm, McKinsey & Company, Inc., indicates that such "core" banks can be quite profitable; although, inevitably, the amount of money in insured depositories would decline as the overbidding for deposits was stopped. Indeed, we estimate $1 trillion would leave the industry. Those activities that would not qualify for the "core" bank could be undertaken in separately capitalized subsidiaries of the holding company. For example, a commercial finance company structure would be used to make loans that were ineligible for the "core" bank, and a "money market investment bank" would be used to undertake foreign exchange, money market, and securities operations. This approach would also embrace the same fundamental changes in the Glass-Steagall Act, the Bank Holding Company Act of 1956, and the McFadden Act that others, including the Treasury, believe are necessary.

Beyond these structural reform proposals, immediate steps are needed to transform the destructive downward spiral threatening the economy into a virtuous cycle of improvement that is built on prompt resolution of failed banks and on proactive steps to save other banks from insolvency.

The key leverage point is in recapitalizing now those institutions that are deeply troubled but are still economically solvent. A similar and successful plan was used by the Reconstruction Finance Corporation to recapitalize troubled banks in the 1930s. However, in many cases, these troubled banks, as they are recapitalized, should also be forced to merge with stronger players.

In this chapter, I have tried to provide the reader with an overview of the case for undertaking fundamental reform of our system along the principles just outlined. In the first part of this book, we will fully explore the deposit and credit anomalies that are destroying our banking system and our economy. We will examine why the S&L crisis happened and how the commercial banking industry went from being a source of strength to a source of weakness for the nation. In particular, we will examine how banks got overcommitted to developing countries, to highly leveraged transactions, and to commercial real estate debt. In the final chapter of this part, Chapter 7, we will explore a scenario of where we are headed, as a nation, if we fail to reform our system fundamentally.

In the middle part of this book, we will examine some of the fundamental economic forces that are at work today, which our regulatory structure must accommodate. Specifically, we will examine how securitization and globalization are affecting all financial markets and how the economic forces of consolidation and disaggregation are affecting the structure of the banking system.

In the final part of this book, a specific reform plan is laid out based on the core bank model outlined earlier. Specific recommendations for reforming the deposit insurance system and for liberating the potentially leading economic forces are proposed. In addition, suggestions are made for how we can handle some of the difficult transition issues. Finally, in the last chapter of the book a scenario is laid out for what could happen if the fundamental reforms being described were, in fact, enacted. In particular, a scenario is provided for how the current vicious downward economic spiral of banking failures and deepening recession can be converted into a virtuous cycle of increasing profitability, confidence, and economic recovery.

I have tried to write a book that can be read not only by financially sophisticated readers, but by the educated general public as well. I have tried to define many of the terms I use as I go along; in addition, there is a glossary of terms at the end of this book, which many readers may find helpful. Even financially sophisticated readers may find it helpful to refer to the glossary of terms used to describe the financial economy in order to understand the precise meaning of the words as used throughout the book.

2

The Theory of a Bank: Postwar Model

═══════

The basic theory of a bank has changed little since its beginnings in medieval Europe. Early bankers started out safeguarding their own money, but quickly found that many in their communities also wanted a safe place to keep cash. As trust grew and communities prospered, it soon became apparent to bankers that at any given time, most of the money they held for safekeeping stayed in their safes. There was always plenty of cash available for any depositor who wanted his money back. It was not long before bankers realized they could lend this idle money out and earn interest, provided they kept enough in the safe to pay off a depositor who demanded his money back. Banks around the world still employ this same fundamental business system.

Of course, the system breaks down if every depositor wants his or her money back at the same time. But in theory, this should never happen, if the pool of depositors is large and diverse. In practice, however, it does happen. And it is quite unpleasant. When depositors as a group lose confidence in their banks for any reason, they naturally all want their money simultaneously, and a bank panic ensues. Throughout the history of banking, up until the 1930s, bank panics were common in the United States and Europe—in fact, they reoccurred with disturbing regularity. Though terrifying, bank panics served a useful economic function: to weed out poorly run banks. Only banks with the soundest credits, most liquidity, and strongest capital positions could survive general bank panics.

The social costs, however, of using bank panics to ensure that only the strongest survived were enormous. It was not only bank managers and stockholders who were wiped out by bank failures. The really tragic losses were felt by the public at large who had entrusted these banks with their savings and by the communities that entrusted these banks with their financial stability. Banks have proved to be incredibly valuable to society through their core functions—deposit-taking and lending. Indeed, it is hard to separate the history of capitalism from the history of banking. Incongruously, we only appreciate how valuable banks are when they fail to function properly.

35

As we examine disintegration of our heavily regulated, post–World War II banking oligopoly, we should always keep in mind the simple source of value derived from these two core banking functions—taking deposits and making loans.

Core Banking

The core function of a bank is twofold, but the most essential function, the one that lies at the heart of the contract between banks and society, is the bank's original function—taking deposits and keeping them safe. Any society worthy of its name should be expected to provide its citizens and businesses with a secure place to keep money. Depositors are not investors; their primary concern is being able to have access to the cash they need for unexpected contingencies. Investors make risk/return trade-offs, depositors do not. Depositors must have quick access to their money and they must be certain that for every dollar deposited, a dollar can be withdrawn. In return for this safety and liquidity, depositors are willing to accept lower returns than they could otherwise earn. As we will see in later chapters, we have suffered enormously as a nation by violating this principle. Many of the problems with our current system have resulted from enabling depositors to have not only liquidity and safety but high returns as well.

By extension, deposit-taking also includes providing depositors with access to their money. In the modern banking world this involves not only providing checking services, but money transfer services, automated teller services, debit cards, letters of credit, and a host of other payment services to settle domestic and foreign debts. Although most of us take these services for granted, the world economy would quickly grind to a halt if these payment services were in any way disrupted. All segments of society: individuals, businesses of all sizes, and governments require these payment services in order to operate.

The second core function of banking is extending credit. Banks add great value to society when they lend money to creditworthy borrowers who are without alternative sources of low-cost credit. Until recently, this included almost all segments of society. Over the last fifty years, and particularly in the last ten years, almost all large creditworthy borrowers (governments and large corporations) have bypassed banks and have issued their debt directly in the securities markets. However, bank credit is still incredibly important for individuals, small and medium-size businesses, farmers, and home builders who have no direct access to the securities markets. Even large corporations, who borrow little, still use bank credit for back-up purposes.

Banks add value to the credit extension process by evaluating each borrower's ability to make interest payments and repay the loan. Credit extension, when performed by experts, involves sophisticated abilities in gathering information, underwriting risks, perfecting collateral, and collecting delinquent loans. As any skilled lender will tell you, it is as much an art as it is a science. A good lender must not only assess the borrower's cash flows and assets but also the borrower's character. Often a key ingredient in the process is personal knowledge of the borrower. Great attention needs to be paid to how the borrower's capacity to repay changes with economic conditions. What if interest rates go up, if oil prices change, or if the economy slows down? Among the highest skills is that of knowing how to work with borrowers who are in trouble so as to preserve their economic value. Successful lenders also pay great attention to the composition of their loan portfolios so that they can avoid any undue concentrations in a single area.

Almost all banks that get in trouble do so through making bad loan decisions. Unlike stocks and bonds, loans are remarkably illiquid. The only way most loans can be converted back to cash is through repayment by the borrower. There is no real market for bank loans; nor could there be. Most bankers are unwilling to buy loans from other banks because they lack the information to do so with certainty. They don't know the borrowers from the other bank personally. They cannot assess how much skill went into the lending decision. Therefore, the value of a loan once made, is highly subjective. As an ongoing concern, most banks expect to be able to recover all of the principal and interest on their loans less their reserves for loan losses. However, when banks make bad lending decisions, they are stuck with bad loans. If they make too many, they go insolvent.

Once a bank goes insolvent, the value of all its loans—both good and bad—plummets since no other lender is willing to takeover the loans at anything close to the original loan amount. Moreover, the personal link with the borrower is broken; few borrowers feel much obligation to repay once the banker they dealt with has vanished. There are often lawsuits involved. It is for these reasons that the market value of a loan portfolio from an insolvent bank may be only 70 percent, or less, of the original loan amount. The value of loans is directly tied to the ongoing health of the bank that made them. When a bank goes insolvent the value of its portfolio is thus destroyed. In some cases, the U.S. Government's losses on failing S&Ls have been over 50 percent of the gross assets of the S&L. In the era before deposit insurance, it was the depositors who bore these losses. Today, it is the federal deposit insurance funds—and the U.S. taxpayer.

The theory of a bank is therefore heavily dependent on keeping the bank an ongoing concern. As long as the banks make good loans, have adequate capital to absorb losses, and have adequate liquidity to always be able to repay depositors, banking provides enormous value to society. Society needs entities that take and safeguard deposits, perform payment services, and provide loans to borrowers without access to the debt securities markets.

One last point on the theory of a bank. Recently, many academics whose research and training have largely taken place in the securities industry have been advocating reforms based on applying concepts from the securities industry to the banking industry. They are misguided.

Some suggest that banks ought to "mark-to-market" their loan portfolios. This is an impossibility since there is no real market for most kinds of loans. Others want to reform the deposit insurance system by creating greater market discipline on banks. They have proposed various measures to create greater market discipline by limiting federal deposit insurance coverage. They have advocated limiting the amount of deposits that can be insured, or allowing partial losses—"haircuts"—like the deductibles on automobile policies.

On the surface, these proposals have great appeal. The discipline of the free market is healthy. Fear of losing money can certainly cause people to weigh risk/return trade-offs carefully. This market discipline has already created strong financial institutions. American Express, General Electric Capital Corporation, General Motors Acceptance Corporation, and IBM Credit are all pillars of financial strength because they are disciplined by investors.

Unfortunately, this approach will not work for banks and thrifts. One major problem is that banks and thrifts are currently blind pools of risk to outside investors. As has already been pointed out, bank and thrift loans are made to borrowers based on detailed understanding of the individual borrower's cash flows and assets. Tailoring these credits to borrowers' particular circumstances are of high value to the economy. However, it is literally impossible for an outsider to have the information to assess the risks in these loans except the way regulators and accountants do—through loan-by-loan examinations. Even regulators and accountants have great difficulty performing this task because of the time it takes and the subjective judgments required. It is unreasonable to expect an outsider to be able to make these judgments, particularly since we have over 15,000 banks and thrifts.

Moreover, because of the illiquidity of the loans, there is nothing a lending institution can do to raise cash when its loan portfolio becomes visibly troubled. Remember, the essence of a bank's value is its ability to meet its obligations to depositors. Since its loans are illiquid and since its role in society is to provide liquidity to depositors, it cannot ever be able to provide liquidity to every depositor simultaneously. This is the reason why throughout the history of banking so-called market discipline is simply another name for bank panic. If there is real risk, *all* depositors want *all* of their money *all* at the same time.

The value of banking to society is, therefore, virtually synonymous with maintaining the public's confidence in banks.

Postwar Era

Against this most fundamental measure, the value of our banks during the postwar era was quite high indeed. Until the S&L crisis, the country's depositors had great confidence in the stability of all insured depositories.

From a safety and soundness point of view, the postwar banking industry performed quite well from the mid-1940s up until about ten years ago. From 1945 to 1980, although banks and thrifts with total deposits of some $5.9 billion failed, no insured depositor lost a cent. Nor did the Federal government need to contribute any funds. The capital of the deposit insurance funds grew continuously during this period. The FDIC fund, which insured the deposits of commercial and mutual savings banks grew from $929 million to $11 billion over the same period. In 1980, the fund amounted to 1.16 percent of insured deposits. There were no bank panics in the country. As providers of safe depositories, the postwar banking model proved to be enormously successful.

In terms of extending credit, the record is less clear. Banks during this era were very conservative about to whom they lent. The average annual charge-offs from the entire industry over this entire period were $1 billion a year. This amounted to an average loan loss of less than 0.25 percent over the entire time period. What is unclear is to what extent banks turned away creditworthy borrowers to achieve this pristine record.

By any measure, though, the industry was very profitable. In one particularly profitable year, 1959, net profits of the banking industry equaled 35 percent of gross revenues! As a point of reference, in 1989, the industry's pre-tax net profits equaled only 6 percent of its gross revenues. Returns on equity were reasonable. They averaged from 11 to 14 percent a year, after tax, while the average inflation rate was under 3 percent a year until the 1970s. Moreover, the returns were relatively uniform from bank to bank. In 1970, for example, among the twenty largest banks in the country, the best had a return on equity of 13.9 percent and the worst had a return on equity of 10.2 percent. The absolute earnings and capital of the industry grew steadily. Bank stocks traded like utilities. Investors expected slow, steady growth, and dependable dividends.

Economic Model

Underpinning this profitable business was the ability to pass on costs to customers, as utilities can. Although there was service competition among banks, there was little price competition. If the industry overbranched, the customers would foot the bill. If regulators required the industry to be overcapitalized, the costs of that capital would again be borne by customers. The post–World War II model worked because the combination of restrictive government regulations in place at the time was very effective in preventing competition—particularly price competition. In effect, the government created and sponsored a banking cartel.

The economic model of a bank, which developed under these circumstances, has some very distinctive characteristics that remain today—even though the oligopoly that justified and encouraged these practices is long since gone. The model is based on "bundling" together customer revenues, bank expenses, and shareholder capital into a single, integrated, economic enterprise. Most bankers today do not question whether or not this bundled economic model makes sense. They know of no other. An understanding of how this model works is crucial to understanding how and why the industry is currently faltering.

The postwar model has three implicit assumptions: (1) each bank will have a stable pool of revenue, known as the net interest margin, sufficient to cover all reasonable costs and to provide reasonable returns on capital; (2) given the net interest margin, each bank can devote most of its operating-cost base to expenditures related to the common service of all its customers; (3) each bank can use a single pool of capital to absorb losses from all risks the institution is exposed to. In combination these assumptions articulate the principle that a bank is a simple, seamless, single, integrated entity. Unfortunately, these assumptions have become less and less valid in the 1980s because of changes in regulation, competition, and technology. Thus the soundness of this model has been seriously undermined.

To see why this has happened, we need to examine each of the underlying assumptions in greater detail. First, let us see how valid they were, and how profitable the model they supported was, from the end of World War II to the late 1970s.

Stable Revenue

Most banks, even today, employ what is know as the "pooled funds" concept. Essentially, they calculate a single net interest revenue number by subtracting interest paid from interest earned. The net interest revenue number for the industry as a whole has historically averaged a little more than 3 percent of assets (or a little more than 4.5 percent of loans). Through the 1970s, net interest revenue dwarfed other sources of revenue. For example, in 1979 commercial bank net interest income was

$57 billion, while total revenues from fees and other sources of income came only to $17 billion.

As we look at the net interest margin numbers for the commercial banking industry in the postwar era, until 1980, it is striking how stable and consistent they were. For example, during the 1970s, the net interest margin for the industry stayed within a range of 3.0 percent to 3.2 percent of assets, despite widely fluctuating interest rates and economic conditions. Even more striking is the fact that the pattern held nationwide, even though interest rates were dramatically different in different regions of the country for most of the postwar period. During the early 1970s, the interest rate of an unsecured consumer loan could have been as low as 9 percent in Boston, but at the same time, as high as 15 percent in San Francisco.

Yet, despite these differences, the net interest margins across the industry remained stable. The source of this stability was not mysterious: it stemmed from oligopolistic pricing. In effect, the nation was divided into a series of local oligopolies. Each local oligopoly charged borrowers whatever rates were needed in the local market to enable all of the players to maintain their stable net interest margin. These rates were not set by direct collusion; bankers chose to follow local market leaders and compete on service rather than price. The only truly national marketplace in the postwar era was the large corporate loan market. In this market the industry also used a single price—the prime rate—as the base rate for pricing all corporate loans. So in this market, the oligopoly operated on the national, rather than the local, level.

Shared Spending Practices

The common pool of net interest income was thus used to cover all non-interest expenses that a bank incurred. Historically, operating expenses such as salaries and rent were dwarfed by interest expenses—but this is becoming less and less true. Another, more important historical feature of non-interest expenses is that they have been only loosely linked to revenues. This is to be expected in an oligopoly, where pricing is determined not by competition, but instead by what the market will bear.

Whenever we at McKinsey have analyzed non-interest expenses in an individual bank, we have seen that the links to revenues are tenuous indeed. Typically, we find that some 20 percent to 30 percent of expenses are for pure overhead and control functions (that is, expenses that contribute neither to attracting nor serving customers—such as finance or personnel departments, auditors, and the like). Another 20 percent to 25 percent are for shared distribution expenses—in particular, branches. Another 20 percent to 30 percent are for shared operations expenses. Only the remaining 15 percent to 20 percent can be attributed to bringing in specific customers and actually delivering services.

One interesting feature of an oligopoly is that participants spend great effort preventing competitors from differentiating themselves. As time passes, "competitors" begin to look more and more alike. Since the members of the oligopoly charge essentially the same prices, they compete based on service and convenience. Therefore, throughout the 1960s and 1970s, bank after bank invested its discretionary funds in nearly identical, service-driven strategies.

The main differences were found between kinds of banks: between money center, regional, and community banks. Within each category, banks tended to be remarkably similar. Money center banks in New York, Chicago, or San Francisco looked much the same. So did regional banks in Atlanta, Denver, Dallas, or Detroit. So did community banks in New Haven, Omaha, or Greensboro. The same regulation, in the same type of city, resulted in the same type of bank.

Same Capital Pool

The final assumption underlying the bundled banking model is explicitly grounded in regulation. The assumption states that banks should have a single pool of capital that is sufficient to absorb all operating risks. These include credit risks, interest rate risks, earnings risks, and payment risks.

Regulators used such requirements to ensure that the system was safe and that depositors were well protected. Capital requirements were allowed to vary by the size of the institution, so that large banks with larger, better diversified loan portfolios were allowed higher leverage than smaller banks. But within a size class, requirements were uniform. This made sense because the difference between the banks with the highest rates of loan loss and those with the lowest rates was relatively minor. As noted earlier, the industry took very little real credit risk during this period, and it was only marginally exposed to interest rate risks (interest-sensitive assets were equal to its interest-sensitive liabilities), to risks in the payment system, or to other risks.

As a result, the postwar banking system was overcapitalized. With loan losses averaging less than 0.25 percent of assets and with equity capital and reserves averaging approximately 7 percent of assets, capital covered annual loan losses by about 25 to 1. There was never a doubt that the industry had enough capital to absorb all loan losses. Many bankers were happy with the environment that had evolved during the postwar era. And why shouldn't they have been? The industry was profitable and it was safe. Bankers had traded off their freedom for a government-sponsored cartel. Banking was a comfortable business. "Bankers' hours" were the envy of the nation.

However, there was a problem. The customers who had been subsidizing the cartel's profits were beginning to grumble and look for cheaper alternatives. All the while, the Federal Reserve was losing its grip on the nation's financial economy.

3

Breakdown of the Social Contract

As the 1970s came to a close, depository institutions were extraordinarily profitable. Our banking industry had never looked sounder. All the while though, the implicit contract between bankers, regulators, and society that had prevailed since the end of World War II was coming unraveled. Massive economic forces were taking over. The healthy profits belied the fact that the framework of regulation and law was losing its potency and relevance. Quietly, but inexorably, the postwar social contract whereby banks had traded off their freedom in exchange for profitability began to fall apart.

Eventually, the contract crumbled in the face of massive economic forces. Bankers wanted to compete and the U.S. government could no longer protect banks from competition. The Federal Reserve lost its ability to control interest rates. And most importantly, captive customers who had been overcharged by the banking oligopoly for years finally fled the system for cheaper alternatives.

The Federal Reserve Loses Control

The stability of the U.S. financial system since World War II was fundamentally due to the stable interest rates that prevailed in the period. The United States had emerged from the war as the overwhelmingly dominant military and economic power in the free world. It was a time of *pax Americana*. The dollar was the world's currency, and, in effect, the Federal Reserve was the world's central bank. The fixed exchange rate system put in place after World War II worked because the United States, in concert with the International Monetary Fund, effectively forced countries to make adjustments in their domestic fiscal and monetary policies in order to maintain the parity of their currency against the dollar. However, the key to making the entire international monetary system work was the relative strength of the U.S. economy and the maintenance of the dollar as a strong currency.

The system worked reasonably well until the mid-1960s when Lyndon Johnson decided he wanted both guns and butter. He would finance the Vietnam War without the unpopular act of raising taxes. As noted earlier, he was merely following in the footsteps of King Edward III of England and a host of other rulers. The Federal Reserve responded by tightening monetary policy, which led to liquidity-induced credit crunches in 1966 and 1969, to restrain the inflation brought about by Johnson's fiscal policies. In both 1966 and 1969, as part of this effort, the Federal Reserve used Regulation Q, designed to limit price competition for deposits, for a purpose never envisioned when the regulation was conceived. The Fed raised interest rates but did not raise the Regulation Q interest rate ceilings. This effectively choked off the banks' ability to raise marginal funds. This also squeezed bank liquidity because corporate borrowers promptly drew down all their existing lines of credit. Thrifts were hit equally hard. The pressured lenders then curtailed credit to everyone else, in particular, the housing industry. The desired effect was achieved. Inflation was slowed. But this was the beginning of an ominous and deadly trend: using bank safety and soundness regulations to achieve government economic policy, not to provide for a safe industry. Note also that the banking industry had to absorb the ensuing loan losses that resulted from the slowdown in the economy.

But the success was temporary. Inflation in the United States kept rising as the Vietnam War continued. As a result, the relative value of the dollar against other currencies declined. This led to speculation against the dollar and other weak currencies. In 1971 the dollar had to be revalued for the first time since World War II. Eventually, in 1973, the United States and the other nations of the world were forced to abandon the fixed exchange rate system. Thus was launched the globalization of the financial economy; another of the fundamental economic forces now at work that will be described in the second part of this book.

Shortly thereafter we were hit by the oil shock of 1973. Skyrocketing oil prices drove the inflation rate to 11 percent in 1974. Again, the Federal Reserve created a liquidity crunch, which peaked in August of 1974. The resulting recession caused the industry's loan losses to soar to approximately $4 billion a year, over 0.5 percent of loans—double the loan loss rates of only 0.25 percent of loans that had prevailed in the 1960s.

Despite this recession, inflation and interest rates stayed relatively high through the 1970s. In 1979 we experienced a second oil shock. This time around, however, the globalization of the financial economy had advanced sufficiently that the Federal Reserve was unable to use Regulation Q as a monetary policy tool. Big U.S. and foreign banks were able to raise as much money as they needed in the Eurodollar markets. This time around we had "expensive" money instead of "tight" money. The Federal Reserve drove interest rates up to levels never seen before in this country. The prime rate peaked at a mind-boggling 20.5 percent in August 1981.

Although not recognized at the time, these extraordinary rates took a devastating economic toll on depositories. Less-developed countries could no longer service their floating rate debt and had to borrow to pay interest or default. The savings and loan industry's capital and earnings power was effectively wiped out because of state usury laws, which still required loans to be granted at uneconomically low rates, and because of low-interest fixed rate loans made in the early 1970s that could not be repriced as rates soared. The back of inflation was broken, but at what proved to be a devastating cost to the financial system.

It was clear that the Federal Reserve cared more about stopping inflation than it did about the profitability and health of the nation's depositories. Although this may have been good economic policy, it was a fundamental violation of the implicit social contract that had prevailed since World War II.

Best Customers Rebel

Under the postwar social contract, banks made money in all sorts of economic environments. From 1961 to 1970, the prime rate was quite stable, moving better than 0.5 percent in either direction only 13 times. The volatile 1970s saw the prime make the same move 57 times. But, despite the interest rate roller coaster of the 1970s, banks' net interest margin remained constant owing to the oligopoly pricing practices described in Chapter 2.

The bundled economic model described in Chapter 2 worked for so many years because regulation had entrapped two groups of customers who paid much more for banking services than was justified by the cost of providing those services. Large depositors in both commercial banks and thrifts were not paid the full value for their deposits because of interest rate restrictions, and high-quality corporate borrowers paid commercial banks much more for their loans than their risks would indicate. In fact, these two groups of customers, who were relatively few in number, not only paid for the vast bulk of the costs of running the entire system, but effectively subsidized other customers as well.

The total subsidy, particularly from depositors, was enormous during the late 1970s. Interest rates soared while regulations limited the amount of interest that banks could pay on deposits. In those high-inflation days this meant that the real return to depositors was actually negative. With inflation at 7 percent, a depositor earning 5 percent effectively earned a return of −2 percent! These depositors were, in effect, subsidizing banks. For example, research conducted by

McKinsey showed that depositors in the commercial banking industry alone contributed a subsidy of over $30 billion in 1979. This is the difference between the interest paid on commercial bank deposits under the regulatory ceilings and the value of those deposits at then prevailing money market rates. In comparison, the commercial banking industry's total pre-tax profits in that year were only $18 billion.

During the late 1970s, McKinsey & Company studied the depositors at different-size banks in different parts of the country. Typically, we found that among every customer set examined, 70 percent to 80 percent of the contribution to profit came from 15 percent to 25 percent of the customer base. In other words, the profitability and stability of the entire system was provided by a small fraction of total customers. In most cases, these customers were found in three segments: the elderly, the wealthy, and corporations of all sizes.

Because of the deposit subsidy, and the fact that regulation forced most of the funds in the economy to flow through the depository institutions, bankers had the advantage over borrowers. They could afford to be conservative in the credit risks they took. They could pick and choose because the bargaining power was in their hands. The power was also used to extract large profits even from high-quality corporate borrowers. In particular, banks required corporations to maintain large compensating deposit balances, which were interest-free by regulation. This cross-subsidy enabled bankers to keep actual lending rates relatively low, which made it difficult for non-bank lenders like finance companies to compete for high-quality borrowers.

Excess profits from deposit-taking were also used to subsidize lending to individuals. Despite usury ceilings, banks kept making loans to good customers in the 1970s as accommodations. In effect, banks were passing excess revenues from one set of customers (depositors) through to another set of customers (borrowers). From an economic point of view, borrowers were being cross-subsidized by depositors. However, from the bankers point of view, based on the pooled funds concept, they were simply maintaining their net interest margin. They were relatively indifferent to the source of that margin.

By the mid-1970s, these traditional subsidies were beginning to disappear. Some of the industry's best retail customers were dissatisfied with the low value they were receiving for their deposits as were many of the industry's best corporate customers who were dissatisfied with the high price they were paying for credit. Many of those contributing the lion's share of the subsidy became more sophisticated and began leaving the banking system. A process called "disintermediation" then, and "securitization" today, was at work. Regulation had not changed. But non-banks, primarily securities firms, saw an opportunity to provide these dissatisfied customers with the services they needed. Crucially, they could under-price the banks and still make an acceptable profit on a product-by-product basis. Unbundled, value-based competition had begun.

On the deposit side, investment management companies began to offer money market mutual funds. These funds offered interest-bearing accounts with check-writing privileges. They were the functional equivalent of an interest-bearing checking account. In the late 1970s, as interest rates rose, large depositors found that they could shift money out of deposit accounts into money market accounts and earn much higher interest (for example, 12 percent to 13 percent versus a passbook savings rate of 5.5 or a checking account rate of zero). In other words, sophisticated depositors were recapturing the subsidy for themselves. From a standing start in 1974, money market mutual funds grew to nearly $80 billion in outstandings by the end of 1979. These funds were then invested either in Treasury bills, commercial paper, or large certificates of deposit, which were exempt from the interest rate ceilings. Although to a depositor these funds looked like they were interest-bearing checking accounts, the Federal Reserve ruled in the mid-1970s that these funds were not checking accounts. This is another example of the government, in effect, backing out of the postwar social contract that protected banks from competition.

On the lending side, large, high-quality corporate borrowers were discovering that they could raise money more cheaply in the commercial paper market than they could from banks. At the time, banks were charging corporations compensating balances worth roughly 1 percent of outstanding loans, and the "prime" rate for borrowings brought in an additional 1 percent margin. In effect, a corporation was paying 2 percent over the bank's cost of funds. Not surprisingly, as alternatives became available, large corporate customers simply bypassed the banks and went straight to the securities markets. The additional liquidity that allowed them to do so came from none other than the nascent and booming money market mutual fund industry. Thus many corporations, with the aid of the securities industry, began to save at least 1 percent on their borrowings by simply issuing "commercial paper," or short-term promissory notes either on their own or with low-cost back-up support provided by commercial banks. Throughout the 1970s, a huge volume of commercial paper was issued. By 1979, some $113 billion was outstanding—much of it provided by money market mutual funds.

Thus the commercial banking industry began losing both the deposits and loans of its most profitable customers. All banks and thrifts would be affected by the loss of the wealthy and elderly depositors. The money center banks would be hit hardest by the loss of the large corporate customers, who were both large depositors and large borrowers. But these changes crept quietly upon the industry; their full impact on profits and industry structure would not be apparent for years.

Decision to Compete

Just as the government, via the Federal Reserve, was beginning to renege on its portion of the social contract, so were many bankers. They wanted to grow and compete. Despite its profitability, the highly regulated banking industry was a somewhat boring place to work. Moreover, it did not pay well. In the early 1970s, a new generation of bankers began to replace those who had grown up in the Depression. Despite the departure of profitable customers and numerous regulatory barriers, the young bankers wanted to make their mark, and their fortune, by expanding their business. Unfortunately, the ambitions of some of these bankers exceeded their skills in competing. This is not surprising since they had all grown up in a government-sponsored oligopoly.

While the new generation understood that they needed to compete more aggressively, precious few understood that they needed to change their approach. After all, the numbers were still strong. As late as 1976 to 1979 the pre-tax return on the industry's assets had increased from about 0.88 percent to 1.13 percent. The source of this change was a huge increase in the net interest margin as a percentage of assets (+0.22 percent). The primary reason for this increase was that the high interest rates then prevailing from the Federal Reserve's desire to restrain inflation increased the amount of the subsidy being earned from the remaining captive depositors (that is, those who had not yet moved to money market mutual funds). From 1976 to 1979, the value of the deposit subsidy on checking and savings accounts went from about $8 billion to $30 billion a year.

Banks began to expand as aggressively as the law would allow. They explored ways to get around regulations, particularly geographic regulation, which once sustained and protected them. In particular, banks expanding geographically went after local banks who were taking advantage of mid-size corporations and wealthy individuals. Competition began to spread. Prevented by regulation from paying depositors more, banks tried to compete with service, adding more branches, or more automated tellers for individuals, or better tailored cash management services for corporate customers. They also tried to expand by adding customers and services to replace the income from the customer business they were losing. By the early 1980s there had been a massive increase in the competitive intensity of the industry, if not in its competitive effectiveness.

These expansion strategies were expensive. From 1976 to 1979, the banking industry's non-interest expenses grew at a compounded rate of 14 percent (from $28 billion in 1976 to $41 billion in 1979). And once one bank started spending, others had to follow simply to prevent any real differentiation in capability. To make matters worse, high inflation rates were driving costs up further.

The banks were working hard and spending hard. But they weren't really strengthening their long-term position. They had increased the *amount* they spent, but had not changed their *patterns* of spending to reflect the fact that now their most attractive customers were beginning to look for value on a product-by-product basis.

These aggressive expansion strategies were plagued by four serious flaws:

1. *Banks assumed, falsely, that all spending could be covered by price increases.* In the old oligopoly, banks had been able to pass all costs along to customers. Managers spent what they felt they had to, and recovered costs simply by allocating them against services. The central assumption was that all spending was justified and that all spending should be allocated to whatever products had sufficient margin to absorb the allocation. Cost accounting might have obscured the truth, but could not change it; costs in most banks were being allocated based on the ability to pay. When non-banks began to compete based on price, however, banks could no longer raise their prices to cover the increased cost, without losing more customers.

   Even in the late 1970s, the ever-dwindling pool of large individual depositors and corporations still borrowing from banks was still contributing the vast majority of bank revenues, bearing an ever-larger burden of the operating costs for the services used by everyone else (such as small depositors and individual borrowers). Shrinking as it was, such subsidy could not go on much longer.

2. *Banks diffused spending over the whole customer base, rather than focusing on customers they needed to retain.* Historically, 80 percent of a bank's costs had been unattributable to any specific product or service; the same pattern applied to additional investment. Money was spent to serve *depositors* better, but no attempt was made to ensure that the elderly and wealthy depositors who were providing what was left of the subsidy felt themselves well served by the improvements.

   Much of the low-value spending was on building computer systems. Few banks considered alternatives such as outsourcing. Rather, each bank tried to build its own. Banks often built very large-scale processing systems that efficiently used computers with enormous power to serve all of the bank's customers for a given product. But they soon found that the needs of individual customers were very different and that it is often very difficult to design a single, large system that cost-effectively meets the needs of all users. Invariably, this caused compromises on service to all users. The high-volume user may want to minimize costs and may want "no-frills" service while the low-volume user may be willing to pay a very high per-item cost and want extra services. If the system was designed for the "average" customer, neither the high- nor the low-volume user will be well served.

   Moreover, once an enormous "serve-everybody" system was built, it often required significant, continuing modification. In many cases, the continuing costs of modification quickly added up to more than the "economies of scale" the larger system was supposed to yield. Despite efforts to fix the system after the fact, the repair efforts were never fully successful, and service to customers was seldom satisfactory.

Massive changes in technology have taken place since most of these systems were built. The costs of computing power have plummeted. Personal computers and work-stations have brought the power of the computer to individual managers. There are powerful new tools that have improved the productivity of computer programmers. Yet even today many, if not most, banks still rely on cumbersome systems that were built up during an era when the objective was to get maximum effectiveness from data centers as opposed to serving individual customers better.

3. *Most banks pursued parallel strategies that tended to cancel each other out.* In an oligopoly, participants work hard to prevent differentiation; banks operated on the same principle. However, as player after player in the 1970s decided to become more competitive, the costs of trying to maintain parity escalated.

   Their head-to-head strategies had long stressed expansion. In the late 1970s many regional banks set up New York and London offices, even though most lacked a customer base, competitive advantages, or even a strategy for making money on such investments. As long as the additional expense could be covered by cross-subsidies from core banking customers, managers did not ask about the potential returns on the investment in expansion.

   Similarly, bank after bank invested in the same services: credit cards, mortgage banking services, interstate loan production offices, expanded cash management services, international departments, merchant banking departments, and so forth. Only a few of these paid for themselves.

   Thus most of the actions banks took to retain customers left them with neither value nor cost advantages — although they did add to overhead.

4. *Banks increased the complexity of the bank, which required an expanded, expensive corporate staff.* Many banks now have large functional departments that report to the chief executive officer. Some large banks have hundreds, and even

thousands, of corporate-level staff people in personnel, economics, control, systems, marketing, credit administration, management information, and so on. What is more, as the banks have grown, they have added layer after administrative layer of managers. At each layer, each manager has wanted his own staff to control and direct. And true to Parkinson's law, all of these layers of staff spent so much time communicating and meeting that more and more staff were required to keep up with the growth in paperwork.

All these spending flaws flowed from the same source: the game had changed, but banks were still playing by the old rules. Bankers were still looking at their overall net interest margin, which obscured the cross-subsidy of customers and products. They were spending for the overall bank rather than for specific products. Meanwhile, non-bank competitors—and increasingly, customers—were thinking in terms of individual product economics and value. What is worse, without a means of understanding where spending adds value, banks often invested revenues from profitable core banking operations into losers.

Deregulating Deposits

By the early 1980s banks and their regulators had mutually abandoned the social contract that had provided soundness and stability of our financial systems for thirty-five years. This was not, however, a conscious decision. Instead, both parties came to deviate from their prescribed roles as inexorable economic forces drove events. The last vestiges of the social contract to remain were price controls on deposits.

By 1982 the volume of money market funds had grown to over $200 billion from a base of under $10 billion just four years earlier. The bulk of these funds consisted of deposits that had left the banking and thrift industries. It was clear that insured depositories were losing their franchise. This flight of capital only added insult to injury for the thrifts, which had suffered so badly from high interest rates in 1980 and 1981; 28 percent of thrifts had been either liquidated or merged into stronger institutions by 1982.

Banks and thrifts, which had rarely agreed on anything for most of their history, united to help push through the Garn–St Germain Act of 1982, which accelerated the deregulation of deposit pricing begun in 1980. Many in both industries had long been active contributors to many members of Congress. Once they united, the industries had enormous political power. The resulting act gave them unprecedented powers to compete— both against money market funds, non-banks, and against each other. Today, it is easy to see that this "freedom of competition" was seriously flawed. The problem was that there was still regulation that prevented the natural consequences of competition: survival of the fittest. These regulations, which once protected depositors, now protected feeble and failing institutions at the great expense of the skilled institutions in both industries. Even worse, as we will see in the next chapter, the act enabled unscrupulous operators in the savings and loan industry to massively abuse the deposit insurance system.

The Garn–St Germain Act had two main features. First, it deregulated deposit pricing, which had been scheduled for 1986, virtually overnight. Now both commercial banks and thrifts could bid for the deposits they had lost to money market mutual funds. Second, the act attempted to revitalize the thrift industry by expanding its charter. In particular, real estate lending and development powers were expanded. Moreover, thrifts could make many more consumer loans than had been permitted before—as well as lend to businesses and offer demand deposit accounts for the first time. To outside observers, thrifts began to look very much like commercial banks, only with greatly expanded real estate powers.

But the regulators did not seem to see it that way. There was no real attempt to unify or even coordinate the regulation of the two industries. The commercial banks and mutual savings banks continued to be overseen by the FDIC, the Comptroller of the Currency, and the Federal Reserve. The savings and loans continued to be overseen by the FSLIC (Federal Savings and Loan Insurance Company) and the Federal Home Loan Bank Board.

The attitudes, talents, and resources of the two groups of regulators also differed. The savings and loan regulators took a *laissez-faire* approach that gave each savings and loan institution almost complete autonomy over lending the federally insured deposits it raised. The savings and loan regulators had little choice; the staffing and skills of the FSLIC and the Federal Home Loan Bank Board were woefully inadequate even to effectively monitor the widespread activities of a booming savings and loan industry. The commercial bank and mutual savings bank regulators were much more active, managing not by exception, but through strict enforcement of their standards.

With federal protection from failure, the freedoms bestowed by the Garn–St Germain Act, ineffective regulators, and a complacent Congress, there is no mystery why the savings and loan industry self-destructed into the most expensive financial crisis in the history of the nation.

4

The Savings
and Loan Debacle

Although this book is about reforming the regulation of commercial banks, it is impossible to write about the subject without also getting into the causes and consequences of the savings and loan debacle.

Savings and loans have always been viewed by commercial bankers as, at best, an unwanted stepsister. Savings and loans were populist institutions whereas banks have always been, first and foremost, commercial concerns. The vast majority of S&Ls were organized, in fact, as mutuals whose focus was on channeling the savings of the community into home mortgages. The movie, *It's a Wonderful Life,* starring Jimmy Stewart, captured the distinction in the public's mind. The local banker in that movie was a direct descendant of Shylock, whereas the savings and loan executive was a friend of everyone. One was heartless, the other, all heart.

Stereotyping is of course always dangerous. Who but a monster could be against an industry committed to providing people with housing? Out of such images came enormous political power for the S&L industry. For the most part, bankers and other knowledgeable, concerned people recognized this power and simply looked away as the savings and loan industry started to go sour during the 1980s.

The Thrift Contract

There is no doubt that the savings and loan industry served a fundamentally useful purpose for the nation. When the savings and loan industry was booming immediately after World War II, commercial banks were unwilling to take either the credit or interest rate risks inherent in channeling deposits into fixed rate mortgages. The savings and loan industry provided the funds needed to finance the rapid growth in the nation's population— particularly in the baby-boom years of 1946 to the early 1960s.

The implicit contract between the government and the savings and loan industry was that the government would provide savings and loans advantages in raising consumer deposits if the industry would invest them in home mortgages. These advantages included the ability under deposit interest rate regulation to pay a quarter of a percent higher interest than commercial banks could pay for consumer deposits (which enabled S&Ls to always advertise that they offered the highest rates) and a friendly regulatory structure. Indeed, the Federal Home Loan Bank Board and the FSLIC (Federal Savings and Loan Insurance Company) often seemed to be as much cheerleaders as regulators. A more subtle clause in this implicit contract was that the government would keep interest rates relatively stable so that the S&L industry could borrow short and lend long—short-term rates are generally lower than long-term rates. This is referred to as "playing the yield curve."

As we saw earlier, in order to combat inflation, the government wound up breaking this critical portion of the implicit contract. During the 1979 to 1980 period when the prime rate soared to better than 20 percent, S&Ls and banks were permitted to pay higher (but still regulated) deposit rates. But while their costs of funds rose, the yield on the S&L's mortgage loans hardly changed because most of them had been made at a fixed rate for periods as long as thirty years. By the middle of June 1981, 70 percent of all thrifts were losing money. Although the available accounting data of that period was somewhat misleading, any careful analyst could see that the industry had almost no real capital left by the end of 1981!

The best thing to have done in 1981 would have been to close the insolvent savings and loans and let the remainder convert to commercial banks. However, that was politically impossible to do given the lobbying clout of the savings and loan and housing industries.

What did we do? The worst thing imaginable.

Money for Nothing

During 1981 and 1982, a plan was hatched by the S&Ls, their regulators, and their supporters in Congress. At the center of the efforts was the industry's trade association, the U.S. Savings League. The idea was quite simple. The industry was going to grow its way out of the problems. Since it could do nothing with its existing portfolio of fixed rate mortgages, which was now largely underwater, the plan was simply to raise a lot of new deposits and lend them out at high spreads, which would increase the net interest margin sufficiently to offset the drag from the old fixed mortgages. Thus earnings would rebound and capital adequacy would be restored. Anyone with any lending experience could have seen a few flaws with this plan, but to the S&L industry the plan seemed to be god-sent.

I talked with a chief executive of one of the best run savings and loans in the country, a major California institution, about the trade association meeting at which this plan was first widely discussed. "It was madness. As word spread, from meeting to meeting, despair turned to euphoria. It was as if the fundamental problems of the industry had simply disappeared."

The plan was realized in the Garn–St Germain Act of 1982. It had the full blessings of both the deregulation-oriented Reagan administration and Congress. In addition to completing the deregulation of interest ceilings on insured deposits, it raised the limits for nonresidential mortgages from 20 percent of assets to 40 percent. It raised the limits for consumer loans from 20 percent to 30 percent and it authorized S&Ls to put as much as 10 percent of assets in commercial loans. S&Ls were also authorized by Richard Pratt, chairman of the Federal Home Loan Bank Board, to make construction loans up to 100 percent of appraised value compared to the 70 percent loan-to-value ratios that had long been the standard in commercial banks. Simultaneously, many states also broadened the powers for state-chartered institutions. California, Texas, and Florida were particularly generous.

Perhaps more importantly, the character of the people managing the savings and loans changed. The community-oriented, conservative residential mortgage lender was replaced in the best case by aggressive managers and in the worst by out-and-out criminals. As regulators took over insolvent institutions, they passed them over to these "eager entrepreneurs." Many were real estate developers, who saw access to unlimited amounts of money. In some states, such as Texas, literally anyone could get a savings and loan charter if he or she wanted one.

The combination was explosive. In essence, we opened up the Treasury to anyone who was willing to pay the highest rates for insured deposits. The removal of deposit ceilings on insured deposits enabled all deposit-taking institutions, whether weak or strong, to compete for deposits on price. All banks and thrifts could back up their deposits (up to $100,000 per deposit) with government insurance; individuals chose where to put their money not on the basis of which was the soundest bank, but which offered the highest interest rate. Too often, the highest bidder turned out to be an incompetent thrift. In some cases, savings and loans with less than $100 million in assets raised money through brokers and grew to multi-billion-dollar institutions in just a few years.

These institutions then started lending aggressively. Because so many lenders were looking for business, loan rates were forced down, and institutions eager for volume often relaxed their quality and lending standards. Inevitably, the weakest institutions took the most risk.

A real estate developer explained to me how it worked. The year was 1982 and an energy-led building boom was in full swing in Texas. He and his partner approached one of the aggressive savings and loans with plans to build a $15-million building. "Why not build a $25-million building?" they were asked. "All we need from you is an upfront commitment fee of 4 percent of the loan commitment so that we can book the fee immediately as profit. That way we will have the capital we need for regulatory purposes so we can raise the deposits to make you the loan. Of course, we will loan you the money for the commitment fee and we will want to build into the loan the interest payments needed to keep the loan current for five years just in case you have difficulty leasing the building up. We can also give you the name of a good appraiser for your property. And we will not require you to personally guarantee the loan. Your building will be our sole collateral."

In other words, the S&L loaned him the money, which he paid back as a fee, in order to give the S&L the regulatory capital needed to raise the deposits to fund the entire loan. And then they gave him a loan commitment sufficient to pay all of the interest on the loan for five years, making it impossible for the loan to go bad during that time period. Completing the process of creating "value" out of thin air, they helped him find an appraiser who would come through with an appraised value high enough to justify the loan. And this transaction was entirely legal. There was no fraud involved. Money for nothing.

Ponzi Scheme

The savings and loan industry was transformed by the resulting credit boom. In a few short years we went from exploiting depositors through interest controls to overpaying them by allowing anyone who owned an insured depository to raise as much money as wanted simply by paying the highest rates. You could even hire a broker to raise the money for you. Through Garn–St Germain, we created an enormous anomaly in the markets for deposits. We provided depositors not only safety and liquidity but ridiculously high returns as well. As noted earlier, depositors should be earning lower returns in compensation for safety and liquidity.

Because of this market anomaly, the savings and loan industry was able to grow at a rapid rate. Their assets grew from $580 billion at the start of 1980 to $1.25 trillion just eight years later—a compound annual growth rate of 10.1 percent even though the industry had no real capital to support this growth.

Much of this money was funneled into real estate construction loans on commercial properties, condominium loans, junk bonds, and other high-risk assets at high nominal spreads over the cost of raising the deposits. The terms and conditions on these assets were ridiculously generous. In other words, we created an enormous anomaly in the credit markets.

Reported earnings grew rapidly at these institutions, which increased their "capital base," which permitted the institutions to raise still more deposits. To a novice examining the publicly available numbers it looked like the "grow-out-of-it" strategy was working.

Of course, as noted, the accounting was absurd. First of all, regulators created artificial capital, called "regulatory goodwill," when it passed insolvent savings and loans to new buyers. This effectively capitalized losses that had already been incurred and enabled them to be written off over thirty-five years or more. They also employed liberal definitions of what loans were performing. As already explained, generally accepted accounting principles allowed lenders to lend to borrowers the interest to be paid back as interest on construction loans. This is fine provided that the construction loan is converted to a permanent mortgage that is paid off through rent payments made by the building's occupants. However, during the 1980s insolvent institutions abused these principles to keep loans "current" that were by any common-sense notion "nonperforming." Specifically, loan agreements were written in the early 1980s that included two or three years of interest payments as well as money for leasehold improvements (that is, improvements demanded by tenants in order to rent the properties).

Many of these buildings sat empty years after construction was finished and yet the loans were kept current by drawing down "interest reserves." The next ploy was to release the money intended to make the leasehold improvements to continue making interest payments. Although these practices delayed defaults, eventual default became inevitable because the loan amount far exceeded the economic value of the building. Eventually, all such loans move from the "current" to "nonaccruing" and finally to "loan charge-offs." Savings and loans used these and a host of other accounting devices to manufacture profits that were never really there.

What is worse, the insolvent thrifts continued to raise even more deposits in an effort to buy time. Anyone who understood these lending practices could see what was going to happen. Liabilities (that is, deposits) rise much faster than earning assets because the cash needed to pay interest to depositors, to pay operating expenses, and to keep loans current will continue to pour out of the institutions while real interest income from true earning assets will fall far short of the cash needed. The gap widens as each day passes.

It was a government-sponsored Ponzi scheme that outdid Ponzi himself. Charles Ponzi was an "entrepreneur" in Boston who developed a scheme in which he promised "investors" high rates on his money (40 percent for forty-five days), then borrowed larger sums from later investors, took a cut, and used the remainder to pay the interest on the first money raised. This pyramid yielded high returns to Ponzi from 1919 to 1920 until the *Boston Post* exposed him, and he was indicted.

The S&L Ponzi scheme, however, lasted most of the decade. Since 1980, thrift regulators had permitted thrifts to use accounting practices that artificially inflated the thrifts' regulatory net worth even above the generous generally accepted accounting conventions. Moreover, even after becoming insolvent under even the most generous accounting, thrifts were able to raise the cash they needed to keep the doors open because of government guarantees. As long as losing thrifts retained these privileges, they had incentives to make very risky loans and to take huge interest rate gambles, because they had nothing to lose. If the risk-taking succeeded, they might be able to generate a positive net worth for their shareholders and continue paying salaries to managers. If the risk-taking failed, the only real loser would be the federal deposit insurance fund (that is, the FSLIC) that would have to cover the thrift's inability to repay its depositors. The perverse incentive that arises when an insolvent insured thrift is permitted to continue operating has been summarized by other observers as: "Heads I win, tails FSLIC loses." While the industry certainly saw more than its share of fraud and abuse, the industry didn't need illegal activity to bring it to its knees. Most of the problems were caused by legal, regulatory-approved activities.

With this perspective it is easy to see why the situation has been deteriorating so rapidly over the last three years. The real underlying cash flow problem has been masked by misleading accounting. While the real problem built up over a decade, the reported numbers only began to reveal the full magnitude of the dismal cash flow reality in 1988 through 1990. This is why most observers, including the Bank Board itself, were caught by surprise at the speed of the deterioration in the late 1980s. What was growing so rapidly was not the problem itself, but rather the recognition of the problem in S&Ls' financial statements.

Politics

Never has a federal agency so dramatically failed to do its job as did the Federal Home Loan Bank Board and FSLIC. Although many individuals at the Bank Board and FSLIC did their best, the net result was a monumental failure of the institution to protect the public interest. And state regulators were even worse. In 1988 and 1989 two-thirds of FSLIC losses were attributable to state-chartered thrifts in just two states—California and Texas.

The regulators were simply reflecting political will. No one wanted to deal with the issues. The Reagan Administration was committed to "deregulation." Much of the Democratic leadership in Congress were friends of the savings and loan industry. The issues were thought to be too complicated to be understood by the public. The numbers reported for accounting purposes masked how bad the problem was. And the clout of the savings and loan/housing industry lobby was enormous.

By the mid-1980s Ed Gray, who was then Chairman of the Bank Board, tried to blow a whistle on what was going on, but no one really wanted to listen. He was not given sufficient staff to track the problems in the industry, let alone deal with them. As early as 1985 the Bank Board requested additional funding to shore up FSLIC. At the time, the GAO (Government Accounting Office) was estimating the problem at $15 to $20 billion. By February 1986 the administration's Economic Policy Council approved a $30-billion plan for the FSLIC to address the thrift crisis: $15 billion in borrowing authority plus $15 billion from the industry. In October 1986, the Senate passed a $15-billion recapitalization bill, but the House, under massive U.S. Savings League lobbying, killed the bill in 1986. The Chairman of the House Banking Committee, Fernand St Germain, and Speaker of the House Jim Wright were instrumental in paralyzing the Congress. Finally, with the Administration's urging, in August 1987, Congress passed a $10.8-billion recapitalization bill. It was far too little, much too late.

Meanwhile, private analysts like Bert Ely, Dan Brumbaugh, and myself were estimating in the press that the economic losses at that time were in the $50- to $100-billion range. I remember going to Washington in 1987 and early 1988 and being dumbfounded at what was going on. The whole atmosphere had an Alice-in-Wonderland quality. Every intelligent person I met acknowledged that we had a massive problem on our hands but everyone was equally convinced that nothing was going to be done about it until after the presidential election.

They were right.

What we got instead was the "Southwest Plan." This plan only compounded the problem. Because the FSLIC was insolvent and had no cash, the Bank Board created a cashless restructuring process. The term "Southwest Plan" was itself a misnomer. In practice, the Bank Board applied the plan to thrift restructurings all around the country.

Given that the government was going to eventually pay for the costs of cleaning up the thrift mess anyway, one of the major problems with these transactions was that they cost the government more than liquidating the institutions.

Essentially, this plan had the FSLIC and the Federal Home Loan Bank Board using a combination of promissory notes, asset guarantees, yield maintenance agreements, and tax shields to absorb all of the risks and most of the operating losses of the insolvent institutions that were "rescued." Unfortunately, very few of these institutions had the franchise value they needed to ever become self-sufficient. Our analysis, at McKinsey, showed that keeping such institutions alive was going to cost the federal government as a whole some 30 percent to 40 percent more, in net present value terms, than outright liquidation. Assuming no worsening in asset quality and no increase in interest rates, we estimated that the liquidation costs of the sixty-three Southwest Plan thrifts would have been about $15 billion, but that the Southwest Plan approach would cost over $22 billion. Taking into account a rise in interest rates or further asset deterioration the cost could almost double to over $30 billion. Over the intervening two years, even this $30-billion figure has proved to be too low of an estimate.

When President Bush was inaugurated, the nation was finally able to begin to address the S&L crisis. In 1989, Congress passed the Financial Institutions Reform, Recovery, and Enforcement Act (FIRREA) along the lines of the new president's proposal. The law was a watershed event. The savings and loan lobby tried its best to emasculate the law, but thanks to committee chairmen like Henry Gonzalez in the House and Donald Riegle in the Senate, and the personal efforts of members of both parties such as Congressman Schumer, Congressman Wylie, Congressman Leach, and the new House majority leader, Tom Foley, the law was passed.

The bill was not a true reform bill, but did provide the funding needed to close down the insolvent S&Ls. It also put the S&L effectively under the regulatory authority of the FDIC and its Chairman, Bill Seidman. With FIRREA we drew a line in the sand. But it was way too late. The healthy savings and loans were caught up in the vestiges of an obsolete regulatory structure. Healthy depository institutions of all kinds were still having to face competing against insolvent institutions for funds. The government began to approach the multiyear task of liquidating the institutions.

With the passage of FIRREA, I got out of the business of estimating the eventual costs of the thrift crisis. By midsummer of 1990, however, Secretary of the Treasury Brady was estimating that the net present value cost was going to be over $150 billion. Chairman Seidman estimated that some $100 billion was going to be needed in 1991 alone. By any measure, the costs are staggering.

Meanwhile, what should be done with the remainder of the industry? None of us would argue with the premise that housing and home ownership is a high national priority. The question is, do we need a separately regulated thrift industry to further the pursuit of that priority?

I believe that the answer is no.

Given the development of the mortgage-backed securities markets and a highly liquid secondary mortgage market, given the broad expansion of commercial banks into mortgage finance, and given the broad national infrastructure (such as, Freddie Mac, GNMA, Fannie Mae) to support housing finance, I believe that mortgage finance is generally available to any credit-worthy borrower in the nation. Remember, the conditions today are in stark contrast to those that prevailed when the savings and loan industry regulatory structure was created in the 1930s. At that time commercial banks were unwilling to take either the credit or interest risk inherent in fixed rate mortgages, and the creation of the savings and loan industry provided the needed housing finance. Today the evidence points to a glut of real estate financing.

Since availability of finance has long been the only constraint on builders and developers, it is not surprising that the removal of that constraint, with the passage of the Garn–St Germain Act, led to the overbuilding of commercial and residential real estate (particularly in condominium form) that we see today. This overbuilding is evident not just in the Southwest and the Northeast, but increasingly in the Southeast and Far West as well. We have now built substantially more residential and commercial real estate capacity than the national economy is willing to pay for. It will take us years to work off that overcapacity. In such an environment, I see little benefit in keeping a separate industry devoted to the housing industry. Indeed, I see enormous risks.

There remains no useful distinction between the savings and loan and commercial banking industries. Commercial banks have become committed to the housing and real estate industries: indeed, real estate loans now exceed commercial loans on bank balance sheets. Meanwhile, savings and loans have used their expanded powers to look more and more like banks. And the securitization of mortgages has dramatically expanded the role of non-depository institutions (for example, pension funds, insurance companies, or individuals) in the finance of residential mortgages. The nation suffers by having two overlapping sets of deposit insurance regulation. Essentially we have two sets of players, both of them funded by federally insured deposits, which play by different sets of rules. This makes no sense.

We should simply allow healthy S&Ls to become commercial banks. Therefore, for the purposes of this book, I am going to assume that the answers for reforming the S&L industry are the same as those for reforming the commercial banking industry.

5

Unleashing Bank
Competition

=====

While much of the savings and loan industry was self-destructing, banks began competing in earnest. By the mid-1980s, banking went from a comfortable oligopoly to one of the most intensely competitive industries in the world. Most bankers entered the battle full of energy, optimism, and enthusiasm. Many emerged somewhat bloodied by the experience.

Competition, indeed, transformed the industry. The image of the tight-fisted banker was replaced by the eager lender who offered you credit lines by mail. Deposits were marketed with techniques borrowed from the fast food industry. The very structure of the industry changed. The terms used to describe different kinds of banks lost their meaning. What, for example, do you call a bank that competes in three different regions? A multiregional?

By the end of the 1980s winners began to emerge, but it soon became clear they were vastly outnumbered by the losers. Ironically, this was despite a great increase in the skills of the average banker. All of the the energy invested into competition was not resulting in a healthier industry. On the contrary, the best participants discovered that it was very difficult to make money. And the mediocre participants discovered that they had developed massive exposures to credit losses. The public, an early beneficiary of a more competitive industry, began to see the dark side of unleashing competition without reforming the regulatory system. Something had gone terribly wrong.

It's Hard to Add Value

As taught in business schools, most industries have an economic equilibrium. Different competitors in an industry maintain or gain share to the extent that they can provide better products at lower prices to customers. If they can do so by operating at low costs, then they can earn more profits. If they cannot do so, then they can gain or maintain share by accepting lower profits. However, in most industries, competitors who do not achieve satisfactory profits are forced to exit the industry. After the exiting, the remaining players gain the profitability they deserve from being able to compete more effectively. If the remaining players overcharge their customers and make excessive profits, they, in turn, will attract new entrants. The winners in a competitive environment should be the companies that add the most value to customers relative to their competition. Yet during the late 1970s and 1980s bank earnings languished. No matter that bankers gave customers better service, better pricing, and better terms and conditions for borrowing money. From 1980 to 1989 average return on equity fell from 13.2 percent to 7.8 percent.

Some observers, including myself, argue that it has been more difficult to add value in banking than in most industries. There are several structural reasons for this. First of all, the history of regulation has filled the industry with institutions that have similar capabilities. Parallel regulation begat parallel skills. Even as banks became more competitive they continued to pursue parallel strategies. If one bank decided to expand geographically, then so would its competitors. If one bank decided to pursue an intensive ATM (automated teller machine) strategy, its peers would follow. When many players pursue head-to-head strategies, it is obviously more difficult for any of them to add value.

A further difficulty in adding value was the tendency of many banks to continue to pursue strategies long after it was clear they were uneconomic. The culprit here was banks' huge shared infrastructure costs. Many banks remained in businesses as long as revenues from that business covered the marginal costs of the business. They were unaware that if they added all their businesses together there was insufficient income to cover all of the shared infrastructure cost and all of the risks they were exposed to and still leave shareholders with reasonable risk-adjusted returns on their capital. Many small and mid-size banks were clearly uncompetitive by the mid-1980s. However, they did not exit the business for the simple reason that they had no place to go; banking was their only business. Even failing banks, like the insolvent savings and loans, were kept in business by regulators long after they had ceased to be economic. The reason is that bank regulators have difficulty taking over failing banks as long as they have a positive net worth using generally accepted accounting principles even though the institutions might be economically insolvent if you marked their assets to their economic (that is, cash flow) value.

Yet another problem is that non-bank competitors have been free to choose whichever banking activities they wanted to pursue without having to incur the heavy shared cost infrastructure that comes with a banking franchise. Among others, AT&T has been free to pursue the credit card business, General Electric Capital Corporation has been free to pursue the commercial finance and leasing businesses, and Fidelity has been free to pursue the money market mutual fund business (that is, the equivalent of the demand deposit business), without being subject to the heavy costs of bank regulation.

Another impediment to adding value is that natural consolidation forces have been frustrated by the regulation that has remained in place. To begin with, the combination of the McFadden Act (barriers to interstate branching) and the Bank Holding Company Act of 1956 (barriers to interstate acquisitions without permission of the states) made it impossible to engage in any interstate consolidation until the early 1980s. In some states it is still impossible to undertake interstate acquisitions. By 1990, there were only thirty-three states, representing 71 percent of the population, which allowed significant interstate banking by all banks outside the region where the bank itself is based.

Even where it has been possible to do an interstate acquisition, the Bank Holding Company Act has made it almost impossible except on a friendly basis; the agony that Bank of New York went through to acquire the Irving Trust is the exception that proved the rule. Inability to do unfriendly transactions has put the bargaining power in the hands of the institution being acquired. This has meant that management selling the institution has often been inclined to favor the acquiror most willing to leave the bank alone. Consequently, many of the acquisitions that have been completed have not resulted in full economic consolidation of the entities.

In contrast to the difficulty of making interstate acquisitions, it has been relatively easy, from a regulatory viewpoint, to expand on a *de novo* basis across state lines in all activities other than branch-based deposit-taking. This led to enormous expansion of new capacity particularly in formerly high-profit lending activities such as middle market banking, credit cards, and leasing. As a result, this type of regulation helped reinforce the industry's tendency to pursue self-defeating parallel strategies.

In addition to the regulatory barriers to adding value, there were internal ones as well. In pursuing their parallel strategies, bankers were simultaneously making their own management tasks far more difficult. As they competed and expanded, most were forced to invest heavily in staff and controls to contain the growing risk as operations became more diverse, more complex, and more geographically diffused. As the geographic scope of the bank expanded, as the customer base changed, and as the product line proliferated, the running of a bank became more and more difficult. Most banks responded by simply overlaying the management of this expanded activity on top of the shared cost management infrastructure designed for a different, simpler era.

Internal staff and consultants (including McKinsey) recommended a variety of management approaches, such as matrix management, which would keep the existing organizational structure and underlying economics intact. Complex management information systems were designed to assist in the management and motivation of employees. But it was a losing battle. Most large banks, except for those with exceptional talent and management capacity, became unwieldy and disorganized. In some large banks, three or four projects were often launched to examine the same issue.

Redundant functions multiplied, and accountability became blurred. New costs were added, while the "essential" old cost base remained. Value was destroyed.

As the large banks struggled with the increasing cost of complexity, many smaller banks struggled with the diseconomies of small size. All were trying to offer the same products, but many smaller banks simply had too little volume to support the costs of "essential" new services, like automated tellers or credit cards. In credit cards, a large player could reduce its non-interest operating costs (excluding charge-off and collection costs) to 3 percent or 4 percent of its credit card loan portfolio. For a small community bank, the same costs could be 8 percent to 10 percent or more.

Unleashing competition among commercial banks was positive for their customers in many respects. We saw a great deal of investment in new capabilities and products. Bankers, in general, worked harder and performed with higher levels of skill than they had in the postwar era. Customers got more services and better prices. Unfortunately, there was something missing: profits. Many banks were finding it difficult to make money.

High-Skill Institutions

Despite such handicaps, some exceptional commercial banks rose to the challenge and implemented strategies that actually added value. There were enormous opportunities: the markets for financial services were very large and growing, the largest institutions had only a fraction of the total market, and the vast bulk of the market share was held by banks that added relatively little value. Among the commercial banks, successes came for institutions of all sizes. What they had in common was an understanding of the unique strengths they possessed and the ability to move fast to translate these strengths into value to the customer—without risk to themselves.

The clear stars of the decade were the "super-regional" bank holding companies. By "super regionals," I am referring to a class of regional bank holding companies that have spread throughout their home regions through acquisition and *de novo* growth. All of the ones I am including as winners now have over $20 billion in assets and are continuing to grow.

By any measure these super regionals have been performing very well. They include such bank holding companies as Barnett Banks, Banc One, NBD (the old National Bank of Detroit), NCNB (the old North Carolina National Bank), National City, Core States, First Wachovia, Sun Trust, and Wells Fargo just to name a few. Bank of America also would have to be included on this list given how it has been restructured. These super regionals are exceptions to many of the trends described in this book. They have grown both in size and profitability and have kept credit losses at minimal levels. In fact, they have had the profit strength to write off or sell off most of their loans to developing countries at the same time less-developed-country (LDC) debt has severely damaged many of the money center banks. Their relative success can easily be demonstrated by looking at the market capitalizations of their stock. In 1980 the list of most highly capitalized bank holding company stocks was dominated by money center banks; today the list is dominated by super regionals.

It is important to understand the source of the super regionals' success. They have succeeded by making the traditional core bank model work far better than their competitors. Most of these holding companies have at their center one or more large banks. These banks typically have a dominant position in one or more important regional city like Columbus, Charlotte, or Detroit, and hold dominant market shares of deposits—25 percent or better in their home cities. Their strength came from serving the core banking needs of individuals, small businesses, and mid-size companies. In addition, entering the 1980s these banks had already developed a broad range of services for the individual correspondent bank and corporate marketplace. They had enormous strength in operations and systems owing to their role in regional check clearing.

As geographic barriers to interstate regulation fell, these banks had the skills and scale to offer more value to customers than smaller regional and local banks. Many of these banks have superior credit skills compared to the smaller regionals with which they compete. During the 1980s these banks discovered that they could acquire smaller banks, even at hefty premiums, and more than pay for the acquisition by eliminating redundant costs. In particular, they discovered they could eliminate the smaller bank's overhead function and use their operations and systems skill to consolidate the smaller bank's operations costs with their own. They acquired distribution and customers while eliminating redundant capacity.

For example, from 1982 to 1985, NCNB acquired eight smaller banks with total assets of $6.4 billion. Prior to acquisition, these banks operated at a noninterest income-to-expense ratio of about 350 basis points. After acquisition, NCNB was able to bring the expense ratio of these banks down to the 270-basis-point range.

Indeed, our analysis of a broad cross section of the industry has shown that large regional banks can operate at significantly lower costs than a smaller regional with the same customer mix. For example, we estimate a $20-billion regional bank might have operating costs as a percentage of assets of 2.5 percent to 3.0 percent, whereas a $3- to $4-billion regional bank might have operating costs as a percentage of assets of 3.5 percent to 4.0 percent.

So these regional bank holding companies have succeeded at old-fashioned core banking. Their net interest margins and fee incomes have grown faster than their shared costs, and as a result, they have had the profitability to avoid the temptations to take excessive credit or interest rate risk. They win because they give customers more value and they operate at lower costs.

But the same barriers to creating value described earlier, over the longer term, are affecting the super regionals as well.

Unless we reform the regulatory structure, they too will suffer. In comparison to all other sectors of the banking system, however, the super regionals, who have avoided the pitfalls of bad lending, stand out for their relative strength. They have strong customer franchises, strong management skills, and are relatively cost-effective. In combination, this has enabled them to enjoy relatively strong profits and to maintain a relatively strong balance sheet when much of the rest of the industry is weak. Some of their stocks still trade at a premium to book value even when most of the industry trades at an enormous discount. They have enormous opportunities to win, but they cannot afford to be complacent.

There have been some clear winners outside the super regional class as well. Bankers Trust and J. P. Morgan have successfully developed sufficient merchant banking and trading capabilities to enable them to convert from being money center banks into leading investment banks. Among smaller regionals, for example, the State Street Bank saw a unique advantage in its longstanding relationship with the mutual funds industry. It built a profitable business on the defection of depositors to money market mutual funds by providing check cashing and custodial services to funds.

There were numerous successes, too, at the community banking level. For example, in 1989 there were over 1,170 banks in the United States with under $500 million in assets with returns on equity above 16 percent. Most of these banks earned those returns by sticking to their local markets and to the core banking businesses of taking deposits and lending to local customers. The New Canaan Bank & Trust Co., in my home town in Connecticut, has done a much better job than many of its larger brethren in avoiding the credit problems of a deteriorating New England economy.

Contrary to popular belief, there were success stories among savings and loans—particularly in California. California-based Ahmanson became perhaps the most successful mortgage banker in the country. Great Western (also based in California) converted itself into an organization that looks today much like a successful super regional.

Problems with the Economic Model

Such relative prosperity is the exception. The vast majority of the industry has been severely weakened as competition has intensified. To understand specifically what happened, let's reexamine the economic model of a bank described earlier.

Banks, indeed, have been having problems with all elements of the model. Their expense base grew rapidly. Their net interest revenues were threatened. Finally, they began to need more capital than they could generate through retained earnings. The fundamental problem is that the unleashing of competition without reform of the regulatory structure undermined the economic model of the bank.

The Expense Base

As the industry became more competitive, its expense base grew enormously. While much of this spending undoubtedly added value to customers, it added little value to the institutions themselves. One good proxy we have found helpful in measuring the productivity of industry-wide spending is to compare spending growth to the growth in the gross national product (GNP). If growth in spending exceeds the growth in GNP, then the industry is adding relative capacity.

From 1980 to 1986, even though inflation had slowed to around 3 percent, bank spending surged. Expenses grew at the same 14 percent compounded rate of the late 1970s, when inflation ran at 7 percent. From 1976 to 1986, the industry's noninterest expenses tripled from an annual rate of $28 billion a year to a rate of $90 billion a year—a 320 percent increase. In comparison, nominal GNP grew only from $1.78 trillion to $4.23 trillion over that same period—a 237 percent increase. Banks weren't alone. Every segment of the financial services industry—broker/dealers, investment banks, consumer and commercial finance companies, life insurance companies, property and casualty companies, and savings and loans—all grew expense dollars much faster than the GNP. The rise in competitive intensity throughout the entire financial services industry was spectacular.

Some of this spending was undoubtedly just a catch up in service levels from having the government limit competition for over thirty years. However, at some point the industry began to overshoot levels of spending that could be recovered from customers. In particular, it was difficult to recover the costs of spending on shared infrastructure within the bank that offered little direct value to customers. The extra spending eventually became unneeded additional capacity.

Over the last four years, from 1986 to 1990, the industry has been much more aggressive in its management of its spending as profit growth came to an end. From the end of 1986 to the third quarter of 1990, bank spending grew only 25.5 percent or at an annual compound rate of 5.8 percent. In comparison, nominal GNP grew only 28 percent or at an annual rate of 6.4 percent. But the damage had already been done in the early and mid-1980s. To offset this enormous growth in spending, the industry needed to find enormous growth in revenues.

Net Interest Spread

Part of the huge increase in spending during the 1980s was recovered from increases in fees. Some of the fees were from price increases and some were from adding new services. For example, the total fee income received by banks grew from $5.9 billion in 1980 to $18.2 billion in 1989.

However, the vast bulk of revenue growth in a bank must come from where it always comes. To cover the growth in spending described earlier requires a massive increase in net interest income. Despite the intense price competition that developed over deposit-taking among banks and thrifts, and despite the loss of high-quality corporate borrowers to the commercial paper market, net interest revenue did grow spectacularly from a level of about $57 billion in 1980 to over $112 billion by 1990 (first half of year annualized). In fact, the net interest margin, as a percentage of assets, for the industry in 1990 was 3.49 percent, up 8 percent from 1980 levels.

How could such growth be possible, when the industry was experiencing intense price competition between banks and thrifts for deposits?

The unfortunate evidence is that many commercial banks maintained their net interest margins by lowering their standards and accepting higher levels of credit risk. High-quality revenue was replaced by high-risk revenues. The results of such practices show only over time. They are beginning to show now, but it is too late for preventive action. We have no choice but to work through the problems.

Unlike savings and loans, most commercial banks did not suddenly decide to take more credit risk. Rather, under the pressure of rapid expense growth and increased price competition for deposits, they gradually loosened their credit standards. Institutions that had been dominated by a conservative credit culture began to see their net interest margin come under pressure. They responded by expanding their definition of which borrowers were acceptable, by relaxing the terms and conditions under which they lent, and by providing more and more generous availability of credit relative to the cash flows of the borrowers. Like a rock climber who goes after steeper and steeper cliffs without improving his ropes and pitons, or his skills, the bankers found themselves overextended with no path of safe return. The economic model had been undermined, so bankers took on more and more risk to keep the model working.

But it is important to remember that it was the system itself that was the fundamental cause of the problem. By allowing incompetent institutions to overpay depositors with excessive rates, regulators channeled money to institutions lacking the skills or the capital—or in some cases the ethical standards—

to properly lend those funds. The massive deposit and credit anomalies were the source of the problem.

Banks were forced by the local competition in the marketplace to charge a certain interest rate, but were left to themselves to determine the quality of each risk, and the potential loss on each loan. The new competition prevented them from using the traditional, conservative standards for acceptable terms and prudent lending limits. New standards had to be developed within each bank, because for most local borrowers (such as individuals, small businesses, or mid-size companies) there are neither ratings nor common information sources that assess the quality of credit risks. Setting and following new standards required sophisticated skills in gathering credit information, underwriting credits, perfecting collateral, and collecting delinquent loans. Only some of the banks—and fewer thrifts—were able to build those skills. Indeed, many thrifts that had been handed a blank check in 1982 to underwrite credit with government-guaranteed funds had never had a credit culture of any kind before.

In the best, most highly skilled commercial banks, more aggressive credits were underwritten with only minimal increases in problem credits and loan write-offs, although these credits are only now being tested by a recession. In less-skilled commercial banks, on the other hand, bad credits were often accepted without real understanding of the risks. The hungriest and least prudent institutions accepted borrowers whose financial condition was so risky that they should have been raising equity instead. In the worst thrifts, there was not only a lack of skill but also fraud and malfeasance as well.

The result was that low-quality borrowers were able to borrow at rates nearly the same as the good credits were paying. McKinsey's research supports this point and demonstrates that, overall, the commercial banking industry clearly has not been able to charge borrowers for the risk it is taking. For high-risk debt, returns are actually negative if one estimates loan losses accurately. The industry underwrote uneconomic credit risk throughout the decade. Risk and return had come unglued.

In effect, the government was subsiding massive risk-taking. Weak borrowers found weak lenders. This government subsidy also hurt the profitability and the health of the stronger thrifts and commercial banks. Well-run lenders were, and continue to be, deprived of the profits they should have earned on lending because their competitors would lend to nearly anyone. Well-run strong depositories were, and continue to be, deprived of the profits they should have earned on deposit-taking because they have had to compete against weaker institutions overpaying for deposits. In turn, this profit pressure caused otherwise prudent lenders to take on more and more risk. Over time, the number of banks taking excessive credit risk grew and grew.

In Texas, for example, banks followed S&Ls over the cliff. Only one Texas commercial bank of over $1 billion in size, Cullen-Frost of San Antonio, was able to survive without outside assistance; that is, Texas Commerce was assisted by Chemical and the others, such as First Republic, First Houston, and most of the banks owned by M Corp. were acquired by other banks with assistance from the FDIC.

At the time, many thought it was just a Texas problem. Today, the Northeast, mid-Atlantic, and parts of the Southeast seem headed down the same track. Even California is showing signs of weakness. In fact, it is only now that we are beginning to realize that our system of extending credit through banks is totally breaking down. In the next chapter, we will examine the particular kinds of loans that are causing the greatest problems. In this chapter, though, we will examine the economic dynamics of the problem.

We should be very concerned about the domestic credit system, which is being destroyed gradually by the giant credit market anomaly just described. The fundamental problem is in the system itself. Unless there are changes in regulation, and in the social contract on which that system is based, many banks and thrifts will suffer more and more as time goes on. And as time passes, more and more of that suffering will be borne by the citizens of this country just as other breakdowns in the credit system have affected the general public throughout the history of banking.

The fundamental problem is an economic one. Banks are now relying far too heavily on credit risk–intensive lending for their profits. In 1980 two-thirds of the industry's net interest income came from core deposits. In 1989 only 45 percent came from core deposits. In 1980 less than one-sixth of the industry's profits were represented by the margins earned on high-risk commercial real estate lending. In 1989 nearly half of the industry's profits came by the margin earned on commercial real estate loans and highly leveraged transactions.

Capital

You may well ask, where have the bank regulators been during all the carnage?

The bank regulators are, and have been, worried about the commercial banking system throughout the 1980s. The U.S. commercial bank regulators, the Federal Reserve, the FDIC, and the Comptroller of the Currency are, and have been, doing everything that they can *with their existing policy tools* to protect the system. They are vigorously auditing commercial banks, stopping unsound lending practices where they find them, forcing the restructuring of banks where that option has the lowest cost to the federal deposit insurance fund, and so forth. Indeed, by most measures, they are doing a remarkably effective job in making the traditional system work as best it can under very difficult circumstances. *But regulators do not make loans.* Few of us would want the government to determine, loan-by-loan, who gets credit and who does not. Instead, regulators rely on several layers of coverage that shield depositors from credit losses, even if they are unsuccessful in stopping unsound lending practices.

First, a loan that is recognized as uncollectible is "charged-off" against reserves. If reserves are felt to be insufficient to cover all losses, they are raised by increasing the loan loss provision. This action reduces earnings. If earnings are insufficient, then the necessary increases in the provision create losses. This is the reason why regulators are particularly fond of requiring banks to have a lot of capital. Well-capitalized banks can absorb unexpected losses. In theory, bank regulators can sleep well at night without having to second-guess individual credit decisions, provided the banks they are regulating are well-capitalized relative to the risks they are taking. In practice, loan losses can quickly destroy capital.

Indeed, if loan losses persist for years, or are truly gigantic, the institution eventually runs out of capital and becomes insolvent. Over the last decade, regulators have closed or restructured over 1,245 banks, including very large banks such as Continental Illinois and First Republic. In closing or restructuring these institutions, federal deposit insurance reserves are used to absorb the losses. These reserves are supposed to be a last layer of protection for the depositors who have put their finds in such institutions. However, in the wake of the savings and loan bailout, it is clear that the U.S. government, and the taxpayer, ultimately stand behind the insurance funds. Neither is particularly pleased with having to backstop these alleged funds of last resort. As will be described later in the book, I am hopeful that if we act quickly, we can avoid a taxpayer bailout of the commercial banking business.

The primary policy tool that regulators have traditionally relied on is to seek more and more equity capital. Over the last decade, they have pushed, consistently, for more and more capital to offset the increased risks they have seen the industry taking. Much effort has been invested in trying to improve the regulatory framework for establishing capital adequacy targets. Our bank regulators, led by the Federal Reserve with counterparts in other countries, have proposed a set of capital adequacy guidelines aimed at raising the worldwide level of required bank capital by 1992 and adjusting those guidelines for risk. The objective of those proposals is to move toward common standards worldwide and a safer global credit system.

This capital adequacy proposal is the single most important regulatory response to the breakdown of the credit system.

But like most recent regulation, it misses the point. This overreliance on capital regulation is an insufficient and even dangerous response to the problems facing the industry. In fact, the proposed revisions have most of the same flaws that our current capital regulations have.

First of all, it is not clear that many of the better banks, even with the catastrophic credit losses facing the industry today, are undercapitalized. Commercial bank regulators have historically required U.S. commercial banks to keep a combination of loan loss reserves and equity capital of roughly 6 percent of assets. In practice, the target number is closer to 7 percent. The capital guideline is a rule-of-thumb approximation of the capital needed for the "average" loan and the "average" bank. This single pool of capital is supposed to provide cross-subsidized protection against *all* risks. First, it includes specific "reserves" for credit losses from specific loans. Second, it includes very substantial equity capital to protect against other, unspecified risks, including interest rate risk and prepayment risk. Finally, it allows for extra reserves to protect depositors against inadequate diversification of credit risk. Regulators believe most banks are too small, serve too narrow a range of customers, or are too geographically concentrated to have safely diversified portfolios, and this causes them to want more capital.

This level of capital would seem to be more than enough, in aggregate, to cover loan losses, since historically most banks have had, until recently, very low levels of charge-offs. However, the rate of loan charge-offs to loans has been rising rapidly. It has grown from 0.16 percent of loans in 1960, to 0.36 percent of loans in 1980, and to over 1.25 percent of loans today.

And in fact, despite the growth of loan write-offs, the industry could still cover them if *all* loan loss reserves and equity capital were available to absorb all its expected losses. In 1990 we estimate that the commercial banks in this country held roughly $52 billion in loan loss reserves and $218 billion in equity capital. They charged-off an estimated $30 billion, thus the total protection was about nine times the charge-offs—*if* all this protection were available to absorb losses.

But the capital and reserves of the strongest banks are not available to absorb and losses of the weakest. A tragic flaw of the new guidelines is that they, like the existing regulations, implicitly assume that all banks are the same. This assumption is clearly invalid; in fact, the evidence is that competition is causing banks to become more divergent. The weakest banks and thrifts obviously need far more capital to protect the deposit insurance funds from loss, but the strongest banks are overcapitalized even now relative to the risks they are taking.

A second major flaw is that the proposed new guidelines make no provision for matching capital requirements to differences in loan quality. Remember, shoddy lending practices have been the downfall of our struggling banks so far. Under the new capital guidelines to be met by January 1, 1992, all loans are to have the same capital requirements, whether the borrower is a triple-A company or a potential bankrupt. Under these guidelines, banks still earn such low spreads on high-quality, floating rate loans that they will be unable to justify the capital needed to book the business. Instead, because the capital requirements for both high- and low-risk loans will be the same, banks with earnings difficulties will continue to be motivated to book high-risk credits.

When asked about the illogic of requiring uniform capital guidelines for highly differentiated categories of loans or for institutions with highly differentiated exposures to risks, regulators reply that a more differentiated system would "be unworkably complex." They do not believe that the government, through capital guidelines, should alter how credit flows to different sectors of the economy. And they are right. It is analogous to government-set price controls that are antithetical to competition. In a capitalist economy price controls always break down. They become too complex to administer, and they force supply and demand imbalances, which adjust through evasion in black markets. But the proposed combinations of capital guidelines and competition will further destroy the industry, forcing high-quality credit (for which the capital guidelines are too high) to bypass the industry, while attracting low-quality credit (for which the capital guidelines are too low) to the industry.

Perhaps the most important flaw with the overreliance on capital regulation is that the laws of economics will not cooperate. Wanting more capital is not enough. Where will banks that need capital find it—lying in the street? Without satisfactory earnings, banks can neither grow the capital they need through retained earnings nor raise capital by issuing new stock.

Capital is not free. Anyone who provides capital expects to earn a satisfactory return on it. However, as pointed out in this chapter, banks are already struggling to earn a satisfactory return on the capital already invested in the business. Given the already great difficulties to adding value, where will the profits come from?

Let me illustrate the point. In early 1989 before the stock market got so concerned about the banking industry that it became virtually impossible for even the best banks to raise new equity, it took a return on equity of roughly 15 percent to justify a market value of a share of common stock that was equal to the book accounting value of the stock. That is, if the book value of a single share of bank common stock was $10, the bank had to earn $1.50 per share to get the stock trading in the marketplace at that book value. Banks that earned higher returns had market values at a premium-to-book value and banks earning a lower return had market values at a discount-to-book value. As pointed out earlier, the average bank earned returns on equity well below this level in 1989.

If you can earn a sufficient return on capital to get the market value of your stock equal to your book value, then you can issue new stock without diluting your existing shareholders, provided you have sufficient opportunities to invest that capital in businesses that are at least as attractive as your current business.

If, as some have proposed, you simply raise equity requirements to provide more equity cushion for regulators, you dramatically increase the amount of profits needed to maintain
your return on equity. For example, with $5 of equity per $100
of assets you need a pre-tax profit of 0.93 percent to earn a
return on equity of 15 percent assuming a 34 percent tax rate.
With $7 of equity, you need a pre-tax profit of 1.51 percent.
With $10 of equity, 2.36 percent is needed. Yet in 1989 the av-
erage bank earned only 0.49 percent of assets.

The problem is that it is nonsensical to talk about how much
capital a bank needs without talking about what risk-taking the
capital is supposed to support. It makes no sense to use the
same pool of capital to support low-risk core banking functions
(lending to individuals, small businesses, or mid-size companies) with high-risk lending (LDC debt, construction loans on
real estate, or leveraged buyouts). The historic equity requirements for the industry are more than are needed to support
core banking functions. However, they are far too low for absorbing the credit risks in high-risk lending. How can you require the same capital requirements for a conservatively run
bank that sticks to the core banking business and a bank with
a large portfolio of high-risk assets? Moreover, if you increase
the capital requirements for everyone, then you simply make
it more difficult for well-run banks engaged in core banking
functions to compete against non-banks.

As we will see later in this book, trying to force banks to raise
more capital when they lack fundamental earnings strength
only causes them to try to earn it by taking even greater risks.
Indeed, many of the large banks in the most trouble as 1990
came to a close were still aggressively expanding their high-risk
lending activities as late as 1988 and 1989 because such lending was supposed to produce the profits needed to meet 1992
capital guidelines. Unfortunately, as we will see, they booked
far more risk than profits. Moreover, as we will see later, en-
forcing capital requirements for institutions with no access to
more capital is contributing to the credit crunch that is causing
our entire economy to deteriorate.

The truth is that raising capital requirements is a destructive blind alley unless other changes are made in the structure of the industry. We must make changes that affect the fundamental economics of banking. Unless we can make it possible for well-run banks to earn healthy profits, we will not cure the problem. Recapitalizing banks is an important part of the answer; however, we will only get adequate capital when the industry's profit problems are cured.

6

Bad Lending

People knowing bankers who have gotten their institutions into trouble are often incredulous when the loan problems are first announced. How could such intelligent bankers, prime products of the conservative credit culture of the 1960s and 1970s, such outspoken foes of lax lending, wind up with such bad portfolios of credit?

Part of the explanation is that these men, despite their training, were simply unprepared for the 1980s. An analogy to the outbreak of World War I is useful. In 1914, thirty-five years had elapsed since the last significant European war, the Franco-Prussian War of 1879. Nearly 100 years had passed since the last pan-European conflict, the Napoleonic wars. Over that peaceful period, generations of politicians and military leaders had come and gone whose only knowledge of battle was from history books. They had lost their terror of war and had become overconfident in their own, untested abilities. When war came, all participants took their *naïveté* into battle.

Similarly, going into the 1980s, bankers had forty years of remarkably low credit losses. By the late 1970s, the last of the bankers who were lenders during the Depression had retired and a generation of managers, who chafed under the old conservative credit culture, came into power. They were not sufficiently terrified of loan losses and when earnings pressures developed, they convinced themselves that they were smart enough to avoid the bad credits while booking only the loans where the returns were high relative to the credit risks taken. They were overconfident of their own abilities.

Another part of the explanation is that these same bankers paid too much attention to the underwriting of individual loans and too little attention to the overall character of their developing credit portfolios. They set precedent and credit policy based on conservatively underwritten transactions and yet continued making loans when terms and conditions eroded. But even then, an individual banker might have been all right if he or she had been the only one who was taking more risk.

Instead, banks competed with one another to give ever more generous terms and conditions. This gets to the fundamental problem; too many competitors liberalized their credit policies simultaneously in response to market forces. And not only did lenders lose their fear of credit losses, many borrowers lost their fear of defaulting on their debt. Banks provided borrowers with credit that was actually exposed to equity-sized risks. Borrowers therefore raised too much debt and not enough equity.

The engine of this systemic problem is made of gross distortions in the competitive environment, what I call "market anomalies." Some were created by the government and some created by the private sector. All drove unsound lending. Otherwise healthy competitive forces turned destructive because of these imperfections in the market. This is the reason why almost all bank credit problems today have been concentrated in three credit categories, each representing a credit anomaly: (1) loans to developing countries (representing roughly $60 billion still on the books of U.S. banks); (2) highly leveraged loans to commercial corporations (representing over $190 billion of loans on the books of U.S. banks); and (3) commercial real estate loans (representing over $385 billion of loans on the books of U.S. banks).

What these loans have in common is that they offered high yields, were easy for banks to originate, and had had long histories of low loan losses. Of course, these sparse loan losses were accomplished by having conservative lending standards.

Lenders in search of higher earnings, however, could convince themselves that they would be able to earn high returns by taking on these risky categories. Meanwhile, the borrowers of these kinds of loans all proved to have no fear of borrowing. What's worse, they proved to have an insatiable appetite for credit.

Let us look, consequently, at *how* the combination of competitive forces and market anomalies transformed the banking industry and *why* banks wound up with portfolios full of a deadly combination of loans to developing countries, to over-leveraged companies, and to commercial real estate developers.

LDC Debt

Led by the New York money center banks, U.S. and foreign banks lent heavily to developing countries from the mid-1970s to the early 1980s. During the late 1980s, it became apparent that much of this debt was not serviceable by the borrowing countries. U.S. banks alone have reserved over $20 billion to cover anticipated losses from this debt. Much of this debt, as now traded in secondary markets, is now selling at about 30 percent of face value. In comparison, most U.S. banks still carry this debt on their books at about 60 percent of face value meaning the market is expecting that further billions of dollars of reserves will be needed on this debt. To understand how this disaster could happen, a bit of history is in order.

During the 1950s and 1960s, under the watchful eye of the International Monetary Fund (IMF) and the World Bank, developing countries borrowed relatively little, at least partly because no one would lend to them. What they did borrow, they carefully repaid because the discipline of the international monetary system at the time enforced prudence. However, the oil shock of 1973 had multiple impacts on developing countries. To producers, like Mexico, Venezuela, and Nigeria, it brought them a huge surge in income and an unsustainable appetite for spending. To others, such as Brazil and the Philippines, it brought huge increases in the cash costs of oil imports, which caused massive current account trade deficits.

But perhaps more importantly, the oil shock added enormous liquidity to the international banking system. The OPEC nations, particularly the Middle Eastern nations, preferred to invest their new-found wealth in floating rate Eurodollar deposits and placements. The banks, in turn, found a willing set of borrowers—the developing nations of the world, who greatly preferred playing eager bankers against each other to dealing with the less-generous IMF and World Bank. International bankers of the day believed that countries could not go bankrupt. This is literally true, since there is no bankruptcy process for countries. What bankers forgot was that countries can default on their debt—and they did—in droves.

In the late 1970s, syndicated bank loans flowed into the developing countries. Some of the money was used to pay for vital imports, including oil, and some was productively invested. Some went into poorly conceived showcase projects with little economic merit; much was simply lost to fraud and graft, leaving the developing countries as "flight capital" headed for Switzerland, London, New York, and other locations to then be reinvested in private banking deposits and other international assets like Eurobonds.

Federal Reserve Chairman Arthur Burns, in 1977, summarized the situation before the House Banking Committee. He was not overly worried by bank lending to developing countries:

> The sharp increase of oil prices, to say nothing of the worldwide recession, caused extensive dislocations in the world economy; but much more serious difficulties would have occurred if commercial banks here and elsewhere had not acted as they did. There simply was no official mechanism in place in 1974 that could have coped with recycling of funds on the vast scale that then became necessary. The supportive role that American and other commercial banks played in this situation thus prevented financial strains from culminating dangerously, and this role continues even now. Certainly, our export trade and the general economy have been helped—and are being helped—by banking's role in international lending.
>
> This is not to say there have been no excesses or that expansion of international lending by American banks can continue at an undiminished pace. Even though losses on foreign loans have been small—indeed, relatively smaller than on domestic loans—the Federal Reserve Board is concerned about the enlarged risk exposure of our banks . . . a slowing must occur—to rates of growth, generally, that are consonant with expansion of the debt-servicing capabilities of individual borrowing countries. Such slowing, it should be appreciated, may well involve some problems for the international economy, since the structural payments imbalances that have occasioned such heavy bank lending to foreign countries are not going

to disappear rapidly. The inference is clear that a strong cooperative effort is more than ever necessary—involving, among others,
official international agencies, the Group of Ten countries, OPEC,
the non-oil LDCs, and the private banks. Unless we succeed in
devising sound financial alternatives, serious strains in the world
economy may develop.

At the time, the nation's leading money center banks were
being hit hard by the shrinking profits from loans to high-
quality borrowers, particularly multinationals. These high-
grade corporations were discovering that they could take advantage of the expanded liquidity in the world's markets,
through securities like commercial paper and Eurobonds and
through heightened competition among banks, to be able to
raise money well below the oligopolistic rates then being
charged. The profitability of the leading money center banks
was being deeply hurt given that these multinational corporations were by far and away their most profitable customers.
Indeed, the U.S. money center banks were losing their franchise.

To these banks, the opportunity to lend to developing countries seemed a gift from God. The fees for syndicating the credits to other banks and the spreads earned on the portions they
retained were very large relative to the out-of-pocket costs of
making the loans, for example a loan officer's time. The fees
on syndicating a billion dollars of credit were $20 million or
more. In addition, the 2 percent loan spread on retaining 20
percent of the billion dollars (that is, $200 million) in your own
portfolio could add another $4 million a year to income. Lead-
ing money center banks were originating over $10 billion of
developing countries' debt a year at the time! Consider what
one leading international banker told me in the late 1970s. "It's
like magic. All I have to do is tell my country managers what
earnings I want from them and the profits come in. I give them
a budget and they meet it."

The willingness of developing countries to borrow was unlimited. And competition drove bankers to offer ever more generous borrowing terms. Like sovereigns throughout history,

developing countries were more than willing to borrow all the money offered to them, particularly if it kept their constituents from having to face harsh economic realities. In theory, the debt of nations should have low risks since governments have the power to tax their entire economy to pay interest and principal. The problem is, like any other debtor, their ability to service debt payments is only proportionate to their nation's income.

But the LDCs did not need debt, they needed equity. Many of the developing countries, particularly the Latin American and African countries, have long resisted foreign ownership of many of their businesses. They have placed massive barriers to direct equity investment by outside investors. They have often restricted foreigners to holding only minority positions of the stock. Or they have often preferred for the nation itself to own key industries. The result has too often been that the developing countries' scarce capital has been inefficiently invested in industries and development projects by unskilled amateurs or in many cases by people who found ways to funnel huge sums into their own pockets. The mismanaged result has often been businesses that require continued subsidies rather than industries that contribute tax revenues. The developing countries would have been far better off allowing highly skilled foreign companies to own major businesses or to use local businesses as captive producers and to then tax the wages and profits of the thriving enterprises. The contrast between the prosperous Southeast Asian nations, which have pursued a policy of working with foreign companies, and many of the Latin American countries, which have often considered foreign companies as the enemy, is stark.

The truth was that the banking system was playing a role it should not have been playing. The recycling of deposits was papering over massive changes in economic flows. If the developed countries of the world, for political reasons, wanted to help the less-developed countries in Latin America and Africa to adjust to economic shocks, they should have done so through direct means by channeling funds through the IMF and the World Bank and by putting pressure on the developing countries to open up their economies for equity investment. But doing so would have meant that both the developed countries and the developing countries would have had to face up to unpleasant political and economic realities. It was much easier to have bankers lend money. Rather than constraining bankers through the regulatory process, the U.S. government actively encouraged its bankers to lend. It other words, the U.S. government helped create the market anomaly.

The official view of the government was that neither the banks nor the developing countries were at risk. For example, Anthony Salomon, Secretary for Monetary Affairs of the Treasury, testified to the Senate Foreign Relations Committee in 1977: "The question has been raised as to whether this rapid and unprecedented enlargement of lending activity and debt has reached a danger point for the monetary system, either in the sense that large numbers of countries have borrowed beyond their capacity to service debt or in the sense that our banks and other institutions are overextended. It is our considered judgment that the system as a whole is not in any such position of imminent danger, either as a result of excessive borrowing by large numbers of debtor nations or as a result of our financial institutions from being overstretched." It is no wonder that many money center banks were not worried. They were being encouraged by their government and told that they were not taking excessive risk.

Then a second oil shock hit in 1979, driving up inflation worldwide. During the next couple of years the Federal Reserve, under Paul Volcker's leadership, sought to bring inflation under control. But, as explained in Chapter 3, the Federal Reserve found that it could not really tighten credit, as it had done historically, given the globalization of the world's financial markets. It could only make it more expensive. The dollar London interbank borrowing rate (LIBOR) peaked at over 21 percent and the desired effect was reached; inflation psychology in the United States was broken as the harsh 1981 to 1982 recession idled plants not just in the United States but around the world.

But the LDCs were in deep trouble. All the money they had borrowed in the late 1970s was at floating rates, and with LI-BOR at 21 percent, their debt service burden was nearly tripled. In 1981 the fifteen most significant developing country borrowers, with debt outstanding of $334 billion, found their annual interest payments rising to $43.8 billion as their exports plummeted because of the U.S. recession and the strong dollar. By 1982 bankers who had been tripping over each other a few years earlier to lend LDCs money had completely lost their appetite for new debt. The banks then began a process of essentially lending the LDCs the money they needed to continue paying interest. This, of course, just added to the debt burden.

During this critical juncture, banks were actively encouraged by the U.S. government to keep lending money. Many commercial bankers received "off-the-record" personal encouragement from the Federal Reserve to "play along" with debt restructuring programs. One of them related his conversation with one of the Governors of the Federal Reserve system. The Governor asked the banker to go along with the rest of the syndicate in lending more money to a particular developing country. The banker resisted but finally asked for the request in writing. The request was, of course, refused. The banker eventually went along. A few years later, his institution sold the debt off—at 50 cents on the dollar.

In 1983 Paul Volcker, then Chairman of the Federal Reserve Board, told the American Bankers Association, in Hawaii, that in effect we have a strong safety net under our own banking system, as do other leading nations. He also said that, if need be, the rules would change to protect the banks.

But the underlying problem was a cash flow problem. When they borrowed in the late 1970s, the LDCs were expecting to pay the LIBOR prevailing at that time, over the life of the loan. When interest rates rose between 1978 and 1982, the additional interest payments required totaled $130 billion. This excess interest was effectively capitalized. The interest on *this* interest, between 1983 and 1986, totaled another $54 billion. So by the end of 1986, some $184 billion of LDC debt represented excess interest from the 1978 to 1982 period.

The total debt to the fifteen most important LDC borrowers went from $334 billion in 1981 to $468 billion at the end of 1986; all of this debt increase represented involuntary lending by the world's banks, who were terrified of letting the countries default. But everyone in the world knew that much of the debt was bad. During the mid-1980s, LDCs were further hurt by developments in the world's commodity markets. The LDCs' primary exports are commodities, and most of them stepped up production in order to get income to help service the debt. This increase in the supply of commodities, when combined with the reduction in demand for commodities because of the recession induced by the high interest rates, led to a commodity glut and to dramatically reduced commodity prices. This helped to make a bad situation far worse. Even the oil-producing LDCs found the income from plummeting oil prices insufficient to cover their obligations.

The strongest banks, with the deepest reserves (the Germans, the Swiss, and the Japanese), began adding loss reserves almost immediately, in 1983, 1984, and 1985. But the world's other banks resisted. Finally, after Brazil suspended interest payments in early 1987, Citibank led the U.S. banking industry into setting aside huge reserves to cover about 30 percent of the LDC debt they held. By year-end 1987 the U.S. banking industry reserved some $14.4 billion. The remainder of the world's banks (the U.K. banks, the Canadians, and others) began making similar reserves of 30 percent or more. Since that time there have been what seems to be an unending stream of debt-rescheduling. In 1989 the money center banks went through yet another round of setting up reserves.

Of course, reserving for a portion of the debt does not mean that the LDC debt crisis is by any means over. The economies of the developing countries are still stagnating. Not only do they lack the infrastructure of plants, equipment, or managers, but their economies need to grow. They now find themselves starved for capital. Since 1982, the Latin American countries alone have paid out over $250 billion in interest, but their indebtedness grew by over $50 billion. What is perhaps worst of all is that the LDCs continue to lose local professionals, critical in building their economies, to better paying jobs in the developed world. The boom times of the late 1970s are long forgotten, and the potential for social unrest, always high in developing countries, is now even higher.

The LDC debt mess seems more and more intractable with each year. Many of the LDCs will never pay off their debt. Indeed, the debt overhang blocks their opportunities to grow their way out of their problems. The international agencies cannot act without funding from the developed countries. International leadership is needed but the nation that has always played that role, the United States, can't take the lead because it can no longer afford to contribute the funding implied by that leadership.

The LDC debt problem, like the savings and loan crisis, shows how profound destruction results when governments distort market forces by encouraging banks to lend money to particular kinds of borrowers, all in the name of some political agenda. The market forces were distorted because U.S. bankers were led to believe that their nation would stand behind them and help out if the developed countries got into trouble. A market anomaly was created because the bankers thought they could earn high returns without taking risk. They were wrong. At the end of the day, the U.S. government walked away from this implicit commitment. As a result, the banks wound up with massive losses. Just like the S&L crisis, there is plenty of blame to go around. The banks, the governments of the developed nations, and the governments of the developing nations all share responsibility. Well-intentioned people distorted market forces with destructive, unintended consequences.

Highly Leveraged Transactions

Of the three troublesome categories of lending described in this chapter, highly leveraged transactions represent the least worrisome problem for U.S. banks today. Indeed, if banks did not have bad credit portfolios of developing country debt and commercial real estate debt, most banks could easily absorb their exposures to highly leveraged transactions. Moreover, unlike the other two categories, it is still too early to say just how bad these kinds of loans may prove to be. Nevertheless, for some banks, highly leveraged transactions may prove to be the straw that breaks the camel's back.

Highly leveraged transaction lending embraces the funding of leveraged buyouts, leveraged corporate recapitalizations and restructurings, and leveraged mergers and acquisitions. While in their early development, these forms of finance were all distinct; the differences tended to blur together by the late 1980s. What they all have in common is that they all involve massive substitutions of debt for equity in the financing of a company.

Leveraged buyout lending was pioneered in the 1970s and early 1980s by speciality firms such as Kohlberg, Kravis and Roberts (KKR); Forstmann Little and Company; and Gibbons, Green, von Amerongen. Originally, leveraged buyouts were exclusively financed by commercial banks. The number of leveraged buyout transactions grew from thirteen a year, representing a value of $1.6 billion in 1981 to an average of over 300 a year in the peak years of 1986 through early 1989. In 1989 deals with a total value of $66 billion were completed. The use of the technique peaked with the completion in 1989 of the $26 billion RJR transaction.

Highly leveraged transaction lending also includes the takeover and restructuring of public companies either on a friendly or an unfriendly basis. For example, Phillip Morris took over Kraft in a highly leveraged transaction that started unfriendly. The highly leveraged Time-Warner merger was formed in a friendly transaction.

At the heart of all these transactions was the ability to take a company that was worth one price one day, and through the magic of financial restructuring, make it suddenly worth much much more on the next. For example, the market value of a share of RJR stock went from $49.75 on June 1, 1988 to $91.75 on December 1, 1988: not from any change in the outlook for the fundamental business, but from the eruption of a bidding war over the opportunity to buy and restructure the company. Similarly, the market value of a share of Kraft went from $59.50 to $102.00 in just twelve days as it was "put in play."

The ability to "change" the value of a company is a classic market anomaly. In a "perfect" market, such changes in value should not be possible. In the real world, they clearly happen all the time. Underlying this financial magic are four distinct factors. The first is an accounting anomaly: the distortion in information flows to stockholders caused by overreliance on historical accounting companies. The second is a tax anomaly: the U.S. tax code biases the financing of a company with debt rather than equity because interest on debt is deductible and dividends on stock are not. The third factor is the ability to make fundamental improvements in the underlying business when control of the company changes. In fact, the tragedy of the excesses in highly leveraged lending is that the backlash against these excesses has forestalled, at least for the time being, the otherwise healthy restructuring of poorly managed companies.

The fourth factor, the one that is directly related to the main points of this book, is the credit anomaly that was caused by the forces described in the preceding chapter. These forces made lenders inordinately willing to take equity-size risks in financing these transactions. However, in order to explain how this anomaly developed, I believe I need to first describe briefly the roles that the accounting anomaly, the tax anomaly, and fundamental improvements played in the process.

By the accounting anomaly, I am referring to the flaws in valuing companies based on generally accepted accounting conventions. Accounting conventions often dramatically misrepresent the value of companies. Generally accepted accounting conventions rely on historical cost accounting to value assets. This distorts the value of many assets, particularly the oldest assets. After the high inflation of the 1970s, many physical assets (such as plants or buildings) were accounted for at a value too low, relative to the replacement cost of those assets. More importantly, historical cost accounting often understated the value of an asset in relation to the cash that can be generated by those assets.

For example, an asset with a historical cost of $100 that will produce $20 of cash per year for twenty years is obviously worth more than an asset with a historical value of $100 that will produce $5 of cash per year for ten years. Yet both these assets have the same historical accounting value. During the 1960s business schools developed techniques to estimate the present value of future cash flows, known as net present value analysis, but these techniques have yet to be reflected in accounting valuation. The pioneers of leveraged buyout and corporate restructuring transactions discovered that historical cost accounting woefully undervalued the equity of companies with strong and predictable cash flows.

One of the major reasons why the net present value of cash flows outstripped the historical value of the assets was the U.S. tax code, which allows interest expenses to be deducted from taxes but double taxes equity. This is the tax anomaly. Let me illustrate this point with a hypothetical example. Assume a company, let's call it the Sleepy Company, makes $100 million in cash earnings before interest and taxes and has a total stock market value of $700 million. Assume that this $700 million was also equal to the book equity value of the company. With today's federal income tax rate on corporate earnings of 34 percent, Sleepy Co.'s after-tax earnings of the company would be $16 million or a return on equity of 9.4 percent. If all of this cash was paid out to shareholders as a dividend, it would be taxed again without benefit to the company or to shareholders.

Assume, however, a new owner came in and bought out the existing shareholders for $800 million (that is, $100 million premium). He provides $100 million of his own money and has the company itself borrow $700 million at 10 percent. In this case, the company's pre-tax earnings would fall to $30 million pre-tax after paying $70 million in interest expense or $20 million after tax on his $100 million of equity. The new owner, though, with a 20 percent return on equity, would be earning over twice as much, after tax, on every dollar of equity invested as the previous owners were—just because interest is a deductible expense, while dividends are not.

However, leveraged transactions were often based on more than just financial finagling. In the postwar era, many companies had been managed more to benefit management than maximize value for shareholders. In particular, many companies had been put together through acquisitions that made no economic sense. Other companies had been managed far too conservatively. Despite the deductibility of interest, many companies with strong cash flows retained almost all of their earnings and borrowed little or no money. This led them to have relatively low returns on equity. Other companies had undervalued assets such as real estate or mineral rights acquired in the 1950s, which represented nonproductive investment of capital.

To see how an entrepreneur could take advantage of these factors, let's return to the Sleepy Company example. If the entreprenuer taking over the Sleepy Company was able to sell off a break-even subsidiary of Sleepy to another company, which could make better use of the assets, for $100 million net of taxes, and if he could sell some land Sleepy Co. had bought in the 1950s for a $100-million gain, net of taxes, he could then repay $200 million of the $700 million in debt he had used to acquire the company. In this case, these transactions would raise the company's pre-tax earnings to $50 million pre-tax or $33 million after tax, plus increasing his equity stake from $100 million to $300 million. In other words, the new owner would now be earning 33 percent on each dollar of his original investment, plus would be $200 million richer just by redeploying the company's invested capital.

There were also real opportunities to make operating improvements in the business. One of the secrets of the success of leveraged buyouts has been the conversion of existing managers into owners. All of a sudden, this converts managers into capitalists who, almost overnight, discover a higher will to manage. Long-neglected cost restructuring opportunities are often soon discovered when completing the transaction.

The leverage from such operating improvements and growth is enormous. For instance, in the Sleepy Company example, improving the pre-tax cash flow by $50 million, in combination with the asset sales just discussed, could increase the company's pre-tax earnings back up to the $100-million-per-year level despite having incurred all the costs of buying the original company's shareholders out. At this point, the new owners might well consider selling the company back to the public and pocketing their gains. If, for example, they could sell the company for the same $800 million they paid, they would have made an eight-fold return on their $100-million investment in just a few years. And in practice, many transactions did result in these kinds of return to equity holders. It is easy to see why so many people were so interested in leveraged buyout (LBO) and corporate takeovers during the 1980s. The opportunities were there to make personal fortunes in the hundreds of millions of dollars.

The opportunities were also there for bankers to make fortunes. Thus was born the LBO credit anomaly.

Much of the debt for LBOs came from banks. When these transactions were first done, in the late 1970s and early 1980s, banks were quite skeptical about financing them. Only a few banks would finance them. Indeed, one of the primary lenders was a non-bank, the General Electric Credit Corporation (now called the General Electric Capital Corporation). In these early days, the debt was usually secured by the company's accounts receivables and inventory. In addition, venture capitalists and finance companies began providing additional financing in the form of subordinated debt and preferred stock.

For example, the largest leveraged buyout in 1982 was the Signode company, a manufacturing company that pre-buyout had a capitalization of $374 million. It was bought out at 1.3 times the accounting book value for $485 million. Pre-buyout, the capital structure was 88 percent equity. Post-buyout it flip-flopped to 88 percent debt with common equity capital equal to 4.5 percent of the transaction and preferred stock equal to 7.5 percent. Sixteen percent of the transaction was financed with subordinated notes and the remaining 72 percent was financed with bank debt.

At the time, the banks involved were very careful in their credit underwriting of these types of transactions, carefully securing themselves and leaving a fat cash flow cushion in case the economy did not fully recover from the recession. The companies involved were generally worth less than $100 million. They were primarily manufacturing companies, and the price being paid was a small multiple to the S&P 500 and to the companies' book value: usually from 1.3 to 1.5. They had stable cash flows. The typical purchase price was only six times earnings before interest and taxes, which meant that only 60 percent to 70 percent of the company's cash flow was needed to service the company's debt burden.

Like all market anomalies, this one was fully exploited. Bigger and bigger companies were taken through the process. Sellers of the equity began to realize how much their company was worth in buyout and began to hold out for higher and higher sums. Takeovers of large, public companies were done with bank debt and junk bonds in intricate combinations.

Just as with the LDC debt, a number of large commercial banks, both money centers and some regionals, began to pursue these transactions as a major source of revenue to sustain their continued loss of profitable, large, creditworthy borrowers. Ironically, it was many of their best corporate customers who were going through these leveraged restructurings. Unless they were to finance them, they would lose the relationship forever. Moreover, the up-front fees, just like with LDC debt, were very large (1 percent to 2 percent of the transaction), as were the interest spreads on the loans (the interbank rate plus 1.5 percent to 2 percent).

If a banker was willing to take a good portion of the credit, much of the remainder could be syndicated to other banks. By the late 1980s, Japanese banks were particularly eager syndicated lenders. A few of the more conservative banks began dropping out of the market as terms and conditions continued to deteriorate.

However, for every participant dropping out, there were dozens of eager lenders and "junk" bond investors willing to replace them. Fed by the abundant credit, there was a boom in leveraged buyouts, leveraged restructurings, leveraged recapitalizations, and leveraged mergers and acquisitions. Bidding groups, and their closely allied banking syndicates, were formed to win transactions. The private sale of the past was replaced by the public auction.

At some point, probably around 1987, banks began pushing clearly beyond prudent levels and began taking equity rather than lending risk. The forces at work driving banks to take excessive credit risk, as described in Chapter 5, were in full swing.

While the stock market crash of 1987 gave the market some pause, by 1988 the frenzy had returned and the market peaked. In 1988, we estimate some $67.9 billion was financed. Excluding the $26-billion RJR transaction, the average deals being made in 1988 were at earnings before interest and taxes multiples of 15.6 versus 6.1 in 1985. At the six-to-one multiples of 1985, the cost of financing the buyout transaction could be comfortably covered by the company's annual cash flows. In contrast, by 1988, the annual cost of financing the transaction significantly exceeded, by approximately

50 percent, the company's cash flows. In other words, substantial restructuring and improvements in operations were needed simply to get the transaction to break even. And if a recession or other misfortune hit, there was no room for error.

Although leveraged financial activity continued into 1989, it began to slow down as the banks that had been buying much of the syndicated debt, particularly the Japanese, began to look more closely at their portfolios. Moreover, by late 1989, it was becoming clear that many of the leveraged transactions done in 1987 and 1988 were in deep trouble. Meanwhile, the "junk" bond market collapsed at least in part because many of the S&Ls that had been working closely with Drexel Burnham were forced by their new Office of Thrift Supervision regulators to divest themselves of the "junk" bonds. With the final collapse of Drexel in early 1990, "junk" bonds lost all of their liquidity and prices collapsed. Since many deals had used both bank finance and "junk" bond finance, it was clear that the bank loans would have had a market value well below their book value if there had been any market in which to sell them.

At this point in time (early 1991), it is too early to see what the ultimate cost of this excessive risk-taking will be. In large measure, it depends on the strength of the overall economy and the strength of the underlying company's cash flows. However, early signs are that many of the highly leveraged credits financed in 1987 and 1988 are going to go bad.

It should be remembered, however, that in these leveraged transactions the banks were always the senior debtors. That is, the transactions were structured so that much of the financing was provided by preferred stock and subordinated debt holders who, in bankruptcy, get paid back after the banks. While this provides some comfort to some transactions, these subordinated creditors are not without power. Upon default on the payments due them, they can throw the transactions into bankruptcy, which can destroy much of the on-going concern value of the underlying companies and can force the banks to put their loans on non-accrual. This puts the banks in a dilemma because they have to either lend more money to the companies or give up some of their security, if they do not want to see the company go into bankruptcy.

Highly leveraged transaction debt is concentrated among relatively few of the nation's larger banks. The ten banks with the highest exposure to highly leveraged transactions had some $44.4 billion in exposure relative to their equity capital of $64.6 billion as of June 1990. It is probably a safe bet that at least half of these loans represent no real risk of loss since they are performing largely as planned (including most of the pre-1987 loans). Of the remaining half, even a worst case scenario would put losses at no greater than 20 percent of the principal amount. Thus only about $4.4 billion would be lost from these transactions or only about 7 percent of the combined primary capital of these institutions. There would seem, therefore, to be plenty of capital to absorb these losses, provided that they were the only problem loans these banks had. Unfortunately, many of the same banks are also heavily exposed to developing country debt. Even worse, as we are about to see, many of these same institutions also lent heavily to commercial real estate developers.

Commercial Real Estate

By far the most overwhelming credit problems facing the nation's banks are in commercial real estate. By commercial real estate debt, I'm referring to all real estate mortgage lending excluding loans on single family homes. It includes loans for office buildings, apartment buildings, hotels, shopping centers, large condominium projects, and so forth. Unlike the LDC debt, which has been significantly reserved against, or highly leveraged transaction lending, which would represent a relatively manageable problem if the rest of a bank's balance sheet was strong, commercial real estate loans could prove to be the undoing of the entire industry. It is not just another credit problem; it is *the* problem.

The direct loan exposure of the nation's banks to commercial real estate mortgage debt is a little over $385 billion. The actual exposure is considerably higher because much commercial real estate debt is made under committed lines of credit that the banks are obligated to make in order to complete the construction of buildings already started. In other words, even if banks stop making new commitments, old loans keep growing as existing commitments are drawn on. Banks also have made personal loans, often unsecured, to individuals, particularly real estate developers, based on the value of their commercial real estate holdings. Finally, mortgage debt on condominium developments is in reality commercial real estate debt even though banks often classify this debt as residential mortgage debt. Although precise numbers are not available, it is safe to estimate that U.S. banks have exposure to commercial real estate of over $450 billion or about twice the combined outstandings to developing countries and highly leveraged transactions combined.

Unlike developing country debt and highly leveraged transaction debt, commercial real estate debt is in the portfolios of banks of all sizes. Even banks with assets of $100 million or less have significant commercial real estate exposure. It was by far the fastest growing component of the loan portfolios of the commercial banking industry during the 1980s. Loans outstandings on commercial real estate grew by over 15.9 percent compounded from 1980 to 1990 as loans to businesses grew at only a 6.5 percent rate, despite the rapid growth in highly-leveraged transaction lending. Consequently, commercial real estate went from 10 percent of the industry's loan portfolio in 1980 to 18 percent in 1990.

When the Texas commercial banks took massive loan losses in their commercial real estate portfolios in 1986 through 1988, a prelude to their government-assisted restructuring, most people in the nation thought it to be a regional aberration. In 1989, New England banks began experiencing similar problems. Now, as the 1990s are starting, it is apparent that commercial real estate problems are spreading throughout the nation. Again, we must look to the past to understand the causes of this now pervasive problem.

Historically, commercial banks have taken very few losses on commercial real estate loans. From the late 1940s to 1970s, banks took almost no losses because of conservative loan underwriting standards. Before a well-run commercial bank would lend money on a commercial real estate project in the late 1960s, it insisted that borrowers meet several strict conditions. Before committing to finance an office building, the bank required that at least 90 percent of the building be pre-leased for at least twenty years. Moreover, the bank only committed to financing for less than 70 percent of the estimated value of the building when completed. This required the builder, in effect, to find equity financing from other sources. In addition, the bank required a commitment from a permanent lender, usually an insurance company, to take the bank out of the construction loan on completion of the project. Finally, the bank was careful to work only with reputable developers, and in order to ensure their good faith, the bank would require the developer, and often his wife, to personally guarantee the loan. This put the builder's entire equity behind the loan.

Developers were thus constrained by the limited availability of financing. Anyone who knows real estate developers recognizes that they are often in need of constraint. In a good market, developers can put together a building worth $100 million that costs only $70 million to construct. Hence, if they are highly skilled and lucky, they can develop a building, even with 70 percent financing, and not have to put up very much of their own capital. Their talent lies in finding the land on which to build, an architect to design the project, the contractors to construct the building, the tenants to occupy the building, and the finance to pay for it. Of these skills, finding the financing was the final part of the process, because banks historically would lend only to developers who had put everything else together first. Real estate, of course, is capital-intensive because it takes decades of income from the building to pay off the costs of construction. Therefore, finding the capital to build has always been the developer's perpetual challenge.

It is easy to see why a real estate developer would rather reverse the historic process and find the financing first. If the developer does so and can then complete the building, it is much easier to find tenants because they can be shown the actual building, rather than blueprints. Moreover, the developer's profits from constructing the building (that is, fees paid to cover overhead, profits from construction workers employed, and the like) are locked in, even if the project fails, provided the developer does not personally guarantee the debt. However, no one was silly enough to provide real estate developers with up-front financing, until there were REITs.

In the early 1970s developers found a non-bank source of finance that would provide them with all the money they could spend: real estate investment trusts (REITs). Investors gobbled up REITs, which financed both the construction and development of real estate. A development loan is one made to acquire and prepare land for construction. In a few short years, nearly $5 billion in equity was raised. The trusts then borrowed another $15.8 billion from banks. At the time, maintaining a financing ratio of three dollars of debt to one dollar of equity was thought to be very conservative. These REITs were willing to make loans to developers without all of the terms and conditions of banks (they did not require personal guarantees, they had few pre-leasing restrictions, and so on). New buildings flooded onto the market—particularly in the Southeast.

But by the mid-1970s the deadly combination of overbuilding, high interest rates, and the recession of 1974–75 brought real estate back to earth. Most of the construction and development REITs went into bankruptcy. Cushioned by the one dollar of equity for every three dollars of bank debt, banks who lent to REITs only suffered mildly. Some banks, particularly in the Southeast, wound up with problem real estate from their own real estate loans. However, the recovery from the recession in the late 1970s combined with resurgent inflation, which buoyed rents, revived the real estate market by decade's end. Few banks had significant problem commercial real estate loans by the end of the 1970s. Sadly, the banks did not learn that over-generous financing to real estate developers is bad business. Just a few years thereafter, the same mistake was made on a far more massive scale.

In the 1980s the nation went on a massive building boom that is only now ending. Fed by the easy availability of finance, it influenced every segment of the real estate industry. Office buildings, shopping centers, apartments, condominiums, hotels, and single family homes were all built at rates far more rapid than growth in either population or GNP.

As if this credit anomaly wasn't enough, another market anomaly, a tax anomaly, was created by the government in 1981. The Economic Recovery Tax Act of 1981 (ERTA), provided incredible tax benefits to the owners of buildings financed with a high level of debt. Essentially, every dollar of equity contributed by a limited partner entitled the investor to savings of three or more dollars in taxes, even if the projected tenants for the building never were found. Thus, a real estate developer could easily line up investors to provide the modest amount of equity needed for a project.

But the far more important market anomaly was the credit anomaly described throughout this book. As described in Chapter 4, the savings and loan industry led the way. The historic approach to lending money to real estate developers was turned on its head. The builder found financing first and then put in place everything else. Once the easy part was over (finding an institution who would agree in principle to lend), the builder would then assemble the right piece of land, the architect, and the contractors for the building; finally, the search for tenants would begin.

Remember that after the passage of the Garn-St Germain Act, the Federal Home Loan Bank Board authorized thrifts to lend up to 100 percent of the appraised value for a construction loan. Remember also that many thrifts had been practically handed over in the early 1980s to real estate developers. All you needed was a friendly appraiser and you could borrow as much money as you wanted. These lending practices placed all of the equity risks with the lender. The developer took most of the upside return, but the downside equity risks went to the lender.

Banks were more cautious but essentially went down much the same path. When their good real estate development customers started to turn toward savings and loans for financing, banks also began to offer more generous terms. While few banks would lend 100 percent of appraised value, many began offering 75 to 80 percent financing and would lend unsecured against the net worth of the borrower. Most banks also required at least some pre-leasing of space. A "conservative" lender might require 50 to 60 percent of the space to be pre-leased before committing to the loan. Many banks were able to convince themselves such liberalization of terms was sensible. As noted earlier, their historic sources of profits were being squeezed. Commercial real estate lending represented a unique market that combined both massive size with high lending spreads. Finally, the construction lending helped build the communities in which the banks operated. It was easy for bankers to convince themselves that they knew the local market better and the local developers better than anyone else. And each banker felt that if he or she didn't make the loan, a competitor would.

Banks were particularly comforted by the rapidly growing net worth of the real estate developers they were lending to. How could you lose money when you were lending to someone worth $100 million? The net worths of developers and prices for everything in the industry were going through the roof because of the building boom. The boom that had been launched greatly increased the price of new construction. The demand for good building sites reached a frenzy and the price of land soared, first in markets such as in Texas and later in Arizona, New England, Florida, and California. Labor shortages developed and so construction wages boomed. Building supply shortages developed and so the prices of construction materials rose. And of course, the interest costs paid to the savings and loan or bank, to finance all of this, were high: front-end fees of 2–4 percent of the loan commitment plus interest at 2–4 percent over the prime rate when the money was actually borrowed. This interest was added to the cost of building. Buildings that would have cost $50 million to build in the late 1970s, cost $100 million to build in the early 1980s.

On paper, this meant that the appraised value of existing property was increasing. If a new building was worth $100 million, then an identical building, built five years earlier, also had to be worth $100 million, didn't it? This was especially true because there was an active market in the sale of existing buildings. Thanks to the Tax Act of 1981 there were eager bidders for all established property; syndicators would create limited partnerships to syndicate the equity in the building to investors seeking tax shelters. Of course, once the equity was found, the needed bank financing was easy to obtain.

And in many markets, rents were also rising rapidly. The real estate bust of the late 1970s had led to a real shortage of space, particularly in markets such as Houston and Dallas, which were propelled by the energy boom of the late 1970s. For example, the demand for office space in Dallas grew from roughly 35 million square feet in 1980 to 80 million square feet in 1986. As a result, rents soared. In Dallas, rents for office space went from $14 per square foot to $22 per square foot from 1980 to 1982. Thus, the projected cash flows from renting the buildings also soared.

Thus, real estate appraisers were able to justify their continually higher appraisals based on the three traditional measures of value in real estate. The cost of new construction justified the appraisal. The market value of comparable properties justified the appraisal. And finally, the projected cash flows from the building also justified the appraisal. But herein lay the fatal flaw in the logic. The projected cash flows, the ultimate determinant in value, were not actual cash flows. Underneath all of the assumptions used by the appraisors, fundamental economic forces were at work.

During the entire 1980s, vacancy rates were rising. For example, from 1980 to 1990 the estimated national vacancy rate for office space rose from about 5 percent to over 20 percent while real rents (rents adjusted for the inflation rate) went from a level of about $22 per square foot in 1980 up to a peak of nearly $30 per square foot in the early 1980s and back down to the $20-per-square-foot level in the late 1980s. In other words, although the supply of available vacant space rose fourfold, real rents at the end of the decade were still as high as they had been in the early 1980s when space had been in short supply. The vacancy rate needed to get real rents to fall (the structural vacancy rate) had increased during the 1980s. Our work indicates that in the 1960s it took a vacancy rate of only 7 percent to 9 percent to get real rents to fall, while in the 1980s it seemed to take 13 percent to 15 percent. Why did the market change?

We believe it was directly because of the changes in lending practices that occurred in the late 1980s. Historically, when a builder had to make his interest payments on his mortgage and he had empty space he would drop his asking price for rents on his vacant space to get cash to pay the mortgage. However, when the original loan amount included enough money to carry the property for years without renting the vacant space, many builders chose to keep the nominal rents high. In fact, both the borrower and the lender had an incentive to keep the asking price for space high because to lower the price would call into question the projected cash flows. This would then lead to a downward valuation of the property that would call into question both the value of the building on the developer's balance sheet and the value of loan on the bank's books. It was simply better to keep the space off the market.

However, this meant that the market for space was receiving bad information about what rents could be expected for new space because much of the available supply was being withheld. This led other real estate developers to overestimate the rents they could get on new buildings, which caused them to start new buildings.

There is another factor at work that also should be mentioned. Once a building has been started it needs to be completed. Raw land is more valuable than a hole in the ground and a poured foundation. A half-built building is not worth half its economic costs—it may even have negative value. That is, it may have to be taken down in order to restore the raw land to its original value.

This helps explain why this building boom continued for such a long time throughout the nation. A large number of projects were started as the building boom began. Next, even though those projects were not fully occupied, even more projects were started because real rents did not fall enough to discourage new developments from starting. These projects take two or three years to complete. This means that new supply continues to come on the market even after it is apparent to everyone that the market is totally overbuilt.

As an example, let's look at the Dallas office market in the 1980s. As mentioned earlier, the demand for Dallas office space increased from 35 million square feet in 1980 to a little over 80 million square feet in 1986. But the supply of office space increased from 35 million square feet to over 100 million square feet in 1986 and then continued to grow to 120 million square feet while demand leveled off at 80 million square feet. There was a 50 percent surplus of office space by the end of the 1980s in Dallas. The same pattern has since appeared in Arizona, Colorado, and in New England. It now appears that the Southeast and California are destined for a similar fate. Only the Midwest seems to have avoided much of the problem largely because, it appears, of the hard times experienced in the mid-1980s, which spared both borrowers and lenders from the excessive optimism that gripped the rest of the nation.

Eventually, of course, fundamental economics take over. Fundamental economics are based on cash flows. Eventually, all of the interest reserves built into the original loan run out and the building just sits there half empty with rent woefully shy of what is needed to cover the mortgage. So now real rents fall out of bed, since developers have no other source of cash other than filling up the empty space. However, by this time more and more space is coming on the market than could ever be absorbed.

In Dallas, the vacancy rate of prime office space almost tripled from 1980 to 1983 (from 8 percent to 23 percent), but real rents went from $14 per square foot to $22 per square foot because most builders were holding out for even higher prices. Finally, after peaking in 1984, rents began to fall rapidly before finally bottoming out around $10 to $12 per square foot in the late 1980s. All the while, vacancy rates continued to rise as buildings that had already been started were still being completed.

Let's examine what this all means to the economic value of a building. First, all of the interest that had been used to keep the loan payments current from the time when the building was completed but was unoccupied is an economic loss because these payments were supposed to be recovered through higher rents. In fact, because rents fell below projections, this empty space reflects lost income, and therefore all of the interest that had been capitalized becomes simply unrecoverable. In addition, the rents that can be earned are less than projected and despite lower rents, some of the space remains unoccupied. It's an unmitigated disaster.

Returning to the Dallas office market, a 30 percent vacancy rate on 120 million square feet of space (which would be 40 million square feet) at a loss of $10 per square foot translates into an economic loss of $400 million a year for as long as the building remained under-occupied. Moreover, because of the perceived higher risk, it is hard to find new investors to buy the building at the current rates of return. All of this conspires to greatly reduce the market value of a completed new building. For example, some buildings in Dallas were sold at 25 percent of the cost of construction. A crude estimate of the economic loss that was incurred just from the construction of prime office space in a single city, Dallas, is some $6 to $7 billion. To put this number in perspective, Dallas represents only about 1.0 percent of the nation's population. And remember, we are not even talking about the economic losses in Dallas on condominium projects, hotels, shopping centers, apartment houses, and less-than-prime office space in nearby cities. Nor are we talking about the economic losses in the rest of the nation as this type of problem spreads.

And it gets worse. Even past projects that were built by top-quality developers under prudent lending standards are affected. New buildings are more atttractive to tenants than old buildings. As rents fall for new buildings, they begin to cannibalize tenants from other buildings. Because many projects were built in the 1970s and early 1980s with tenants agreeing to only a five-year lease, tenants either would extract lower rents from the existing landlord or move as their leases rolled over. Tenants occupying Class B space in older buildings further from town, move to new Class A space in prime locations. Tenants occupying Class C space, very old buildings in bad locations, move to Class B space. This, of course, economically obsoletes this Class C space even though it may have twenty or more years left before it becomes physically unusable.

Some of this cannibalization takes place nationwide. Companies and people are often willing to relocate if they can save enough money. For example, prime Dallas space became so cheap that it could draw renters from around the nation. As a result, this exacerbates the problems of other regions who are now finding that they, too, overbuilt.

This cannibalization has further depressing impacts on the health of even the strongest real estate developers. Much of their cash flows and net worth is coming from property they developed in the past. As space cannibalization proceeds, their cash flows from old property begin to disappear even as the cash flows from their new property fall well short of projections. It is for this reason that some of the most prominent real estate developers of the 1980s, whose projected net worth was in the hundreds of millions, or even billions, are now facing insolvency.

But at the end of the day, the economic losses on bad commercial real estate lending fall to the institution that made the loans. With over $450 billion of loans and commitments on commercial real estate already on their books, it seems inevitable that many banks face terrifying losses on commercial real estate loans in the 1990s. It turns out that we built commercial real estate capacity not only for the growth of the nation in the 1980s but for the 1990s as well. Indeed, in markets such as Texas, Arizona, or parts of New England, as much 20 percent or more of the growth in employment was from the real estate boom itself.

It seems that we have fundamentally overbuilt our real estate capacity relative to our ability to pay for it. Bank portfolios of commercial real estate grew from $132 to $385 billion from 1982 to 1990, or by nearly 300 percent. Thrift commercial real estate lending grew even faster. In comparison the population of the nation grew 7 percent and the GNP grew only 83 percent. The eventual loan losses resulting from the economic cost of this massive overbuilding of real estate capacity will be enormous.

7

The Costs of a Bankrupt
Regulatory Structure

═══════

As we entered into 1991, the nation was beginning to feel the full effects of having allowed market forces and obsolete regulation to interact destructively for nearly a decade. We are now well on our way to destroying not only our banks, but also are harming our economy.

The bad lending practices of the last several years are now coming home to roost. As much as 25 percent of the banking industry, representing some $750 billion in assets, faces loan losses of sufficient size that they will be left without sufficient capital to operate. Indeed, at least half of this total, representing some $300 to $400 billion in assets, face economic insolvency within three years if nothing is done to check their decline. This, in turn, means that the Bank Insurance Fund also faces insolvency unless it is recapitalized, raising the specter of another taxpayer bailout of a deposit insurance fund.

But, most seriously of all, the banking industry's troubles are spilling over into the real economy. Banks fighting for survival are squeezing the availability of credit. In turn, economic activity is constricting. As the economy weakens, credit losses rise causing more banks to post even more massive losses. Credit constricts further—and so on. The prospect for an out-of-control downward spiral suddenly seems very real. Even if we are lucky, and if accommodative monetary policy prevents an economic freefall, the economy will be far weaker than it should be.

I believe the path we are on is simply unacceptable. I believe we need to take proactive, immediate action to transform the vicious downward spiral that has been developing into a virtuous upward cycle. But before describing, in the later chapters of this book, what actions I believe we should take, let's first examine in this chapter the unmanaged outcome of the path we are on.

Structural Damage to Profitability

How much structural damage has been done to the banking industry's profitability over the last decade? What are the prospects for the industry's profitability even without regard to the potential for a devastating recession?

To bring the points home to the reader, I am going to share with you some of the analyses we have undertaken at McKinsey & Company to determine just what condition the industry's profitability is actually in.

The risky loans of the 1980s, made because of the deposit and credit anomalies, were already resulting in massive loan charge-offs, even without benefit of a recession, as the 1980s came to a close. Loan charge-offs are the nonperforming loans that banks actually write off. The median rate of charge-offs to total loans and leases for the industry has gone from 17 cents per $100 of loan in 1980 to $1.25 per $100 for the industry—a sixfold increase. Moreover, the average volatility of earnings due to the increased risk of high loan losses has also dramatically increased. In 1980 loan losses represented only 23 percent of earnings for the industry. By 1989 it had reached over 120 percent.

These numbers reflect the declining quality of the industry's earnings. In 1980 two-thirds of the industry's net interest income came from low-risk core deposits. By 1989 that percentage had slipped to roughly 47 percent. Meanwhile, net interest income from commercial real estate loans and highly leveraged transactions grew from less than 5 percent to over 12 percent.

In 1980 the spread from these high-risk loans represented about 15 percent of pre-tax profits for the industry. By 1989, however, the net interest income from these commercial real estate and highly leveraged transaction loans contributed nearly 50 percent of the industry's $27 billion in pre-tax profits. The reason why these loans are theoretically so profitable is that they have high rates and incur practically no operating costs because they are large wholesale loans.

What is most striking about these numbers is that reported earnings for the industry have been weak despite booking the earnings from these loans. Because the bulk of the losses from these loans are still to come, earnings should have been much higher.

The industry's earnings grew at a mere 3.1 percent compounded from 1980 to 1989. During the same period, the banks' return on equity declined dramatically from about 13.5 percent to about 8 percent—a decline of over 40 percent.

Given the high risk in these earnings and the relatively low returns, it is not surprising that the stock market has given bank stocks relatively low values recently. As 1990 came to a close, less than one-third of the largest banks had a stock market value for their stock greater than their book value and a good many were selling at less than 40 percent of book. Moreover, bank stocks were selling at only 35 percent of the relative level of the S&P 500. In other words, the stock market was clearly saying that the industry's earnings prospects were poor.

And we agree. Taken together, all analyses seem to indicate that the industry's earnings prospects combine high risk and low returns.

If all that was at stake was the banking industry's profitability, it would be an issue largely of concern only to the industry's stockholders. However, far more is at stake. In fact, given the low stock prices in the industry, it is probably safe to say that the public now has a greater stake in the profitability of the industry than do the industry's shareholders. That is to say, the potential losses to the banking industry's shareholders if all bank stocks went to zero is no more than $150 billion. However, as we will see, the potential losses to the nation from a crippled banking system are massively higher.

FDIC Solvency

The first issue that we face as a nation is whether taxpayers will be forced to bail out the Bank Insurance Fund, as the FSLIC (the now defunct insurance fund for the savings and loan industry) was bailed out.

When you talk about insurance you need to focus on the potential for credit losses because they are almost always responsible for bank failures. The insurance problems occur when credit losses are so great that they wipe out reserves and capital and thereby force the FDIC, through its Bank Insurance Fund, to make up the difference between what depositors are owed and what the marked-down assets are worth.

What then is the outlook for loan losses and how will they be concentrated?

During the some thirty-four years the FDIC kept consistent records, from 1948 to 1982, the banking industry wrote off about $28 billion in loans. In 1982, the Garn–St Germain Act was passed and loan charge-offs have risen steadily ever since. In just the last four years, the industry has charged off over $75 billion or nearly three times total charge-offs from 1948 to 1982. Some portion of these loan charge-offs is LDC debt, although much of the LDC debt, though reserved against, has not yet been charged off. The great majority of these charge-offs has been domestic debt.

What is the most disturbing about these numbers is that the $75 billion in charge-offs came during a period of sustained economic growth. Our analysis shows us that charge-offs have doubled during recessions in the past, for example, in 1969 to 1970, 1974 to 1975, and 1981 to 1982. After each doubling, loan charge-offs continued to rise more slowly.

If the first half loan charge-offs of 1990 are annualized, a record $30 billion in loan charge-offs can be expected when that year's final results are in. Based on history, this means we can expect charge-offs to soar to $60 billion a year for both 1991 and 1992 if the recession we are now in is of average severity.

Whenever we do the analysis we also discover that loan charge-offs are concentrated. In 1986, for example, 57 percent of the charge-offs in the industry occurred in banks with 20 percent of the assets of the industry. In 1989, roughly the same phenomenon occurred: 55 percent of the charge-offs were focused in 20 percent of the banks by assets.

The significance of these analyses, taken together, is that we can expect roughly $120 billion of charge-offs to occur in the banking industry and that roughly $65 billion of these losses will occur in some 20 percent of the industry. The total capital of these troubled banks is no more than $40 billion. In other words, we can expect the capital of almost all of these institutions to be exhausted if we continue on our current path.

What kind of losses can the FDIC expect from this projection? What kind of reserves does the FDIC have to absorb those losses?

The Bank Insurance Fund (BIF) has been very busy for some time. Over the past decade, roughly 1,200 banks with $130 billion in assets have failed and required some form of FDIC assistance. Since 1985, an average of approximately 1,300 banks with an average of almost $240 billion in deposits have been on the FDIC's troubled bank list.

For a long time, the FDIC fund grew roughly in step with the insured deposit base, maintaining a ratio of FDIC funds to insured deposits of at least 1.25 percent. The absolute size of the FDIC fund grew steadily until the middle 1980s when it peaked at about $18 billion. But then it went into a steep decline in the late 1980s as the full impact of bank failures began to take its toll on the FDIC. The insurance fund began to report its first net losses in its history. Since 1985, the FDIC fund has represented a sharply falling percentage of total deposits, now well below 0.50 percent of insured deposits. Thus there are less FDIC funds available today to back more insured deposits, and it seems obvious that additional resources will be required in the near future to bolster the FDIC. The chairman of the FDIC, William Seidman, and Treasury Secretary Nicholas Brady have confirmed that the fund is "under stress."

How much stress? Depending on what assumptions are made, we estimate the unmanaged outcome of events will be the insolvency of the BIF over the next 24 months.

We have attempted to build realistic assumptions into an analysis of how the BIF is likely to fare during the next year.

We start with a fund of $15 billion in 1991, which is before losses and after assessment and investment income. Our analysis has two key drivers: (1) marking the bank's loan portfolio (primarily commercial real estate) to its economic value (that is, the net present value of its cash flows) and (2) imposing a test for positive real capital and positive operating income after the write-down of the portfolio. We tested our analysis against past bank failures and found that it accurately predicted the "economic" failure of the Continental Illinois, large Texas banks, and others in the 1980s.

We then developed a bank failure model to simulate probable bank failures over the next few years. Running this model indicates that anywhere from $100 billion, to well over $300 billion, of assets are in the hands of commercial banks that are headed—in an unmanaged outcome—to being restructured by the FDIC in the next two to three years. In addition, there are another $400 billion of assets in the hands of commercial banks that would then be vulnerable to being restructured. In other words, from $750 billion to $800 billion of assets are in the hands of banks that would be significantly undercapitalized if we had a severe recession. The great unknown in estimating how many institutions will fail is the depth and duration of the recession we have now entered. Another critical unknown is when these banks will fail in a regulatory sense, and whether or not the government will undertake a fundamental reform of the banking system.

Given these uncertainties, we estimate that if we continue on our current path, the Bank Insurance Fund will need a range from $20 billion to $40 billion in cash, if it uses its historic procedures, over the next couple of years to resolve its expected caseload of troubled banks. The $20 billion number assumes that there is a 20 percent markdown in commercial real estate loan values (the Texas experience was closer to 35 percent) in banks in regions of the country experiencing severe real estate recessions. It also assumes that it costs the FDIC 9 percent of assets to resolve the cases of banks with greater than $10 billion in assets and 16 percent of assets for banks smaller than $10 billion in assets. The historic experience of the FDIC is closer to 11 percent and 20 percent, respectively.

The $40 billion number assumes that there is a 25 percent markdown of commercial real estate values. It also assumes that it costs the FDIC 11 percent of assets to resolve the cases of banks greater than $10 billion and 19 percent of assets to resolve the cases of banks with less than $10 billion in assets. Finally, it assumes that the recession is severe enough to cause a doubling in the loan losses in the commercial loan portfolio of all banks (that is, an extra 1.5 percent of all commercial loans).

As stated, the FDIC's recent actual experience of the cash costs of resolutions is close to 11 percent for large banks and 20 percent for smaller banks. These large cash costs result from the loss of ongoing concern value of the bank being restructured. This loss of ongoing concern value includes having to sell assets at distressed prices, loss of goodwill, loss of tax carryforwards, loss of good managers due to uncertainty, loss of employee morale, loss of maintenance spending to protect the customer franchise, and so on. One very important cost of loss of ongoing concern value is that borrowers tend to lose their moral obligation to repay their debt when a troubled institution is taken over and, indeed, begin suing everyone they can find. They are often able to tie up assets that could otherwise be liquidated to resolve their indebtedness.

Against these cash needs, the Bank Insurance Fund has approximately $9 billion in net assets and is already under-funded against its target reserve level by some $15 billion. It therefore seems likely that some $35 billion to some $55 billion of new cash will be needed both to meet a "base-case" scenario of funding needs for the next two years and to get the BIF up to a level that is reasonably prudent (1.25 percent of insured deposits). If the recession we have now entered proves to be severe, we may need even more.

One proposal to bolster the FDIC's resources is to increase the deposit insurance premium under the FDIC's authority granted in the budget accord of 1990. Such an approach is consistent with the theme that any solution to recapitalize the FDIC should come from the banking industry and avoid the taxpayer.

The FDIC, however, has already more than doubled premiums, up to a level of 0.195 percent of insured liabilities, since enactment of the Financial Institutions Reform, Recovery, and

Enforcement (FIRRE) Act of 1989. Significant further increases from today's levels will begin to make it impossible for even the best run institutions to make enough money to earn their cost of capital, let alone raise capital in the equity markets. At an assessment level of 19.5 basis points, less than one-third of the industry can maintain an ROE greater than 15 percent. Assuming for a moment that the cost of capital currently is 15 percent as well, two-thirds of the industry are already destroying shareholder value—that is, not earning their cost of equity capital—at current assessment rates.

And in fact, a further premium increase would probably cause more pain than it was worth to the FDIC. An additional 50 percent rise in premiums to 30 basis points would increase the FDIC's income by only $2.5 billion. This small amount is far short of what we have predicted will be necessary in the next year or two to handle economic failures. For this reason, in early January, it was reported that officials were considering a huge premium increase, of 1 percent of deposits, or $25 billion.

We think premium increases of this magnitude would be a tragic mistake. It is possible to analyze the impact of further premium increases on the health of the FDIC fund itself. There is a clear trade-off between premium increases and FDIC income—since the higher the premium, the more banks will fail. Remember, any bank that fails costs the fund at least 10 percent of its gross assets. Based on our analysis, the fund is still marginally positive up to about an annual 38 basis point assessment rate. Beyond that rate, additional bank failures caused simply by premium increases make the FDIC fund decrease (rather than increase) the capital of the fund. A 1 percent premium increase, as was proposed, would, by itself, bankrupt the FDIC fund. Apparently, Washington has come to realize that a premium increase of this magnitude would be disastrous since it has abandoned this particular proposal—at least for the moment.

There are alternative ways to recapitalize the FDIC without increasing bank assessment rates further or driving the fund into insolvency. Our preferred approach is found later in the book and is a critical transition issue as policymakers contemplate how best to reform and restructure our banking system to ensure a profitable and competitive industry going forward.

Counterproductive Capital Pressure

Not surprisingly, bank regulators have long focused on increasing bank capital as one means to backstop the FDIC. And there is no doubt the industry needs more equity capital. But equity capital is just another name for increased profitability. Without reforming the banking system so that it becomes possible to increase profits, increased capital pressure can have devastating results.

Remember that a bank has only two potential sources of equity capital. Either it can raise more equity through newly issued stock or it can retain earnings. Given the risks the industry faces, the near-term ability of most banks to raise significant amounts of equity is close to nonexistent. Indeed, the prospects for retained earnings is also severely limited. If the prospects for anything approaching $120 billion of loan charge-offs in the next two years projected earlier were to come true, even the 80 percent of the industry facing only 45 percent of the charge-offs would still have loan losses so great as to reduce their earnings to close to break-even.

How do you respond to capital pressure when you can't raise capital from either new issues or from retained earnings?

The only alternative that remains is to contract. However, there is a problem with contracting in today's environment. You cannot reduce high-risk problem loans. The borrowers have no source of repayment. The only loans you can reduce are to relatively strong borrowers.

Curtailing credit extension has little economic impact on the nation as long as only a fraction of the industry is under capital pressure; the reason being that if other institutions are still lending, strong borrowers that face a reluctant lender simply switch banks. This is one of the major reasons why there was no immediate economic fallout from the capital crunch put on the savings and loan industry after the passage of the FIRRE Act. Borrowers turned away simply switched to commercial banks.

What happens, though, if all lenders turn reluctant to lend? In this case you have a credit crunch.

Credit Crunch

In normal times, banks are eager to lend to all borrowers they feel are creditworthy because lending is ordinarily profitable. However, in order to lend money, you must first have funds available to lend. There have been three occasions over the last twenty-five years, in 1966, in 1969–1970, and in 1974–1975, when banks were short of the funds needed to continue lending. All three of these funds shortages were the result of deliberate tightening of monetary policy combined with use of Regulation Q (the regulation that formerly allowed the Federal Reserve to control rates paid on deposits) to deprive banks of available funds. In all three occasions there was a credit crunch as almost all banks, at once, curtailed credit extension. The 1969–1970 and 1974–1975 credit crunches resulted in significant recessions.

Now, however, we have a credit crunch that is spreading and growing in severity that is not a result of deliberate Federal Reserve policy. To help the reader understand what is going on, let me explain what it was like to be managing a troubled bank in late 1990.

Running a troubled bank is a nerve-wracking experience. When loan losses reach the point where the bank must begin making massive loan loss reserves that are greater than earnings, then those reserves must come from reducing equity. As equity capital falls, both regulators and outside investors get more and more nervous. Not only does the stock price fall, but the prices of the holding company's bonds fall as well.

Most seriously, though, deposits become both more difficult and more expensive to raise. All of a sudden, liquidity begins to become an issue. Liquidity pressures and capital pressure from regulators then combine to induce the bank to restrict credit. Not only are no new loans being made to high-risk borrowers, such as real estate developers, but credit extension is reduced to other kinds of borrowers as well. In particular, credit begins being denied to even creditworthy small businesses and mid-size companies. Most troubled banks, however, work hard to continue to extend credit to creditworthy individuals because these loans are so very profitable. Even for these loans, however, terms and conditions are tightened.

When enough banks become troubled, a credit crunch begins to develop. And as of the time this book was written (February 1991) we had had enough of a credit curtailment to have helped cause the economy to fall into a recession.

In February 1991, new lending to the commercial real estate markets and to the highly leveraged companies had been stopped, nationally, since about March 1990. Moreover, in New England, credit had been significantly curtailed to small businesses and mid-size company borrowers, and even to some categories of individual lending, since early 1990. Meanwhile, banks in New York, New Jersey, and Pennsylvania were also beginning to curtail credit to small businesses and mid-size companies as well as tighten up terms and conditions to individuals. In the Southeast, the Far West, and the Midwest, the banks had really only begun to curtail credit beyond the high-risk loan categories. In other words, the credit crunch of early 1991 was only a partial credit curtailment. All of the nation's banks had essentially stopped lending to the commercial real estate sectors and to highly leveraged companies. In addition, perhaps 25 percent of the nation's banks were curtailing credit to small borrowers and mid-size companies. Finally, nearly all banks were applying more conservative terms and conditions to all kinds of borrowers. Yet even this modest tightening was enough to make a major contribution to the economic slowdown of late 1990.

And this gets us to the real danger. The health of our economy and the health of the banking system are directly linked.

Credit Contraction

Tightened credit produces recessions. When credit is less available, borrowers without access to borrowing alternatives curtail spending and economic activity declines. In the past, when credit was tight because of restrictive monetary policy, simply loosening monetary policy was sufficient to increase lending activity and thereby to restart the growth of the economy. Once it was clear, in early 1991, that we were in a recession, the Federal Reserve has again attempted to restart the economy by increasing liquidity and lowering interest rates.

This time is different, however. This time the recession, though being significantly caused by tightened credit, is not reversible by simply loosening monetary policy. Increased liquidity may not increase lending very much at all. At best, new lending caused by easy money may only offset credit curtailment by weak banks, leaving us with a stagnant economy.

At the worst, we face the danger that the recession we are now in will turn into one that feeds upon itself and persists for an extended period of time. The problem is that the recession itself, by causing more and more loan losses, creates more and more troubled banks that curtail credit further. As incomes fall and defaults mount, more and more banks become severely undercapitalized and begin curtailing credit to more and more borrowers. As the recession spreads, more and more healthy lenders will further tighten the terms and conditions on which they will lend, out of caution. Many of them will be able to be quite choosy, because they will have the pick among customers denied credit at more troubled institutions.

My guess is that in contrast to most postwar recessions, this one may drag on. In past recessions, the national tightening of credit by the Federal Reserve affected most regions of the country, all at the same time. But this time, the diversity of the regional economics and the wide divergence in the health of different banks means that the credit tightening process has been inconsistent. For example, though New England and the mid-Atlantic are well into declines, the Far West and the Southeast declines have barely started, and the Southwest is actually growing again. Similarly, while $750 billion of assets are in the hands of deeply troubled banks, there is another $2.1 trillion of assets in the hands of banks that are still, by all conventional measures, healthy.

The good news from this is that there is much strength to draw on as the economy declines. The bad news is that the recession has become reasonably severe already despite the health of much of the economy as we entered into it.

How bad is the economy going to get?

Most economists expect that the recession we have entered will be of relatively short duration. However, these are the same economists who did not see it coming. Most economists have no experience that is relevant in observing what is happening. In all of their business experience, the nation has had a strong banking industry. Most of them do not really understand how banks work. They take for granted that credit will flow.

But the truth is that none of us know how deep and how long the slide we are entering can last. It is not clear what will stop it because we already are running a major budget deficit. More fiscal stimulus is hardly likely. Most economists assume that the Federal Reserve will continue to lower interest rates dramatically if the economy continues to tailspin, and they assume that it would help. But to be effective, monetary policy relies on banks that are willing to lend, and to do so requires that bankers be confident in their own institutions, in themselves, and in the economy. On this last point, I can speak with personal knowledge. I have never known my banking friends to be less confident than they are now. As loans go bad, as their earnings and stock prices fall, as the economy sinks, it is hard to be optimistic. Even very healthy banks are worried by what is happening to their more troubled colleagues.

Let me share with you an excerpt from a 1951 book by Jesse H. Jones, *Fifty Billion Dollars: My Thirteen Years with the RFC (1932–1945)*, which illustrates the dangers of having bankers who lose their confidence. The RFC, or Reconstruction Finance Corporation, was the government agency that was used in the 1930s to recapitalize the nation, and particularly the banking system, to help pull the nation out of the Depression.

> It was patent that if the bankers didn't provide credit to accommodate agriculture, commerce, and industry based on a going country, the government would have to. No community can prosper if its banks fail to supply local credit. Yet during that period bankers, scared by what they had been through, went to extremes on keeping liquid. A few even solicited deposits with the boast that they were 75 percent liquid. One bank, which had amassed an uncommonly large surplus, bragged of being 110 percent liquid.
>
> Some banks of excessive liquidity strove for even higher liquidity. They called loans, thereby forcing liquidation by the borrowers. This was breaking men's hearts, destroying values, sometimes snuffing out a lifetime's savings. And it was creating more unemployment.
>
> In 1934, with deposit insurance in operation, there was no longer any valid excuse for a bank to cram its vault with idle cash which borrowers could be using with profit all around. The cheapest deposit insurance, it seemed to me, was ample capital, and the government was offering to provide it by purchasing preferred stock.

Over time, there is a real danger that as more and more borrowers run out of alternative borrowing sources, as more and more regional economies decline, and as the credit crunch migrates to consumers as well as businesses, we wind up with a multiyear recession. Under such conditions, unemployment could rise to double digits; asset values, particularly real estate assets, could completely collapse, and real prices could begin to drop. We, of course, have not seen such economic conditions since the thirties. Once started, deflationary conditions feed upon themselves. With deflation, interest payments of even 3 percent or 4 percent represent enormously high real interest rates so no one with any options is willing to borrow. Credit therefore contracts as borrowers either repay their borrowings or default causing even further weakness in the banking system. In other words, if we get ourselves into such an economic morass we may remain in it for a very extended period. The costs to the nation could be enormous. For example, if the GNP were to decline 5 percent per year for two years, the lost output would be over $500 billion.

Lest we forget how bad it can get, let me share with you another quote from Jesse Jones.

> Amid the prosperity which now suffuses the country, the bleak conditions which blighted the lives of millions of Americans in the early 1930s have almost been forgotten. They certainly have been by the younger generation. The then agonizing days and nights of fear and insecurity now seem a bad dream, but dimly remembered. In those dire days, between ten and fifteen million employable Americans disconsolately walked about without a means of livelihood. Other millions, whose incomes had been reduced, worked in daily dread of being dismissed or furloughed, or of having to suffer still another cut in the necessities of life. The national income had fallen from eighty billion dollars in 1929 to forty billion in 1932. This meant very simply that the income of every individual in the United States, every farmer, businessman, industrialist, clerk, wage earner, or whatever, on the average had been cut in half. But many had no income at all because they had no work, and, in countless cases, family savings had been swept away in the collapse.

Although I do not believe we are headed to another Depression, I do believe we are risking the health of our economy, unless we alter the course we are on. Even if the combination of lower interest rates and lower oil prices combine to produce a weak recovery, any new shock could send the economy back into a tailspin. We are playing with fire. The sickness in our banking system will not miraculously disappear. We need a comprehensive plan that restores both the confidence of the public in its banks and the confidence of its bankers in themselves.

In February the Treasury proposed the administration's plan. In a two-inch-thick report entitled *Modernizing the Financial*

System: Recommendations for Safer, More Competitive Banks, the Treasury outlined sweeping proposals for reform. It is by far the most thoughtful, most courageous attempt yet made to reform the system. And it is headed in the right direction. It is based on the premises that the government should not absorb risk that should be borne by the market and that obsolete laws and regulations should change.

As you will see in the final part of the book, I disagree with many of the specifics of the Treasury proposal. In particular, I do not believe that the Treasury proposal goes far enough in reforming the deposit insurance system. I also believe it relies too heavily on regulatory supervision. Most importantly, I believe it does not adequately address what we must do to recapitalize and restructure troubled banks and to ease the credit crunch. Yet, despite these reservations, the Treasury proposals are remarkably sound, given political realities. A careful reader of both the proposals made in this book and the Treasury proposals will find them to be in substantial agreement on perhaps two-thirds of the key issues. Unfortunately, I believe the Treasury proposals are weakest on the core issue of deposit insurance reform. I believe the proposals are an inadequate reform of the deposit and credit anomalies.

This chapter concludes the first part of this book. Up to this point, we've focused on how the banking system got itself into its present sorry state. Before describing the fundamental reforms that are needed, in the third part of this book, we need to first look at some of the fundamental economic forces that are transforming our entire financial system. Specifically, we need to examine three different economic forces that are at work. Without understanding these economic forces, the reader will find it difficult to understand what reforms are needed.

First, we need to explore how the securitization of the flow of funds is redefining what we mean by banking. Second, we need to explore why the globalization of the world's capital markets is making it impossible for us to control our own economy and why we need strong banks in order to remain competitive as a nation. Finally, we need to examine the economic restructuring of the banking industry resulting from the unleashing of competitive forces and how that is leading to both consolidation of the core banking business and the disaggregation of other parts of the bank.

History teaches us that trying to resist these economic forces is both futile and destructive. We need to reform the system in a way that works with these forces instead of at cross-purposes to them.

PART II

IRRESISTIBLE
ECONOMIC FORCES

8

Securitization

The securities business is a natural outgrowth of banking. Large merchants, forerunners of modern corporations, would present early European bankers with very promising profit ventures that the bankers, however, found too risky to fund. In order to be able to always meet the demands of their depositors, these medieval bankers always had to keep a lot of cash on hand. They were unwilling to finance, out of the bank's funds, illiquid investments, with unknown returns, no matter how attractive they appeared to be. So the response was the creation of the joint stock company, which divided up ownership into equity shares that were, in turn, sold to investors willing to take on more risk. Most often it was natural for the banker who wanted to help a client find equity money to seek out among his other clients those interested in investing in promising ventures. It was also natural for these bankers to arrange trades of the stock thereafter. Similarly, governments and businesses often wanted to borrow for periods of time longer than were appropriate for the balance sheets of early banks. Bankers responded by helping them sell debt securities, bonds, to investors and, as with stocks, established the after-market.

The kinship of the commercial banking and the securities businesses is quite natural, although there have always been firms who have been exclusively in either the securities or the banking business. In the United States, commercial banking and securities were a part of a single integrated industry until the early 1930s when the Glass-Steagall Act forcefully separated them. For example, the House of Morgan was cloven into the Morgan Bank and into Morgan Stanley. All of a sudden, the commercial banking and securities businesses became separate industries. The purpose of this was twofold: (1) to protect bank deposits from exposure to the risks of underwriting public offerings of debt and equity and (2) to prevent conflicts of interest. These were certainly valid aims because some commercial banks had gone bust from securities underwriting risks in the 1929 crash, and others, after discovering credit problems in their own loan portfolios, had packaged and sold

155

these loans as securities to an unsuspecting public. However, forced separation seemed like overkill. It was a bit like mandating divorces for everyone just because some couples had been found guilty of adultery. Divorcing all married couples does, of course, make adultery impossible, but it does seem draconian.

Nevertheless, during the 1940s, 1950s, and 1960s, the resulting legal separation worked reasonably well as the commercial banking and securities industries stuck to their new well-defined charters. With the exception of trading and underwriting of Federal government and municipal bonds, which were exempted under the Glass-Steagall Act, banks stuck to core banking activities: lending short-term money, taking deposits, and running the payment system. Securities firms, who were regulated by the Securities and Exchange Commission, stuck to the traditional securities businesses: underwriting, trading, and selling securities to retail and institutional investors.

The reason that such forced separation worked was that the regulation was effective at keeping each industry out of the other's business. In turn, this depended on the ability of the Federal Reserve to control the economy and on the limitations of the existing technology to evade regulation. However, when the Federal Reserve lost control of inflation and interest rates (as described earlier in this book), customers began to develop powerful economic incentives to bypass banks. Once technology became available to make this possible, securities firms were quick to exploit the economic incentives of customers to earn higher rates on their funds and to borrow more cheaply. In other words, when securities firms discovered in the 1970s that they could divert funds, which would have otherwise been deposits or loans, into securities, the Glass-Steagall Act became obsolete.

A word, securitization, has been coined to describe the process of using securities instruments to displace bank deposits and loans. Securitization is one of the most powerful economic forces at work in the financial services industry. As such, any new regulatory model we develop must be built to accommodate this force or else it, too, will fail.

What Is Securitization?

As described earlier in the book, securities firms created products like money market mutual funds and commercial paper that fulfilled the needs of customers far more cost-effectively than competitive products offered by banks. Large, creditworthy corporations found that issuing commercial paper through a securities firm was far cheaper than borrowing from a bank. And individual investors discovered that money market mutual funds offered far higher yields than price-regulated deposits. In fact, much of the money flowing into money market mutual funds was, in turn, invested in the commercial paper market.

Such direct, simple forms of securitization are powerful by themselves. However, such direct securitization is limited to products with relatively simple risks (for example, commercial paper sold by highly rated large corporations). In particular, many loans are not easily securitizable. Nevertheless, Wall Street has found ways of packaging some loans together, generally those loans with the most standardized terms, such as mortgages and credit cards, into securities.

Advantages of Securities over Banking

There is a powerful economic logic behind securitization. Given an option, it will always be cost-effective to securitize an asset rather than place it on a bank balance sheet. Securities have a natural economic advantage over banking for any financial assets that can be bundled together, chopped into uniform bits, and sold to investors. Putting loans and deposits on a bank's balance sheet is very expensive partly because of the way banks are regulated and partly because of the economic model they use. In terms of regulated costs, for every $100 it loans, a typical bank must kick in roughly 20 cents for required reserves, 20 cents for insured deposit premiums, which are headed higher, and another $1.20 of pre-tax profit to support its regulatory equity requirements. In addition, as noted in earlier chapters, it costs an average of $3 per $100 in assets, in largely shared costs, to operate a bank. Put together this means that a bank must earn an average spread of 4.5 percent between the interest it charges to borrowers and the interest it pays to depositors. In other words, a bank needs roughly $4.50 of income for every $100 put on its balance sheet.

In comparison, a money market mutual fund can serve institutional investors with a total spread between what the investor receives and what the issuer of the securities invested actually pays of less than 25 cents for every $100 invested. Even if it gets its funds from small investors, a money market mutual fund can operate at a total spread between what investors receive, and what issuers pay, of no more than 70 cents for every $100 invested.

It is easy, therefore, to see why the securities industry was easily able to bypass, or disintermediate, banks once it became possible to do so. When the Federal Reserve ruled that money market mutual funds were not demand deposits, firms such as Shearson and Merrill Lynch (not to mention Fidelity and Dreyfus) were quick to offer their customers the opportunity to invest in these funds. As this new source of non-bank money became available, it was relatively easy to match high-quality borrowers wanting to issue commercial paper with money market mutual funds wanting to invest by eliminating the middleman—the bank. Goldman Sachs and A.G. Becker, now part of Merrill Lynch, were quick to expand their commercial paper programs by pointing out to major corporations how much money they could save by leaving banks. Other securities firms also began selling corporate and municipal bond funds directly to retail investors, luring even more deposits away from banks and thrifts. In other words, once it became possible to do so, banks were doomed to lose easily securitizable loans and deposits.

As if direct cost advantages are not enough, securities also have other advantages over bank loans. Securities are liquid and tradeable, while loans are illiquid; there is only a very limited market in which loans are bought or sold. The value of a debt security is determined every day by the market. In contrast, the value of a loan is based on all manner of subjective valuation. What, for instance, is the economic value of an equipment lease at a 14 percent effective interest rate, on a computer, to a company that has just undergone a leveraged buyout? Eighty percent of its face value? One hundred and twenty percent of its face value? Who knows?

Another advantage of debt securities is that they are rated by credit agencies, whereas loans are not. Most investors, be they individuals or pension funds, have little ability or desire to assess credit risk. By investing in securities whose risk has been quantified by rating agencies, these groups theoretically can better avoid the trouble and expense of analyzing cash flows, assessing credit worthiness, or working out problem loans to avoid large losses. Investors have historically been willing to pay for the greater liquidity and credit transparency of securities over loans by accepting lower returns than the equivalent loan would provide. This, in turn, has led borrowers who raise money through securities to have even lower financing costs than a comparable bank loan.

Given all of these advantages, it is not surprising then that any asset that can be securitized, has been securitized.

Mortgages and Other Loans

It is not surprising that the securities industry did not stop with restructuring the easy-to-securitize assets. Starting with mortgages, the industry has proved that it could securitize all sorts of assets.

Mortgages were the easiest to securitize because there are federally sponsored enterprises, most notably "Fannie Mae" and "Freddie Mac," which guarantee residential mortgages and cause all mortgages they guarantee to conform to a set standard. This uniformity makes it relatively easy to package them into securities. In the mid 1970s firms such as First Boston and Salomon Brothers pooled large numbers of these mortgages together and passed the interest from them on to investors who bought the securities. As the years passed, Wall Street found ever-better ways of repackaging these loans to provide investors with ever-more predictable returns. These mortgage-backed securities have eliminated much of the value of holding an unsecuritized mortgage loan on the books of a financial institution. A player who simply originated mortgages and got them off the books by securitizing them, a mortgage bank for instance, could out-compete banks and thrifts that held loans on their books. Given equal costs for originating the mortgage, a mortgage bank could avoid the cost of reserves, deposit insurance premiums, and capital that a bank or thrift would have to pay to keep the asset on its books. The securitization of mortgages all but eliminated the value that could be created by conventional depository institutions making mortgage loans. As noted in Chapter 4, this innovation made the classic thrift business sytem obsolete since the value of holding mortgages was lost.

By the mid-1980s, investment banks had found means of securitizing automobile loans, credit card receivables, and other assets with high credit quality and predictable cash flows. Unlike mortgages, however, there are no government-sponsored enterprises that guarantee the credit of these assets. The additional guarantee came from what is known in the industry as "credit enhancement." For a fee, a financial institution agrees to guarantee the cash flows that underlie the new security. These guarantees have come often from the institution that made the loans in the first place, although in many cases, a foreign bank or an insurance company has reinsured the credit. This means that the bulk of the value added from securitizing these kinds of assets has remained with the institution that originally made the loan. So far, securitization has not eliminated the role of the institution originating assets, although eventually, if volume continues to grow, some of the savings from the process will have to be passed along to the borrower. In particular, as non-banks continue to buy the assets and as non-banks continue to originate the assets, it will be harder and harder for banks to charge borrowers for their special, regulatory-driven costs.

The force of securitization is unstoppable because it is driven by fundamental economics. Bluntly put, the securities business system is more efficient than the banking business system. As a nation, we should accept the fact that in the future anything that can be securitized will be securitized.

The Banks Battle Back, Sort Of

By its very nature, the securitization process erodes much of the historic franchise of banks. In contrast, it expands the historic franchise of the securities industry. The sight of long-time customers fleeing led many of the most competitive banks to try to adopt the securities business system themselves. They were, however, frustrated at every turn by the Glass-Steagall Act, the Federal Reserve, the FDIC, and the Comptroller of the Currency, which prevented them from fully competing for the emerging business. Although their franchise was at stake, banks were basically powerless to protect it.

Within the constraints of the law, bankers did as much as they could to lure and please high-quality customers. They created a "loan sale" market for high-quality corporate loans that resulted in instruments that looked a lot like commercial paper. The money market deposit account authorized by the Garn–St Germain Act operated much like a money market mutual fund. Banks that could, went offshore to the London market, where they were free from Glass-Steagall limits, and underwrote bonds. Finally, in 1989, bankers were given permission by the Federal Reserve to underwrite corporate bonds in the United States and in 1990 the Federal Reserve gave J.P. Morgan permission to underwrite equities.

When permitted to do so, by regulators, thousands of banks set up discount brokerage operations. However, all this increased competition for the low-margin discount business accomplished was to undercut the margins of the full service brokers. It added little to the banks' profits. All in all, many banks entered the securities business but did it in a way that only helped drive the securities business itself into overcapacity. Instead of banks being able to migrate their customer base into the securities business or securities firms being able to acquire banks for their customer base, both industries expanded and in the process created enormous overcapacity that still exists today.

With hindsight, it was clear that Glass-Steagall was not an effective barrier to competition. It clearly was unable to keep banks out of the securities business or securities firms out of the banking business. Although the law was created to prevent banks from being exposed to securities underwriting risks, those risks are trivial compared to the risks banks have been allowed to take in underwriting credit risks. Also, the insider trading abuses of the 1980s (that is, Boesky, Segal, Milken, et al.) showed that Glass-Steagall didn't solve the inherently difficult issues of conflicts of interest in the securities business. All Glass-Steagall accomplished was prevention of the natural convergence of the two industries at great cost to both the industries themselves and the general public. We will never know how much pain could have been avoided if, instead of passing the Garn–St Germain Act of 1982, we had simply allowed banks and thrifts to sponsor money market mutual funds so that they could protect their customer franchise through selling securities, rather than raising deposits. Glass-Steagall represents an unnatural attempt to separate two industries that are in fact two sides of the same coin.

However, I am not arguing that we should have simply let banks enter the securities business. As I will argue later in the book, I believe banks should perform their securities activities in separately capitalized and separately regulated subsidiaries. The problem with Glass-Steagall is not that it forced the segregation of banking and securities activities; indeed, given potential conflicts of interest and the differences in how the businesses add value, there is much merit in such segregation. The problem with Glass–Steagall is that it forced the legal separation of ownership of banks and securities firms. This prevented any one firm from being able to exploit the natural linkages between the businesses. Because these linkages are profound, Glass-Steagall, in effect, drove participants in both industries to try to find ways around the regulation and law that separated them. This, in turn, led to the development of significant overcapacity in both industries and, moreover, has prevented the economic consolidation of participants. But perhaps most seriously, the Glass-Steagall Act prevented progressive banks from being able to adjust, smoothly, to the massive impact on their historic franchise by the economic force of securitization.

Distorting the Flow of Funds

If you step back from the details, you can begin to see how the combination of the economic force of securitization, when combined with our obsolete regulatory framework, led to massive distortions in what economists call the flow of funds.

The securitization process effectively led to the removal of the highest quality assets from banks. It also led to the removal of the most valuable deposits from banks and thrifts. The securities industry was able to offer people and institutions who wanted liquidity and safety higher returns through money market mutual funds. With the development of securitization, the assets and liabilities of depository institutions should have shrunk back to their remaining core functions. So as commercial paper was issued, as money market mutual funds and bond funds grew up, as mortgages were securitized, the balance sheets of insured depositories should have shrunk. Instead, they grew because weak banks and thrifts chose to raise deposits and put them into risky loans. The retail securities industry was, of course, an enthusiastic participant in this process.

When the interest rate ceilings on deposits were lifted through the passage of the Garn–St Germain Act, they were able to offer something even better than a money market mutual fund. Specifically, they were able to offer federally insured, brokered deposits—in effect, a securitized deposit that offered safety and high rates. These brokered deposits were a major part of the deposit anomaly. When combined with banks and thrifts which were also exploiting the deposit anomaly through simply selling high-rate deposits to their customers directly, the result was a massive distortion in the flow of funds, which caused money to flow to our weak institutions that would have otherwise been unable to get these funds. This, in turn, led to the credit anomaly, causing banks and thrifts to offer overgenerous terms for the credit they were extending so they could replace the revenue lost through the securitization process. Indeed, banks and thrifts began taking the massive equity risks in highly leveraged transactions and commercial real estate transactions, described earlier, which are now destroying the industry.

The fundamental economic force of securitization, when combined with an obsolete regulatory structure, has transformed the money of investors who want liquidity and safety into assets that are neither liquid nor safe. From a macroeconomic point of view, this has resulted in an enormous waste of capital and labor. As a nation, we wound up allocating credit to borrowers who made poor use of it and now, as we face up to the resulting mess, are reducing the credit available to worthwhile borrowers.

Are Banks Obsolete?

Is it inevitable that as securitization proceeds the banking business will become obsolete? Although I used to believe that banks as we know them might well disappear, I have now come to believe that there is a core banking business that is likely to remain viable far into the future if we have the will to reform our regulation of the financial services industry. To some extent, the question of the future of banking is a moving target because innovation and changes in law and regulation continuously expand the variety of assets that can be securitized. However, the securitization process clearly has some limits.

For example, in the near future, it seems clear that only very high-quality borrowers, such as governments and investment-grade corporations will be able to raise money directly by selling public debt. While Drexel Burnham was able to convince a number of investors that directly issued "junk bonds" were acceptable investments, the subsequent collapse of that market in 1989 and 1990, and of Drexel Burnham itself, shows that "junk bonds" were an unsustainable market anomaly. Indeed, without the deposit anomaly that allowed a number of savings and loans, with which Drexel had close working relationships, to hold "junk bonds" on their balance sheets, it is doubtful that the market would have ever taken off the way it did. The rapid collapse of "junk bond" prices in 1989 when savings and loans were forced, in the wake of the FIRRE Act, to sell these bonds out of their portfolio, certainly indicates that the thrifts were an important part of this market's support. Thus it seems likely that going forward it will only be possible to securitize high-quality assets. This means that assets with very complex risks, such as highly leveraged transactions or commercial real estate construction loans, are unlikely to be securitized. Either equity will need to be raised to finance these assets, or the risks will have to be structured and absorbed by participants other than an investor who wants to hold a debt security.

Another limit to the securitization process is that direct securitization (that is, issuing debt that is sold directly to investors), is only an option for large borrowers. No matter how creditworthy a small borrower, it is impossible for them to access the securities markets directly. For small borrowers, the costs of issuing securities exceeds the interest savings from issuing debt. This generally means, in today's market, that a borrower needs to be able to borrow at least $100 million at a time, because issues below that size are too illiquid to appeal to investors and the costs of issuing are too great relative to the cost savings.

As described earlier in the chapter, this size limit can be overcome in some kinds of assets by pooling together such loans as mortgages, auto paper, and credit card receivables. However, this process only works where the terms and conditions of the underlying loans and the information available on those loans allow investors to be able to make risk/return trade-offs. If the cash flows from the underlying loans are unpredictable or if the information needed about the cash flows is too difficult or too expensive to obtain, then the loans cannot be securitized.

At this point in time, this means that there are many categories of loans that are impossible to securitize. For example, it is impossible to package unsecured lending to individuals or loans to individuals with nonstandard terms into securities. It is also presently impossible to securitize almost all small business loans and loans to mid-size companies.

There is, of course, another limit to the securitization process. To the extent that depositors want to keep their money in an insured depository, the insured depository must have a place to invest those deposits. Indeed, many of the banks that have refused to take excessive credit risks have found that they can raise deposits far easier than they can originate high-quality loans. These banks then find that they need to buy securities to keep their balance sheets in balance. What this means is that if we find ways of reforming the deposit and credit anomalies, insured depositories are likely to have much of their deposits invested in securities. To the extent that this takes place, the depositor will have to bear the entire regulatory burden for the government's safety net. The result will be that depositors will have to accept lower yields on their deposits to pay for the regulatory-imposed reserves, insurance premiums, and capital to support the investment of his or her deposits. Of course, those borrowers who have no choice but to borrow from an insured depository, like small businesses, would also be paying for the costs of keeping their loans on a bank's balance sheet through the higher interest they pay.

Securitization, though it diminishes the role of banks, does not eliminate the need for banks. At least for the intermediate future, we still need banks to perform core functions that cannot be securitized. These core functions include much of the lending to individuals, small businesses, and mid-size corporations and the safekeeping of assets, the payment system, and the federally insured deposit-taking function, particularly through branches. These core functions are still vitally important to the nation. Clearly, what is needed is reform of the regulatory framework to accommodate the economic force of securitization while still allowing banks to perform their remaining core functions and still make a profit. This involves not only reforming the deposit insurance and credit anomalies but rewriting the Glass–Steagall Act as well.

9

Globalization

No one set out to create today's global capital market. It grew spontaneously after the major nations of the world abandoned fixed exchange rates in the early 1970s. Lack of financial discipline, mostly on the part of the United States, made a fixed rate system unworkable and inefficient. In the twenty years since abandonment, the resulting financial freedom, in combination with a boom in technology, has produced an ever-expanding global marketplace for financial instruments of all shapes, sizes, and denominations. As trading volumes soared and the variety of instruments multiplied, this global marketplace has acquired awesome strength. But the boom is only half complete. The markets for money, bonds, and credit have already become truly global; however, the globalization of stocks and real estate has just begun.

Despite its importance and power, few Americans outside the world of banking and securities understand much about global capital markets. Yet the integration of our national capital markets into the global capital markets has profound implications on the contract between our society and its banks. In fact, it is useless to talk about reforming the U.S. banking system without first gaining a thorough understanding of the history and workings of global capital markets.

The Birth of the Global Market

From the end of World War II until the early 1970s, the major nations of the world maintained an international monetary system that was based on maintaining fixed exchange rates and direct controls on capital flows. As a result, the economies of the various nations of the world were, for the most part, connected only through the flow of traded goods and the capital flows required to finance them. There was no global financial marketplace; there were only national financial markets that were largely independent of one another. The returns to

171

be earned on financial investments were largely determined by the particular conditions and circumstances within each country such as: regulations, laws, taxes, the structure of the local financial services industry, cultural patterns, and any number of other purely national factors. The dominant force in most countries was the nation's central bank, which controlled both the supply of money and interest rates and was often also responsible for regulation of the financial system. This localization of national capital markets led to significant differences in how similar financial instruments were valued from one country to another. For example, in Germany, in the postwar era, the stocks of companies have often been valued at six or seven times earnings; whereas in Japan, the stocks of companies in the same industries have often been valued at fifty times earnings or more.

A Sure Thing

When foreign exchange rates began to float in the 1970s, clever international banks found that they could make profits by linking these previously unlinked markets together. Banks found risk-free market anomalies they could exploit through a trading practice referred to as "arbitrage." This type of arbitrage should not be confused with arbitrage in takeover stocks practiced by Ivan Boesky. Here arbitrage refers to taking advantage of the fact that the same commodity does not have the exact same price at every moment in every corner of the global market.

This arbitrage process drives the global capital markets. Understanding how the global capital markets work first requires some understanding of how the arbitrage process works itself. Let me, therefore, ask that readers who are not deeply versed in finance hang on through the next few pages even if things get a bit rough. The effort is worth the trouble.

Let's go back to the mid-1970s for an example of arbitrage in the global money markets involving the foreign exchange markets. Let's assume that, at the time, the interest rate for borrowing U.S. dollars for *12 months* in the London interbank market was *8 percent* and yet, at the same time, the *12-month* rate for lending Italian lira was *20 percent*. So if you could convert dollars into lira, you could earn 12 percent higher interest. Unfortunately, you would also be exposed to the lira declining in value, relative to the dollar. The decline could more than wipe out the 12 percent extra in interest you were earning. However, if you could fix the future rate of exchange of lira back into dollars, you could protect yourself from this risk. This is known as a forward exchange contract: an agreement between two parties for exchanging a specific amount of currency at a specified future date at a specified rate. Let's say that at the time the conversion between dollars and lira was at a rate of 10 lira to the dollar. And let's further suppose that through a forward contract, you could guarantee yourself a price of 11 lira to the dollar in 12 months time. You now have a risk-free profit opportunity!

You get the forward contract at 11 lira to the dollar for 12 months hence. You borrow $1 million dollars at the 8 percent London rate. You convert the dollars into 10 million lira. You lend the lira out at the prevailing 20 percent rate. At the end of the 12 months you reconvert the 12 million lira (10 million of your original money, plus 2 million in interest) back into dollars at the guaranteed rate of 11 to 1 and receive $1,090,000. You pay off your original $1 million loan, plus the 8 percent ($80,000) interest you owe, leaving you with a $10,000 profit, absolutely risk-free.

The arbitrage process just described is known as "covered interest arbitrage." It is a very complicated, but very effective way to make money. If you can do thousands of these transactions in a year, you can make more than enough to make the effort worthwhile. A wide variety of similar arbitrage strategies also were opened up, once exchange rates floated and capital controls were lifted. As long as the revenues from undertaking such transactions exceed the costs, institutions will continuously arbitrage these cross-market differentials as long as they persist.

In the mid-1970s, most of these kinds of complicated arbitrage transactions were originally undertaken by investment bankers using slide rules and rates quoted to them by brokers. It used to cost $2,000 or more to complete such a transaction. But at the time, the arbitrage spreads between the markets were more than large enough to support these costs. Today, traders use computers and the Reuters and Telerate global information systems to find arbitrage opportunities. Fifteen years of technological innovation and regulatory change has eliminated most of the physical and regulatory barriers that used to preserve pricing anomalies between markets. However, arbitrage remains profitable for high-volume participants because high-tech telecommunication and computer systems have cut transaction costs. Most of the major participants have automated systems that continuously search for arbitrage opportunities through the simultaneous analysis of data for multiple markets. Some participants even use systems that can complete routine arbitrage transactions with little or no human intervention.

All of this has led to huge surges in volume. To put this in perspective, the number of money market and foreign exchange payments settled annually, just through the New York Bank Clearing House CHIPS system, expanded from 13.2 million to 36.5 million between 1980 and 1989. The volume of dollars settled per day increased from $147.9 billion to $758 billion during the same period.

In today's gargantuan and highly efficient market, covered interest rate arbitrage opportunities in the foreign exchange market persist for only moments and then disappear; but because of the enormous trading volumes involved, the profits for the leading players, major commercial and investment banks, are still frequently large. In the process, the foreign exchange and money markets of the major industrial countries have become quite tightly linked. Changes in the price of any one instrument in one currency affect the price of other instruments in other currencies, almost simultaneously.

If It Can Be Globalized, It Will Be

All of these linkages have driven the old national capital markets into a single, integrated, and often overwhelming global capital market. The strength of global pricing linkages appears to depend on the complexity of the risks influencing the price of a financial instrument. That is, the simpler the market, the stronger is the linkage; hence the strong global ties between straightforward markets like foreign exchange and money markets. Cross-border linkages are far less strong in the markets with more complex risks—real estate and equities—where massive pricing anomalies still persist.

The foreign exchange and money market were the first to globalize because they were the easiest to link up. Over the last fifteen years, linkages in the foreign exchange markets have become quite tight for many reasons: the simplicity and short life of the instruments traded; the lack of restrictions; the increased liquidity of foreign exchange, forward, futures, and options markets; the ready availability of market information; and the low cost of telecommunications and systems technology. As already noted, traders and arbitrageurs today take advantage of even small, transitory misalignments in the prices of financial instruments and, in doing so, tightly link the world's foreign exchange and money markets.

Next in line were the bond markets, especially government bonds. This process took place through much of the 1980s. Linkages between bond markets are somewhat weaker than in the foreign exchange and money markets, because the risks of bonds are more complex and harder to quantify. Corporate bonds are subject to default. They are often not actively traded and therefore can be expensive to sell. And corporations often have the right to prepay the bonds if rates fall. In contrast, government bonds issued by major nations are not thought to have credit risk, are very actively traded, and usually cannot be prepaid. For these reasons, the global linkages in the pricing of government bonds have become quite strong whereas linkages in corporate bond pricing are somewhat weaker.

There are two kinds of bond markets; the market for newly issued bonds, called the "primary market," and the market for bonds that are traded after they have been issued, called the "secondary market." Both the primary and secondary markets have been globalized. In the primary markets, links between domestic markets and the broader pan-European market known as the "Euromarket," have been forged mainly by corporate borrowers issuing in the Euromarket in London. In the secondary markets ties between domestic bond markets have been mainly established by investors trading government bonds outside their home market—primarily in London, New York, and Tokyo.

In the primary markets, globalization is driven by issuers looking for cheaper or less-restrictive financing across national borders. The discrepancies—and they were often quite large during the early 1980s—were created by differences in each country's accounting standards, access to information, regulatory constraints, tax system, financial services industry structure, cultural patterns, and investor preferences and expectations.

For example, enormous foreign investments have been built up in Switzerland—partly because tax evasion is not a criminal offense there and partly because of Switzerland's tough privacy laws, which enable investors who avoid their local national laws, known as "flight capital," to be protected from detection. These investors create a huge demand for unregistered instruments that do not identify the owner, known as bearer bonds. Eurodollar bonds by U.S. issuers are in "bearer" form, whereas United States corporate bonds and equities are registered. United States issuers found in the 1980s that they could place their bonds in the Eurobond market, with private banking clients of Swiss banks, at far lower rates than they could get in the United States, because portfolio managers working for private investors via Switzerland often cared more about privacy for their client than obtaining the absolutely highest yield.

Issuers have also taken advantage of the fact that Eurobonds are priced largely on the "name" recognition of the issuer. The reason is that U.S. investors have historically been more sensitive to nuances of credit risk than Eurobond investors. These offshore investors have only recently begun to use ratings to evaluate credit risk and are not yet comfortable with the process. Therefore a U.S. single-A company with a well-known name has often been able to raise money in the Eurobond market at AA or even AAA rates, thus saving one quarter to half a percent on its borrowings.

Similarly, Japanese companies found that in the late 1980s they could issue convertible bonds in the international markets at very low interest rates. Because of the sky-high multiples prevailing in the Tokyo markets at the time, the bonds actually increased earnings per share of the issuer when they were converted into stock!

It should come as no surprise that there was an explosion of international corporate debt issuance throughout the 1980s. From 1980 to 1989, some $1 trillion of international debt was issued by corporations.

The borrowing did not stop with corporations. Governments around the world also took to the international debt markets. The U.S. government, in particular, borrowed enormously from international investors to finance its out-of-control trade and budget deficits. Since 1985, the U.S. government borrowed an estimated $1.9 trillion from international investors who bought their bonds through dealers based in New York.

Although the boom in the primary market for international bonds has gathered most press coverage in the 1980s, the tighter linkage of the national secondary markets is perhaps more important economically. Bonds and notes remain outstanding until they are redeemed, are called, or default. With maturities ranging from two years to twenty years or more, the only way for an investor to get money back on demand is to sell it in the secondary market. Historically, domestic secondary markets were self-contained, but they have become increasingly linked through the same technological changes that have enabled the foreign exchange and money markets to be linked. There is even a trading practice equivalent to covered interest rate arbitrage that uses bonds and currency swaps, rather than money and foreign exchange market instruments.

In addition to direct arbitrage linkages, the prices of all bonds are linked through the efforts of expert investors searching for the best risk-adjusted yield. Such linkages have long existed in national markets. Local investors are always trading off the risks and returns of money market instruments with medium- and long-term corporate and government bonds, thereby moving up and down the yield curve and trading off various credit, liquidity, and prepayment risks against differences in yield. In the process, pricing relationships between instruments change continuously.

Increasingly, investors make such pricing trade-offs between the Eurobond secondary market and national secondary markets. As a result, Eurobonds sold by Japanese corporations are increasingly winding up in the portfolios of Japanese investors, while Eurobonds sold by American corporations are winding up in the portfolios of American investors.

Investors are also trading off the yield spreads between bonds issued in their own currency and bonds issued in other countries' currencies. One of the reasons why Japanese investors, such as the large life insurance companies, were willing to take the currency risk implicit in making unhedged investments in U.S. Treasury bonds during the early 1980s, was the low real yield (that is, after adjusting for inflation) available to them in domestic ten-year Japanese government issues, around 2 percent, at the time. Compare that to the real yield in ten-year U.S. Treasury issues of around 5 percent at the same time and you can understand why Japanese wanted to invest in U.S. Treasuries. Bond investors are always looking for the highest real yields available to them.

The combination of arbitrage, cross-border, cross-instrument, and cross-currency trading is leading to a convergence in bond volatility across the world. In many countries, including the United States, bond yields have become highly correlated with changes in the value of the dollar against other currencies. Bond prices in all markets are simultaneously affected by global events, although the linkages will never be as strong as in the foreign exchange and money markets because of the complexity of the bonds themselves.

Globalization has moved more slowly in some other markets. Price linkages, for example, still remain weak among equity markets. Here significant differences in valuation exist across different markets, even for comparable companies in identical industries. Yet there is no simple technology that allows multinational corporations to take advantage of these radically different valuations available in different markets. Few U.S. companies were able to take advantage of generous Japanese valuations by selling stock on the Tokyo Exchange. In the secondary market, cross-border equity investments require very sophisticated analytical skills and research capabilities, given the enormous complexity of equity pricing and subtle differences in accounting and market regulations.

But the sympathetic rise and fall of the world's equity markets in recent years does demonstrate that, despite the hurdles, cross-border equity markets, too, are indeed becoming linked—if by nothing more than investor psychology. During the October 1987 stock market crash, most of the world's national stock markets declined to varying degrees. Japan fell the least. During the 1987 recovery, most of the world's stock markets recovered again with Japan leading the pack. During the 1990 "bear" market, most of the world's stock markets declined. Japan was off 41 percent. Germany declined 23.6 percent. The United States fell 10.6 percent. Much of this market reaction in the second half of 1990 was due to Iraq's invasion of Kuwait and the rising cost of oil.

The linkage of equity markets is likely to remain much less perfect than linkages in bond and foreign exchange markets. Indeed, many studies have shown that well-diversified international equity portfolios are less risky than purely domestic portfolios. But equity linkages are clearly developing, and will continue to develop, as cross-border information on management quality, hidden reserves, cash flows, accounting, and so on improve and as techniques for valuing stocks converge.

If worldwide equity markets are only loosely linked, then worldwide real estate markets are linked by a long leash, indeed. One look at Tokyo and New York tells the story. In 1990, a well-located 1,200-square-foot apartment in midtown Manhattan was worth some $350,000 to $400,000. The same size apartment in Tokyo, even after real estate prices had softened during the early part of the year, was still selling for over $4 million. However, it seems likely that even real estate values will become more closely linked as time passes.

What Has Been Done Can't Be Undone

It would be hard to imagine a more convoluted, haphazard, jury-rigged system than the one just described. Of course, no one designed these markets. They just came into being as the result of millions of individual decisions made by investors seeking higher returns: fund raisers seeking cheaper funding; intermediaries seeking profits; all facing the physical and regulatory barriers designed to thwart them.

Nevertheless, amid all this complexity and imperfection, the global capital markets exist and function, even if the process is only half complete. Demands for funds in one nation affect the prices for funds in all linked nations and vice versa. All of the capital providers and users in all of the participating nations are now directly linked together. If a nation's borrowers find that its own domestic savers want higher returns than demanded in world markets, then they in effect draw on the world's savings until a new pricing equilibrium is reached. Or conversely, if a nation's savers find that the world's markets offer higher investment rates than domestic investment markets, then they invest in the world's markets until prices equalize. In the 1980s the United States drew on the world's savings and was thus able to finance its demands for funds more cheaply than if it had been forced to finance its borrowings entirely domestically. At the same time, savers in the globally linked countries, particularly in Japan, earned higher returns than would have been available if they had only been able to invest in domestic markets.

It is hard to imagine how the integration of the world's capital markets could ever be reversed. Indeed, global pricing linkages of all types are sure to continue growing stronger, because the underlying forces at work are structural, rather than cyclical. The evolution of telecommunication systems for both voice and data has significantly reduced the transaction costs of global financial operations and expanded cross-country financial flow volumes in the same way that a reduction in transportation costs opened the way for international trade to flow in response to patterns of competitive advantage. Supply and demand forces that were previously confined to national borders (the liberalization of deposit ceilings in the United States or the high savings rate in Japan are two good examples) are now spilling over and affecting prices of financial instruments worldwide.

In 1990 this truth hit hard in the United States. After a decade in which we financed our ever-increasing consumption by borrowing well beyond increases in gross national product, we suddenly realized that our economy was significantly driven by the global capital market flows. During the 1980s the United States imported over a trillion dollars of net foreign capital to finance its trade deficit. These capital flows, in turn, enabled us to finance our even more massive government fiscal deficit. What's more, our indebtedness to the world will grow until we are able to shrink these twin deficits.

We recently began to feel the pain of our decisions to borrow rather than save. Early in 1990 long-term yields on government bonds rose, even as our economy began to soften, because of rising rates in Japan and the need for capital in Eastern Europe, and in particular in East Germany. Our dependence on other nations' savings to finance our spending resulted in higher rates for us, once these other nations began to need the funds for themselves. Late in the year as the credit screws tightened, the unwillingness of foreign banks (particularly Japanese) to lend deprived many of our over-leveraged borrowers the credit they needed to keep liquid. Moreover, our dependence on foreign capital left the Federal Reserve unable to lower interest rates as the economic slump deepened. Any attempt to lower interest rates would have probably just triggered a rapid depreciation of the dollar, which—given our dependence on oil and other imports—would have accelerated inflation, which in turn would have increased rates. The truth is, in an integrated global financial economy, a debtor nation's interest rates are largely shaped by the demands of the global marketplace, not by central banks.

I would not be surprised if the worldwide tumult, as the 1990s begin, leads to calls for re-regulation and the return to national markets. But there is a scant chance that regulators can overcome the amount of financial interdependence that already exists between the nations of the world. It is the enormous volume of cross-border instruments already outstanding that creates the greatest structural interdependence. The alternative to globalization is self-containment, but it does not appear that self-containment is even an option.

Even if each nation were miraculously able to run a balanced current account from now on and there were no new cross-border capital flows, the existing stock of cross-border financial instruments, already outstanding, would still remain and the prices of those financial instruments would need to continue adjusting to all the differences in the various domestic economies. As investment rates, savings rates, and inflation rates fluctuated, so too would prices in the global secondary market. Because the opposite is likely to be true—that is, since cross-border capital flows are likely to continue growing and current accounts surpluses and deficits seem likely to remain— we can expect to see the interdependence of national financial markets increase, rather than decrease.

In the face of such interdependencies it would be difficult to re-erect national financial boundaries no matter how strong the desire. Like it or not, the United States is now a net borrower to the tune of roughly $1 trillion from the world, and no one can regulate that interdependence away. And even if the United States could immediately convert to a constantly improving current account balance, it would take until well after 2000 to get back to the degree of self-containment we had in the early 1980s.

History shows that regulation designed to control market forces is seldom successful. As this book has tried to illustrate, such efforts to control markets and use them as a tool for government policy usually have destructive consequences. History has also shown that financial innovation can overcome almost any regulatory barriers. In fact, much of the globalization existing today is the result of regulatory barriers, which drove borrowers and investors to find ways around national regulation.

Globalization has thus significantly changed the rules of the financial world. So long as there are persistent benefits for borrowers and investors, globalization will proceed largely unabated and will be irreversible. Economic agents seldom surrender newly won opportunities voluntarily, and market forces, once unleashed, can rarely be successfully reined in. The alternative to globalization, self-containment, would cripple the citizens of our country. It is no longer even an option.

Closed Mind, Open System

We are now tragically mismanaging our integration into the global economy. We need to completely rethink how the United

States and other nations manage their national financial markets and their national financial economies. An analogy to design engineering illustrates the gravity of the problem.

Design engineers often talk about "closed" and "open" systems. A "closed" system is one for which the designer tries to think through how *everything* should work in *all* circumstances, anticipating *everything* that could possibly go wrong, and devising solutions to each and every problem. Much of the design work, therefore, involves insulating the system from the outside environment. For example, engineering a nuclear power plant is a classic closed system design problem. A closed system engineering approach is designed to thwart Murphy's Law (anything that can go wrong, will go wrong, at the worst time).

In contrast, for an "open" system the designer tries to think through how everything should work in response to *changing conditions*. Open systems usually rely on an individual at the controls to respond to new information and make appropriate adjustments. In a car, for example, the steering wheel, brakes, gas pedal, windshield wipers, and lights all are tools to be used by the driver to respond to changes in road conditions, weather, flow of traffic, and so forth.

Since the Depression, the government and the Federal Reserve have attempted to use the banking system as one of their tools to control our economy. As described in Chapter 2, this worked fine, as long as the government was in control of the whole system—in other words, as long as we had a closed national financial system, we dominated the world's economy, and so the system could work. However, now that we are part of a much larger open system, it is no longer possible to control all of our financial economy through banks. We are like the driver careening down a road who no longer has use of the steering wheel. It makes little difference that we still have perfect control of the gas pedal and the brakes. The car is no longer under our control. By acting as if we still had complete control, we will do great harm to ourselves and others.

We have lost our ability to control our financial economy as the flow of funds has become securitized and as the global capital marketplace has been born. We will never get it back. Throughout this book, I show that our government's attempts to use the banking system as a vehicle to meet our political and economic objectives has been a disaster. Although the social objectives of helping developing nations or promoting real estate development are important to our national interest, the unintended consequences of promoting these objectives through the regulation of banks and thrifts has all but destroyed our financial system.

We have not been alone. All the governments of the world have tended to manipulate the financial economy, to some degree, in order to help finance governments' expenditures or to meet national political objectives. Evidence suggests that political leaders must pay more respect and attention to the power of the global financial economy. Over the last twenty years, the various nations of the world have used the freedom of floating exchange rates to pursue widely divergent economic strategies.

The United States used the freedom of the global financial marketplace and the liberation of its own national financial economy to finance enormous trade and fiscal deficits and to keep its real economy growing for nearly the whole decade of the 1980s, even as productivity lagged. Japan, on the other hand, used its financial economy to gain a competitive advantage in trade markets, but kept domestic inflation moderate despite high growth rates and high savings rates. Japan achieved this end by channeling the resulting excess liquidity into the markets for real estate and equities rather than into domestic demand for real goods and services. Germany also pursued an export strategy. Germany kept domestic inflation moderate by maintaining very heavy regulatory control over its domestic financial economy. Neither Japan nor Germany could have pursued these strategies without the United States running its massive fiscal and trade deficits.

For the last twenty years, the globalization of financial markets has represented a "free lunch" to the political leaders of nations. The globalization of financial markets has let them pursue widely divergent political and economic strategies, without significant consequences. Now, however, it appears that the so-called free lunch has, in fact, been expensive, and it is now time to pay the tab. The walls that these countries and other major nations of the world have used to contain their financial economies are cracking; ironically, they are under pressures from the global financial economic forces unleashed when they floated exchange rates twenty years ago.

Part I of this book described one of the costs of our free lunch—the breakdown of the U.S. credit system. Japan is now developing credit problems as well, but with some very important differences. Because the Japanese system effectively prevents defaults, the consequences of credit excesses are different in Japan than in the United States. In Japan, credit excesses have led to massive speculation and overvaluation of stocks and real estate, rather than waves of loans going bad. I must confess that I am unconvinced by arguments that Japanese valuations are rational, if I would only take the time to understand them. I have and they are not. How could the market capitalization of Japan Airlines (JAL) in 1989 be over $15 billion when Lufthansa, British Airways, and Delta (each with higher earnings than JAL) were worth only $3 billion or $4 billion each? Indeed, it is totally absurd that in 1989 the entire land mass of Japan was allegedly worth four times more than the land mass of the United States, which is twenty-five times larger! The ludicrous overvaluation of stocks and real estate in Tokyo has placed enormous stress on the Japanese social system. Older people in Japan who owned property before the rapid run-up in values took place are rich. Younger people, with little hope of ever being able to afford to buy a place to live, feel like paupers. Such overvaluations are not sustainable in an increasingly global financial world. The 45 percent decline in value of the Tokyo stock market in 1990 could be only a prelude to what adjustments may be needed to get Japanese valuations of stocks and real estate back to reality. And since massive amounts of credit have been extended against these excessive valuations, the resulting economic loss could be huge. I will not speculate on how this economic loss will be absorbed, but my guess is that it will involve considerable pain, both for Japanese banks and for Japanese society.

In Europe, the liberalization of financial markets has only just started. On the surface, European banks look quite sound. Most European bankers, like their U.S. counterparts during the late 1970s, find it inconceivable that a breakdown in lending practices could occur in their countries. Yet the same forces that have brought our banking system to the brink are being unleashed in Europe. Non-bank competition such as money market mutual funds are growing. Borrowers are increasingly bypassing banks in favor of securities markets. Bank after bank is gearing up to compete outside its national boundaries, just as U.S. banks during the early 1980s prepared to compete outside their states and their regions. In fact, I believe that in the next few years, price competition for deposits will become as intense in Europe as that which developed in the United States during the 1980s.

As in the United States, these competitive forces are being unleashed in Europe without reform of the fundamental regulatory structure. Pan-European liberalization of rules is taking place without fundamental reform of national safety and soundness regulation. I do not know where the weak links are in the European safety net system, but I will bet that market forces will find them. Competition will not just be over the price of credit, but also over terms and conditions. Weak borrowers will find weak banks. Credit excesses will take place in those nations with the weakest regulatory systems. Just as in the United States, I fear this will lead to concentrations of credit risk in the weakest institutions.

In some ways, the adjustment to the liberalization of regulation may be more difficult in Europe than in the United States. It will be more difficult in Europe to lay off workers in response to profit pressures. Moreover, national banks in Europe are more clearly seen as instruments of national policy than in the United States. They may be asked to finance essentially uneconomic activities to further national interests in a drive for share in an increasingly pan-European economy.

The existing regulatory structures for banks in the United States, Japan, and Europe are fundamentally unsound. Competition and market forces have been unleashed, worldwide, without reforming the various national regulatory systems. What is needed is proactive reform, worldwide, before we destroy our banking systems and do fundamental damage to the economies of the societies they serve. The financial disasters of the last few years merely presage cataclysms that lie ahead, as we move into the next century.

As the world's real and financial economies continue to become more closely integrated and interdependent, we face inevitable clashes in the different financial, cultural, and political values of nations. The truth is that the eventual price to be paid for the freedom to pursue independent national economic strategies is the creation of a global financial system that is beyond the control of any individual nation, and which ultimately has the power to discipline bad policies through destructive financial shocks.

If nations cannot control the global financial economy, then who should control it?

I believe the only answer is to let Adam Smith's "invisible hand" of the marketplace control the allocation of the flow of funds. However, if we want the financial marketplace to do its job of allocating resources through setting prices, the financial marketplace has to work better than it does today. Let me hasten to say that making markets work better does not mean completely deregulating them, because financial markets require regulation or they self-destruct. Making markets work better, however, does mean eliminating all of the destructive market anomalies caused by obsolete regulation or a government's desire to meet political or social objectives. It also means building the public and private infrastructure needed in each nation to make the financial markets in each nation more "perfect." A specific plan for reforming the U.S. banking system along these lines is contained in Part III. A plan for the world's banking systems is far beyond the scope of this book.

If we reform the system and make global and national financial markets more "perfect," then the inevitable clashes in the different financial, cultural, and political values of nations can be worked out by relatively small, continuous changes in market prices. If we fail to reform the system, then these clashes in values will be worked out through the destructive manias, crashes, panics, and credit crises that characterized the six hundred years of the banking industry's history.

What Can We Do?

It is obviously in our nation's interest to have financial institutions that have the skills needed to operate in the global marketplace and the capital required to absorb the risks of operating in the global marketplace. Moreover, it is clearly in the nation's interest to have an industry that is healthy enough to finance customers lacking direct access to the global capital markets. The United States has a disproportionately large share of its gross national prouct produced by small- and medium-size companies, that depend on banks. Most fundamentally, given our nation's continued dependence on foreign capital, we need highly skilled institutions that can ensure that capital will flow when it can be most productively employed.

Against these measures, we have some problems. Although many U.S. banks and securities firms have built the capabilities to play global roles by making enormous investments in systems, telecommunications, staff, and premises in London, New York, Tokyo, and elsewhere, a number of these institutions are retreating from the global marketplace. Part of this is a healthy shake-out of excess capacity. However, much of it is not.

Many U.S. money center banks are cutting back their overseas branches, simply because they can no longer afford to invest, given their massive losses from the developing country's debt and commercial real estate debt as described earlier. Moreover, to operate in the global capital markets requires unquestioned strength as a counterparty; a loss of 0.125 percent to 0.25 percent in spreads caused by higher perceived credit risk can wipe out much if not all of the profits from arbitrage transactions. Finally, banks struggling with credit problems and capital guidelines may lack the capacity to take even normal trading risks. As a nation, we need a number of powerful global capital markets participants. As of the early 1990s, we had only a very few who still retained unquestioned ability to operate as full participants in the world's markets.

One of the reasons is that in world terms, many of our banks are pygmies. Despite the fact that our nation has the world's largest economy, we have very few banks that are large in world terms. Only two of the world's 50 largest banks, as measured by earnings, are U.S. banks. By national policy, we have maintained a fragmented banking system, and as a result most of our banks lack the muscle to compete in the world's markets.

Most fundamental, however, is the issue of having a financial system that is effective in doling out capital and credit. Given our national fiscal and trade policies during the 1980s, we are going to be dependent on foreign capital for the next decade, at least. Getting capital where it is most productively used will require high skill. Like it or not, we have miscommitted hundreds of billions of dollars to high-risk developing country debt, to unsoundly underwritten, highly leveraged transactions, and to commercial real estate projects. As a nation, we are going to need institutions that can deliver funds— that is, credit, debt, and equity—to their most productive uses. Although non-U.S. institutions will play some role, perhaps a significant role, the credit environment today makes it unlikely that many foreign institutions will be able, or willing, to provide the funds needed to any but the largest, most creditworthy borrowers.

Frankly, many foreign banks have their hands full with their own nonperforming loans in the United States to highly leveraged corporations and to unsoundly underwritten commercial real estate projects. Foreign capital directly invested by foreign institutions is far more likely to find its way into Treasury bills and publicly rated securities rather than to finance businesses and customers with whom they have had no historic relationships. Moreover, given our nation's need to recapitalize many of its companies and regional economies, we would be foolish as a nation to become completely dependent, not only on foreign capital, but on foreign financial institutions, as well. All things being equal, such a situation would tend to disadvantage our private sector's ability to compete in the global real economy as well as in the global financial economy.

Taken together, it should be a high national priority to have a thriving, highly skilled, highly profitable, and highly confident financial sector. Right now, much of our financial sector is sick, and our economy has already begun to suffer. Unless we fix it and fix it soon, our real ability to compete globally will waste away as the new century dawns.

10

Consolidation and Disaggregation

The banking industry is being radically reconfigured. Paradoxically, the forces of restructuring are pushing the core banking functions together into ever-larger and fewer institutions, and yet simultaneously pulling all nonessential functions away from the core bank. The classic, bundled, banking model I described earlier in the book is being reshaped. The industry is consolidating and at the same moment it is being broken apart.

Understanding the forces that underlie this apparent paradox are terribly important as we think about reforming the relationship between banks and society. If we allow these forces to act, they will naturally heal many of the economic flaws that now cripple the industry. But if instead we adopt a muddle-through approach, both the industry and our economy will suffer.

Compressing the Core

Let me first clarify what I mean by a "core bank." The core bank takes deposits, lends primarily to individuals and to small- and medium-size businesses and is responsible for the retail payment system. At the heart of a core bank is the shared cost structure discussed earlier in the book. All things being equal, it costs relatively little to add more revenue to a core bank because most of the costs of being a core bank are both fixed and shared. When core banks in the same geographic market join together, as when Wells Fargo acquired Crocker in 1986, the cost savings are enormous.

Wells Fargo was able to save $240 million per year through this merger. All told, the combined results of Wells Fargo in the first full year after the merger were $843 million; in comparison, the combined earnings of Wells Fargo and Crocker in the year before the merger were only $283 million. Simply allowing strong institutions to take over adjacent institutions in neighboring states has also brought savings through combining overhead and processing functions. If the acquiring bank is more highly skilled than the bank being acquired, which is often the case, there are also enormous opportunities to increase profits through better pricing and better marketing of products. Super regional banks like NCNB, NBD, and Banc One are the natural result of allowing top-notch banks to take over smaller, less-competitive banks.

The concentration of core banking functions has been remarkable. From 1980 to 1989 the share of domestic deposits held by medium and large regional bank holding companies grew from 25 percent to 46 percent of the industry. These banks are primarily engaged in core banking activities, but are large enough to have economies of scale. Far more telling is the fact that the share of deposits at money center banks, which are not as deeply committed to the core banking functions, declined slightly throughout the decade from a level of 11.7 percent in 1980 to 9.9 percent in 1989.

The explanation for this consolidation among regional banks is simple: reinterpretation of the Bank Holding Company Act of 1956 by individual states. Under the act, permission to acquire banks across state lines was granted to the states. And from 1956 to 1980, all states essentially prohibited cross-state acquisitions. However, in the 1980s, the unleashing of competitive energies put the act under pressure. Small regional and community banks realized their disadvantage and began to sell out to stronger players. Larger regional banks sought to acquire smaller banks, so they would be too big to be acquired by even bigger players. And even the largest institutions feared being acquired by New York money center banks. The result was the so-called regional compacts of the early 1980s, which permitted interstate acquisitions within defined regions like the Southeast or New England. Only now, in 1991, are many states permitting full interstate acquisitions; indeed, many states still have important barriers to interstate mergers.

Unfortunately, much of the consolidation that took place in the 1980s was non-economic. Often large institutions merged simply because the respective chairpersons wanted to run bigger companies or to prevent their respective companies from being acquired by someone else. In my experience, at least half of all the large mergers that took place in the 1980s took place for non-economic reasons. In these mergers, little changed except ownership. In many cases, almost no integration took place. The acquired banks operated almost as if no change in ownership had occurred. This type of consolidation adds no value to the nation. Indeed, it may prevent or delay economic consolidation, since it protects poorly run institutions. In some cases, it fuels bad lending. Not coincidentally, many regionals with the worst credit problems were the results of these non-economic mergers. Interest and fees from taking excessive credit risk enabled these mergers initially to report significant profit gains. Predictably, the gains were followed by massive losses.

In contrast, economic consolidation benefits the public and rewards well-run banks and their shareholders. Economic consolidation occurs whenever the long-term profitability of the resulting merged institutions is greater than the profit of the institutions as separate entities. Economic consolidation is a merger in which value is increased, through either providing better services to customers or lowering costs. In general, economic consolidation has been driven by large, well-run super regional banks that have taken over poorly run, smaller regional banks. Of course, these well-run institutions have also succeeded by simply being better and improving their market share. About half of the growth of well-run super regionals has come from growth, and half has come from acquisitions. Although, in truth, it is hard to separate the two. Acquisitions can give an institution the critical mass to dominate a market. In the best case, a virtuous cycle begins. Growing profits lead to growing share price, which leads to expanded acquisitions, and so forth.

The process of healthy economic consolidation should continue to accelerate. There is no shortage of failing S&Ls and failing banks waiting to be taken over. By our estimates, roughly $1.5 trillion of deposits and other funds are currently in the hands

hands of undercapitalized banks and thrifts. Most of these institutions need to be placed into stronger hands. Only the most robust players can raise the capital, either through issuing stock or retained earnings, to recapitalize these failing players. Also, interstate barriers continue to fall. California and New York bank holding companies will be able to acquire one another in 1991. Finally, few banks can afford the continuing investment required in technology and information systems. Technology continues to displace labor in banks at an accelerating rate. Tom Steiner, a banking and technology expert at McKinsey, estimates that roughly 65 percent of the banking industry's expense to upgrade and expand systems are made by the largest thirty-five bank holding companies. Most smaller players lack the base of business to be able to afford the huge investment required.

This consolidation is a natural healing process that can help correct many of the problems described throughout this book. By allowing winners to win, we not only rid ourselves of the poorly run institutions, but we help restore the profitability of those that remain. The result will be institutions of the size and scale needed for us to remain competitive as a nation, as banking continues to globalize.

It is possible to envision ten to fifteen very strong multi-regional core banks, each with 3 percent to 5 percent of the nation's deposits, or more. These institutions would be the natural outgrowth of today's super regionals and most would be headquartered in regional centers like Columbus, Charlotte, Detroit, and San Francisco. Each could have from $100 to $200 billion of deposits and earn from $1 billion to over $2 billion per year. These banks would be formed primarily from consolidation of the largest 120 bank holding companies, which already account for two-thirds of the industry's deposits. They would earn these profits by lending to individuals, small businesses, and mid-size companies; by making the payment system work; and by providing a safe depository for all—the core banking functions. There would be no excessive credit risk. There is still room in this future world for thousands of well-run local and community banks, and dozens of well-run smaller regionals, as well, who would continue to succeed through providing superior service to customers at the local level. The poorly run institutions would disappear, replaced by institutions with clout to take on the mammoth European and Japanese institutions, which have emerged in the last decade.

There are all kinds of barriers that currently thwart the creation of such institutions. The most important of these are the remaining regulatory and legal barriers. Let's examine what some of these barriers are and how they came into existence.

Sneaking Past the Road Blocks

It is remarkable that consolidation of core banking has gone as far as it has, given the legal barriers to acquiring banks. Since the late 1700s, the nation has continuously distrusted concentrations of financial power. Remember, much of the disagreement between Hamilton's Federalists and Jefferson's Democratic Republicans was over the power of the national bank. Throughout the nineteenth century, the westward pioneers distrusted those in the east who provided them with money. The resulting populist spirit is still strong in many western states.

As the nation grew up during the industrial age, so did the movement toward the use of bank holding companies to buy up financial institutions. These forerunners of the modern bank holding company were then called "group banks," because a company would control a whole portfolio of smaller banks. These group banks developed for both economic and regulatory reasons. The nation was growing rapidly, mergers were in vogue, and the new large regional manufacturing companies needed access to a wide variety of financial services. In a regulatory sense, the various restrictive state branching laws forced bankers who wanted to follow their customers' expansion to adopt the holding company structure. The use of state law to protect local banking interests from what was viewed as unfair competition from big city banks has thus been part of the fabric of the regulatory system for over a century. Many of the state laws still in place can be traced to state laws written before the Civil War. In 1927, the federal government passed the McFadden Act, which reaffirmed state preeminence over intrastate branching by out-of-state banks. McFadden remains the primary obstacle to interstate banking.

During the Depression the industry did not consolidate much. It mostly just shrank. Because of bank failures, we went from 31,076 banks in 1921 to only 14,776 banks by June 1933. It was not until after World War II that bank holding companies resumed the rapid growth that had characterized the 1920s. Part of this came from the growth of the domestic economy. But much came from the desire of larger bank holding companies to raise capital and have enough shares of common stock outstanding to be publicly traded. Small banks have such small stock market capitalizations that they are, in effect, private companies. As consolidation under bank holding companies proceeded, many in Washington, particularly at the Federal Reserve, began to fear unchecked consolidation in the banking industry.

As always, the fears were manifested in new legislation: the Bank Holding Company Act of 1956. This law essentially prevented interstate acquisitions without the permission of the states and made the Federal Reserve the primary overseer of bank holding companies. This newfound concern about the concentration of economic power was viewed by many as simply an excuse by the Federal Reserve to extend its already considerable power over banks. A Federal Reserve staff report, "Concentration of Banking in the United States," played a prominent role in the congressional debate. It pointed out that since 1921 the total deposits of the 100 largest commercial banks had risen from roughly 32 percent in 1921 to over 46 percent by 1951. As an aside, the largest 100 bank holding companies represented 71.0 percent of total deposits as of the end of 1989, despite the limitations of the Bank Holding Company Act of 1956. It is hard to stand in the way of fundamental economic forces.

The lead witness in favor of greater federal regulation of bank holding companies was William McChesney Martin, chairman of the Board of Governors of the Federal Reserve System. Chairman Martin had been pushing for such regulation since the early 1950s. In testimony he said that he was concerned about situations "in which a large part of the commercial banking facilities in a large area of the country may be concentrated under the management and control of a single corporation." He also was concerned that "there is nothing in existing law which prevents the combination under the same control, through the holding company device, of both banking and non-banking enterprises controlled by the holding company." These sentiments were shared by a majority in Congress. Since that time, the Federal Reserve Board has had both the authority and the responsibility for deciding what are proper activities for bank holding companies.

The Bank Holding Company Act of 1956 had one major loophole. Holding companies with only one bank were allowed to own any other enterprise. The Federal Reserve had opposed this one-bank exemption from the beginning, and by 1970 was joined by the Nixon administration in its bid to eliminate the exemption. Wright Patman, chairman of the House Banking Committee, promoted legislation to directly deal with "the problem of conglomerate activity in our corporate system." The result? Yet another law and more power for the Federal Reserve: the Bank Holding Company Act Amendments of 1970.

Thus it was only twenty years ago that the functions of banking and non-banking were officially separated from one another by legislation. In ruling on permissible activities, the Federal Reserve has taken a "go-slow" approach, to say the least. It was not until 1989 that the Federal Reserve ruled that savings and loans were "closely related to banking and a proper incident thereto" even though the man on the street could see little difference between making a deposit in a commercial bank branch or at a savings and loan branch.

Over the intervening twenty years, the Federal Reserve has used its powers under the 1970 act to exercise enormous control over bank holding companies. In particular, it has imposed its own capital requirements on the acquiror in a bank merger. The Federal Reserve requirement trumps those requirements defined by the FDIC or the Office of the Comptroller of the Currency (OCC). Moreover, the senselessly protracted approval process effectively made it all but impossible to do hostile takeovers as amply demonstrated by the endless agony that Bank of New York went through to acquire Irving Trust.

But the real problem was that the 1956 and 1970 acts created a fundamentally unsound financial structure. Because the only major asset of most bank holding companies were banks, the only source of strength came from the bank itself, not the holding company. To mitigate this problem the Federal Reserve permitted banks to "double leverage," which means that bank holding companies were allowed to raise long-term debt at the parent and invest it in subsidiaries as equity. Although this practice put more equity in banks, it left the holding companies groaning under huge debt loads—a source of weakness rather than a source of strength. The banks were stronger than the holding company rather than the other way around. Therefore, if a bank got into trouble, it had no where to turn. Moreover, holding company activities had to be financed off the bank's strength. So if a holding company's non-banking activity gets in trouble, the whole enterprise is in trouble. If the bank holding company was regulated so that each non-banking subsidiary was capitalized as if it were a standalone entity (that is, if there was no implicit support from the Federal Reserve), the marketplace would demand that each non-bank subsidiary be appropriately capitalized for the particular risks it was taking. Moreover, if "double leverage" was not permitted, the holding company would be a source of strength, not a weakness.

In combination, the McFadden Act, the Bank Holding Act of 1956, and the Bank Holding Company Act Amendments of 1970 have proved powerful barriers to consolidation. Indeed, it is remarkable that the consolidation described earlier has even taken place. Throughout our history, Washington has insisted that we have small, relatively weak banks. And now it has got what it wanted. In world terms, our banks are puny. We no longer have to fear the concentration of financial power in New York City. Instead, we can rightly fear the concentration of financial power in Tokyo, Frankfurt, and London. I personally believe the time has come—now that we have major banking organizations growing up in such cities as Columbus, Charlotte, Detroit, and San Francisco—that we allow the economic consolidation of the industry to begin in earnest.

But even if we were to drop the McFadden and the Bank Holding Company Acts tomorrow, there would still be a major barrier to consolidation. Given the credit problems described in Part I, many banks now have a "poison pill"—bad loans that effectively block mergers. As a result, merger activity among banks has come almost to a complete stop. Most banks can no longer agree to terms because neither party can agree anymore to what each other's loan portfolios are worth. Moreover, few banks can raise the capital needed to acquire and recapitalize failing banks or thrifts. And no strong bank wants to take over a weaker bank's loan portfolio because it now represents a blind pool of unknown risk. Sadly, until some means is found of separating out the high-risk assets that are now bundled together with the core banking functions, the continuing economic consolidation of the banking system will be stymied. Later, in Part III, I'll suggest such a means for separating good assets from bad.

Breaking Up the Bank

The core banking business is consolidating, but all the while the classic bundled bank is being broken apart and recon-

figured through subcontracting, spin-offs, mergers, joint ventures, and shared production. In particular, non-core banking
activities are being separated from core banking functions. In
addition, economic pressure is causing bankers to reexamine
each step in their business system. Today each step in the de-
livery of a bank's services is being reexamined to determine
who can perform the function most cheaply. Often it's not the
same bank. In fact, it may not even be a bank at all.

What is going on is that large, complex banks are being converted into several simpler, easier to manage businesses. This
entire process, known as "disaggregation," is the natural economic response to industries experiencing intense competition
and overcapacity. We have seen it in the automotive industry,
where even the largest manufacturers use parts manufactured
by specialty companies and distribute cars through independent dealers. In the petroleum industry, exploration and production are increasingly separated from refining and marketing. What was once a single business breaks up into many
businesses.

In the last few years, many functions within the banking
system are being disaggregated, too. Particularly important to
this process is the bundling together of loans into securities
described in Chapter 8. Those types of loans that can be securitized are easily broken away from the core bank. The business
of making mortgages has been transformed. Historically, the
local bank or thrift made a mortgage loan and placed it on its
own balance sheet. But with the advent of mortgage-backed
securities, this business has come apart into a number of separate businesses: making the loans, guaranteeing the cash flows,
packaging the loans, placing and trading the mortgage securities, and servicing the mortgages (taking and processing payments). In the process, the institution that makes the loan does
not have to hold the loan. Depending on the economics of each
individual business, the appropriate level for success may be
local, national, or even global.

For instance, making loans is, first and foremost, a local
or regional business. Servicing is a national business. Trading

mortgage-backed securities is a global business. In those businesses with national or global scale, this process creates very large enterprises that operate to do just one thing. For example, Fannie Mae and Freddie Mac are enormous enterprises even though they are essentially involved in only one activity: guaranteeing mortgages. This trend creates more large players, not less. Many regional banks have been selling off their credit card portfolios to competitors who are building national market share.

Banks are also breaking up through the use of subcontractors. At the simplest level, many banks have shed their own economics departments, and are now being served by outside consultants. At more complex levels, some banks now subcontract their entire back office functions. A service business owned by General Motors and based in Dallas, EDS, is now performing all of the processing for First City (Houston) and First Fidelity.

Much of the breakup that needs to take place in the industry simply involves the shedding of unnecessary, or low-value, work. As described in Chapters 3 and 5, much of the industry's cost simply grew up, based on thousands of decisions made with little thought or analysis. Bankers flocked into businesses like discount brokerage or mortgage banking without having any competitive advantages. Many banks have continued in such businesses out of pride, even though the economic rationale for entering the business is long gone. Many medium-size regionals still maintain large corporate banking departments even though they make very poor returns from that business. Moreover, the overhead functions built up to control these businesses still remain. Some banks are finally beginning to leave bad businesses and to redesign their overhead costs, aiming for expense reduction of 20 percent to 30 percent, or more.

The trend toward breaking up the bank can often benefit participants even when they do not actually sell off the business. Many large banks today are very difficult to manage. Indeed, one of the major reasons why a number of money center banks are so deeply troubled is that they became impossible to manage as they are currently structured. If you simply organize the bank into its individual businesses it can be much easier to manage the very diverse portfolios, which were often lumped together with core banking activities under common management. Bankers can match the capital needed in a particular business to the requirements of the business rather than forcing all activities into the classic bundled structure. If you then do want to sell businesses, having already carved the bank up into pieces makes the process much easier. Or in other words, disaggregation increases the liquidity of a bank's investment in its diverse businesses.

Barriers to the Breakup

Although regulators and legislators have historically had far fewer objections to breaking banks apart than bringing banks together, they have inadvertently created barriers that impede the process anyway.

The Bank Holding Company Acts of 1956 and 1970 are perhaps the most significant barriers to breaking up banks. The false safety of the holding company structure has enabled banks to operate many businesses together using the same pool of capital. This creates a very serious problem. Bankers know they would need to raise $10 or $15 of equity to support a freestanding $100 portfolio of high-risk loans. But why should they bother when they only need $4 or $5 of equity to support the same $100 portfolio on the bank's balance sheet? Naturally, bank holding companies prefer to lump high-risk activities in the bank subsidiary because they are able to operate with less capital and lower funding costs. Over time, however, banks have put so much risk on their balance sheets that their funding costs are now significantly higher than those of the big non-banks despite the "too big to fail" doctrine of regulators.

This disadvantage is greatest at the holding company where the financial stress of large banks winds up being concentrated. In late 1990, for example, the average bond rating for the largest sixty-seven rated bank holding companies was single A. The average yield on the long-term bonds of these bank holding companies was in the 10.5–13.5 percent range compared to the 8.6–9.6 percent yield on such strong financial companies as General Motors Acceptance, Ford Motor Credit, General Electric Capital Corporation, or IBM Credit.

But the real impediment to breaking up the bank are banks and bankers themselves. Many of them lack the will, the skills, and the financial capacity to restructure themselves. The curse of the bundled, shared cost structure of the industry means that if you sell off a business, you may well shed more revenue than costs. True cost savings only come if you redesign the entire enterprise. It is not just a matter of headcount reductions. The work itself needs to be redesigned; however, few banks even remotely possess the skills needed for this radical procedure. What's worse, restructuring often means write-offs of bad investments. Given the poor earnings and capital position of much of the industry, many are loathe to take the additional hits required to restructure. Sadly, the greatest problem is that many bankers are totally overwhelmed by their problems. Saddled with troubled loan portfolios, lacking the fundamental skills, will, and capital to restructure, many small and large banks are literally wasting away. Their franchises are disintegrating. And not only their shareholders are losing. It is the nation itself that is losing.

Consolidation and breakup are the natural healing economic forces that can enable our banking system to recover. A more compact industry of large, robust banks will be able to compete in the global marketplace for financial services. An appropriately disaggregated industry will guarantee that customers will be served most efficiently and at the lowest possible cost. Both forces, however, are being arrested by the malaise that has settled over the banking system, the economy, and the nation. Our current approach to regulating banks is bankrupt.

The time has come to break the gridlock. The time has come to rewrite the fundamental social contract between banks and the nation. We stand now at a crossroads. If we enable fundamental economic forces to take over, then I believe the industry can heal itself. If we continue to resist those forces, we will surely destroy the industry and do great damage to our nation.

PART THREE

RESTORING THE HEALTH AND PROFITABILITY OF THE BANKING INDUSTRY

11

Core Banking

The essential dilemma of banking reform is simple: how to protect the payment system and small depositors through government safety nets without creating massive flaws in the financial market. This is a tough problem. In fact, this is my second attempt at an answer.*

The approach I'd like to suggest is one that limits the government safety nets to what I call "core banking" functions. In today's world, these core functions primarily include serving the needs of individuals, small business borrowers, and mid-size companies. Most of our existing banks would be converted into banks that would be limited primarily to performing these core functions. These core banks would then be run as segregated, regulated, FDIC-insured banks with some significant limits on how they would be operated in the future. As we will see in the next chapter, these banks would be segregated sufficiently that they could be owned by holding companies pursuing widely divergent activities. The key would be to carefully regulate intercompany transactions between the core banks and their affiliates. The government's safety nets must never be extended to non–core banking functions.

However, for the moment, we want to focus on what steps should be taken to eliminate anomalies from the government safety nets in the core bank itself.

What's a Core Bank?

Core banking is a common sense notion. Ask a few people on the street what banks do, and my guess is that you would get a

---

* Some three years ago I wrote a book called *Breaking Up the Bank*. Although my opinions presented here have some conceptual similarities with that book, my thinking has progressed significantly since then.

rough description of what I like to call a core bank. It includes all of the activities that go on in your local branches: checking accounts, savings accounts, money market deposit accounts, and other deposit services. It includes lending to individuals, small businesses, and mid-size companies. It includes trust and custody services. This is the everyday stuff that has been the traditional province of banks for better than a century.

The core bank would not include highly leveraged transaction lending, lending to developing countries, or lending on large commercial real estate projects. Nor would it include the global money market activities of the money center or large regional banks. Nor would it include securities underwriting activities or real estate development or any of the other activities into which bank and thrift holding companies have diversified. There is nothing wrong with these businesses. It is just that they have risks that should not be underwritten by government-insured institutions. Instead, if they are performed at all, they should be undertaken in subsidiaries of a holding company outside and totally separate from the core bank.

My objective is to return banks to those traditional activities that have proven, over time, to be relatively safe and where banks have a demonstrated advantage over non-banks. These lines of businesses are all close-cousin to the "safe place to keep your money," which is the essence of the social contract between banks and the societies they serve. What's more, in our work at McKinsey, we have found that most of our banking clients make the overwhelming bulk of their profits from these core banking functions. Indeed, core banking activities now account for over 100 percent of the industry's current earnings due to the large credit losses being incurred from commercial real estate, highly leveraged lending, and developing country debt. The government's safety nets would no longer encourage senseless, wasteful investment, because the safety nets would only stand behind the core bank where the chance to take excessive risk would hardly exist. All the more important, we would then create a strong core banking industry that would be a source of strength in financing the nation's communities—particularly individuals, small businesses, and mid-size companies.

It would also be a significantly smaller industry. Of the some $4 trillion in assets now held by insured depositories, we estimate that at least $1 trillion would migrate to other financing sources.

Safe Lending

A "credit anomaly" exists whenever a lender offers rates, terms, and conditions out of step with risks being incurred. The "credit anomaly" fueled the commercial real estate booms and highly leveraged transactions of the 1980s. The anomaly occurs and can be sustained because the government is absorbing risk by guaranteeing the lender's liabilities. To eliminate the credit anomaly we must limit the risks a core bank is allowed to take.

A core bank would have significant limits on its ability to take credit risks. These limits would be of two kinds. First, a core bank would be limited to the kinds of customers to whom it would lend, and it would be limited in the terms and conditions—things like interest rate paid, the length of the loan, when the principal and interest were due—it could offer. Core banks would not be permitted to make large loans to developing countries, highly leveraged transactions, or large commercial real estate loans.

The primary customers of a core bank would be individuals, community businesses, like the local hardware store, and mid-size companies. If you exclude commercial real estate loans, borrowings from these customers already represent over 90 percent of the loans of all non-money center banks. Very few banks have gotten into trouble with these kinds of loans, although the recession we are in may test these credits. Included in the lending to individuals would be residential mortgage debt, home equity loans, credit cards, installment loans, automobile loans, and so forth. Loans to small businesses and mid-size companies would include accounts receivable lending, leasing, commercial mortgages, unsecured lines of credit, and so forth.

How would we enforce these limits? I favor the relatively simple approach of limiting the size of the loans core banks could make as a percentage of their primary equity capital. Currently, most banks can legally lend up to 10 percent of their equity to a single borrower (that is, one obligor). This rule, by itself, keeps very small banks (those with less than $10 million in capital) from lending more than $1 million. There is no need to put further restrictions on banks of this size. If you then applied a sliding scale, you could restrict bigger banks to lending to smaller customers as well. For example, banks with between $10 million and $100 million of capital could lend only 5 percent of their equity capital, above the first $10 million, to one obligor. That is, a $100-million equity capital bank would be able to lend 10 percent of its first $10 million of capital and 5 percent of its next $90 million of capital for a total limit of $5.5 million. Banks above $100 million in equity could be limited to lending 2 percent of their capital, above the first $100 million, to a single borrower. It may also make sense to allow large core banks to make loans up to 5 percent of their equity to very safe (double A–equivalent) large corporations. These limits would ensure that all significantly sized core banks would have a reasonably well diversified loan portfolio.

Given the atrocious record in commercial real estate lending, it seems reasonable to ask whether or not core banks should be allowed to make these types of loans to local real estate developers. I think the answer is a qualified yes. There is a strong, pragmatic reason for allowing banks to make such loans. Who but the local bank can finance a mid-size company's warehouse or a small medical office building? Core banks should be allowed to make these loans, provided that the terms and conditions are limited by regulation. The legal lending limits just described are a good start by themselves, since they foreclose the ability of core banks to finance large commercial real estate projects. However, I believe there should be other limits as well. For example, it would be reasonable to require that builders provide 30 percent of the equity in a project, that the building be 90 percent pre-leased (if it was a construction loan), and that committed leases provide at least 100 percent coverage of principal and interest payments. Such limits would ensure that core banks, once again, would be taking credit risks, not equity risks, in the financing of commercial real estate projects. Common practice during the 1980s flaunted these minimal, prudent rules.

Furthermore, there should be some restrictions on *all* of the terms and conditions used by core banks that extend credit. As explained later in the chapter, I believe the private sector should take the lead in setting these terms and conditions. The core bank's lending activities must be safe. For example, it is appropriate to place limits on the amount of a home equity loan you can make as a percentage of the appraised value of a house. Without such limits, a struggling core bank will be driven to take excessive risk with home equity loans, just as banks were earlier driven to compete on terms for commercial real estate loans. If it tried hard enough, a bank could go bust in any kind of lending activity.

Talk of limits on terms and conditions goes against the grain of many people, especially those bankers who have avoided credit troubles. But remember, the objective is simply to ensure that all core banks, protected by safety nets, adhere to conservative lending standards and are limited in their ability to give over-generous terms and conditions in order to get business. In other words, the credit anomaly would be eliminated. Limiting competition on terms and conditions is the price we need to pay to rid ourselves of the credit anomaly once and for all.

Remember that all core banks will be in the same boat, so all will be on equal footing. Remember also, this model anticipates that holding companies owning core banks will also own other non-insured subsidiaries, which will have the power to lend to anyone they want, under whatever terms and conditions they want, provided they raise their funds in the market without any access to government safety nets.

One major advantage of this model is that it limits the ability of noncompetitive banks to take ever more credit risk to pump up current earnings, as they did in the 1980s. Instead, it will make them confront the reality of their competitive weakness and force them either to improve or to sell to another player.

Another major advantage is that this approach will reduce the amount of equity capital a bank needs in order to operate. By limiting risk to safe assets, a core bank needs far less equity than it would otherwise need because it is exposed to much lower risks. For example, our analysis shows that a core bank would need only about $4 of equity per $100 of assets to be rated AA; in contrast, the same bank with some 30 percent of its assets in high-risk lending needs at least $7 of equity per $100 of assets to achieve a similar rating. Similarly, the cost of the equity will fall. In today's market, even a reasonably well-run large regional bank must earn from 16 percent to 18 percent to be able to have the market value of its stock equal its book value with a clean loan portfolio. Our work indicates that a core bank would probably need to earn only 13 percent to 14 percent return in today's market to have the market value of its stock equal its book value. The reason is that the earnings of a core bank would be of greater quality and would be far less volatile than the earnings of today's typical risk-laden lender.

Safe Deposits

The "deposit anomaly" occurs when weak banks overpay depositors for their deposits. This overbidding provides depositors with too high returns relative to the risks they are incurring. The risk for federally insured deposits is basically the same as for U.S. Treasuries of equivalent maturity.

Let's approach this complex problem from another direction. Because it has less risk, a bank backed by the government's guarantee should be able to raise money more cheaply than an uninsured institution. The insurance, in effect, is providing a government subsidy of the deposit-taking function. Historically, this subsidy was the *quid pro quo* for enduring government regulation. As a result, the industry historically paid much less than the Treasury rate to its depositors. However, in the early 1980s, many commercial banks began to lose high-quality income because of the growth of the commercial paper market and money market mutual funds. Much of the industry replaced this lost income by taking more credit risk. As they did so, the amount of effective subsidy from the government increased. After all, without the government guarantee, depositors would have demanded far higher rates from these risky banks. At the extreme, a deeply troubled institution only has to pay a depositor a little more (1 or 2 percent) than a rock-solid institution because of the government safety net. If it had to raise deposits in the open market, the rates it would have to pay would go "off the map." However, even the 1–2 percent premium paid by the faltering institution hurts the industry. It erodes the profits of even the rock-solid competitor because every institution has to offer higher prices to keep its depositors from switching over to its troubled, but still insured, competitor.

We must eliminate this deposit anomaly directly. How? By limiting the interest that core banks can pay on federally insured deposits to the rates paid by the U.S. Treasury. This has great intuitive appeal. Treasuries are guaranteed by the government just as a core bank's deposits would be. Unless core banks can add additional value to the Treasury guarantee through convenience, through greater service, and through offering payment services, why should they be allowed to pay more? A core bank would, under this model, be only permitted to pay the rate paid for U.S. Treasuries for equivalent maturities.

In other words, if the 6-month Treasury rate was 7.5 percent, core banks would only be allowed to pay 7.5 percent.

Again, talk of re-imposing interest ceilings on deposits bothers many people, especially bankers who remember the problems caused by Regulation Q. But because deposit rates would move freely with Treasury rates, the forced disintermediation caused by the old Regulation Q deposit price ceilings would not be a problem. The objective is simply to ensure that core banks can't offer depositors over-generous returns for the risks they are incurring. In other words, the objective is to eliminate the deposit anomaly. Banks would be free to compete for deposits through terms and conditions, convenience, service, and price—up to the Treasury ceiling. In fact, over 80 percent of banks' deposits already pay interest below Treasury rates. Nevertheless, we estimate that $600 billion of price-sensitive deposits would leave the banking industry and $400 billion of price-sensitive deposits would leave the thrift industry to alternative investments if this proposal were enacted. Much of it would go to money market mutual funds. I think it would only be fair, therefore, to allow core banks to offer uninsured money market mutual funds out of their branches (with appropriate conflict-of-interest regulation to prohibit investment in, for example, the securities of affiliates). This would ensure that banks do not necessarily have to lose the funds of customers who want full money market yields unprotected by government insurance.

This system eliminates the ability of poorly run core banks to stay in business simply by raising more money through continuing to overbid for deposits. Note that most companies become illiquid (run out of cash) before they become insolvent (the value of their liabilities exceeds their assets). This is why it is possible for secured creditors to be able to recover most of their loans made to a bankrupt company by orderly liquidation of a company's assets. But insured depositories are the opposite. Because they can never run out of cash as long as they can continue overbidding for deposits with the government's guarantee, they never go illiquid; you have to wait for them to go insolvent. As a result, they can keep operating as long as they have accounting equity left. Because much of their reported equity is only equity if the bank is an ongoing concern (because the equity includes such intangible assets as goodwill, capitalized software expenses, and so forth), by the time an insured depository becomes insolvent and the government steps in, the institution's assets are worth considerably less than its insured deposits and so the taxpayers must bear the losses.

What Would a Core Bank Look Like?

The typical core bank that emerges after all these regulatory changes actually looks similar to how retail-oriented regional banks like NCNB, Banc One, or NBD look today, but with some important differences. One such difference shown by our analysis is that the amount of available deposits is likely to be far greater than the amount of loans to individuals, small businesses, and mid-size companies that qualify under the new stringent rules. These excess funds will need to be invested in securities and interbank placings. It would probably be wise to limit these investments to securities rated AA and above, including such instruments as Treasuries, mortgage-backed securities, commercial paper (which would have to be within the one-obligor limit), and so forth.

This asset structure raises two critical questions about core banks. How safe would they be? How profitable would they be?

Given the kind of limits to credit risk-taking being proposed, core banks should be quite safe. It is hard to find any commercial bank of significant size that has encountered trouble lending to individuals, small businesses, and mid-size companies. If the imposed limits on the terms and conditions are reasonably conservative, it would be hard to imagine a core bank getting into trouble from bad loans. The one point of vulnerability, other than fraud, would be the possibility that some banks might take excessive interest rate risk in their securities port-folios or in fixed rate mortgage lending. This means that some rules would also need to be developed to limit the ability of core banks to take excessive interest rate risk; the FDIC and the OCC already have been working on rules for both banks and thrifts. Government insurance would return to its proper role as a backstop and no longer be the main pillar of confidence it is today.

But would core banks make money given their loss of high-margin loans? The answer is a resounding "yes!" In fact, they would certainly be more profitable than today's commercial banks, because the evidence is clear that commercial banks have been making uneconomic loans. The high interest spreads on risky loans have been "devoured" by loan losses. The prof-itability of high-risk loans has been illusory; the accounting income taken in at the time the loan was made has turned into a loss by the time the loan has been collected.

Moreover, safety has economic value. Individuals and busi-nesses need a place to keep their money safe and are willing to pay for it. Limiting the pricing on deposits to Treasury rates will increase the profitability of all core banks because the overbid-ding by weak competitors would be eliminated. Our estimates indicate that limiting deposits to Treasuries rates as we propose would increase spreads on the price-sensitive deposits that re-mained in the core bank (that is, were not converted to money market mutual funds) by at least a half a percent. Some of the credit and deposit business lost from the core banks could be picked up by non–core bank subsidiaries of the holding com-pany.

The flip side of this is that borrowers will have to pay more for credit on less-generous terms, and depositors will earn less-generous returns on their deposits. But this is what fixing the credit and deposit anomalies is all about. Borrowers will have to pay the economic cost of borrowing and depositors will only receive the economic returns due them from investing in fed-erally insured deposits. Of course, the same individuals and businesses, as taxpayers and as participants in the economy, will be far better off than they would have been if we simply try to "muddle through" this problem with piecemeal quick-fixes.

Not that core banks would be without competition. In extending credit, non-banks such as consumer and commercial finance companies would compete with core banks as lenders, and non-banks such as money market funds would compete with core banks for deposits. But in the long term, well-run core banks would be viable, profitable entities because the core functions are still valuable to society—particularly for all those customers that lack direct access to the securities markets.

The core bank's competitive advantage is its ability to share costs such as branches and overhead among a group of naturally related customers. If existing regulations are lifted, permitting national consolidation and restructuring, the industry's cost base can be significantly pruned. I believe core banks will be able to prosper. However, there is no way to prove whether core banking will be viable in the very long term. If core banks are able to add sufficient value, they will be able to prosper. If core banks fail to add sufficient value, they should be closed down without cost to the government.

Protecting You and Me

This gets us the most pressing issue in deposit insurance reform. How can the taxpayer be protected? In the aftermath of the savings and loan debacle, this is a painful point both to taxpayers and their representatives in government. Much of the debate in Washington centers here. I believe the core bank approach makes this thorny issue quite manageable.

Let's explore a number of key questions in the debate and how the core bank concept answers them.

1. *Should we limit deposit insurance coverage?* Much of the debate today centers around deposit insurance coverage.

What is the appropriate level of coverage? Is $100,000 per account too much? Should individuals be treated the same way as corporations? Is there a role for some form of private insurance to complement FDIC coverage?

My starting premise is that people need a safe depository and a safe payments system. Since 1933, deposit insurance has become part of our social contract. It is inappropriate to use depositors to instill greater market discipline. *Depositors are not investors.* You cannot use the fear of bank failure as a means of setting market rates for deposits. Investors make risk/reward trade-offs; depositors want a risk-free rate of return.

We must recognize that retail depositors, like you and me, are incapable of exerting market discipline on depository institutions. Banks are blind pools of risk. We can't look inside of a bank. As described in Chapter 8, one of the most enduring functions of banking is the extending of credit to those who lack direct access to credit through the securities markets. Credits that are in a core bank are, by definition, those which can't be securitized and therefore cannot be made transparent to the markets cost-effectively. Essentially, the market would have to duplicate the costs of regulatory examiners to get an assessment of the credit risks in a bank. The government safety net adds value to banks, not the least of which is that less equity capital is needed than would otherwise be required. Moreover, the rates paid on deposits are lower than they would otherwise pay. If we were to require banks to keep enough equity capital to provide for real protection to depositors, we would destroy much of the economic value of the safety net. In other words, banks would have to bear the economic burden of paying for the safety net (in terms of deposit insurance premiums, costs of complying with regulation, and so on) but they would be deprived of the economic benefits of the safety net.

Therefore, I believe that attempts to promote market discipline by depositors by lowering the levels of deposit coverage are misguided. I believe the fundamental value of a bank is derived from the fact that the bank is a safe place to keep your money. Any perceived increase in risk by tampering with the safety net will result in immediate increases in the rates paid to depositors, which will decrease the profitability of banks. Moreover, I do not think you can have it both ways. Either banks are safe or they are risky. If banks are risky, then they are subject to bank runs. Indeed, I believe market discipline by depositors is another name for bank panics.

With this in mind, it is far more worthwhile to spend time and energy devising ways to limit risk-taking in a depository institution (for example, interest rate risks) than it is to debate proper level of coverage in any single account. Is $100,000 per account about right? Should it be $75,000 or $40,000, or $10,000 as it once was? While I would not want to see the level increased beyond the current statutory amount, I believe these are the wrong questions. We should focus our attention on the fundamentals; that is, ensuring that the government does not absorb risk that should be borne by the marketplace. This is the essence of the core bank approach being advocated.

2. *How quickly should the government move to close or resolve failing depository institutions?* Early intervention to close or resolve failing depository institutions is critical as we think of ways to strengthen our financial system and reduce the overcapacity that plagues the industry today. We are now paying the price for all of the thrifts (and some commercial banks) that were kept afloat in the 1980s, when economic forces were working to drive them out of existence. Had a clearly defined early-intervention policy been in existence at that time—with sufficient financial resources to back it up—we would be far better off today.

Because the government is the ultimate guarantor of the liabilities of a bank, the government has a responsibility to remove the capacity of failing competitors from the system. No other party can do it. The natural outcome of competition is that somebody fails. In the United States, however, the government safety net has kept losers alive, who then overbid for deposits with government guarantees, thus raising the costs to everyone else. Rather than keep these failing institutions alive, the government should move to resolve them quickly.

In other words, since the deposit guarantee removes the discipline of the market, the government can rely on nothing but itself to guarantee that the government is not exposed to loss from its safety net. Practically speaking, this means that the financial regulators should have to use a combination of tools (bank examinations, capital requirements, or insurance premiums) to protect the government from loss. Not the least of these tools is a credible and known policy on the early resolution of troubled depository institutions. Such a policy would place limits on uneconomic risk-taking and insulate the government from such practices.

If we were to adopt the core bank proposal outlined in this chapter, early intervention would become automatic. The government should intervene whenever banks become either illiquid or insolvent. In most cases, illiquidity would hit first. Core banks who were becoming illiquid would be unable to raise money by bidding more than Treasury rates. They would have no alternative but to borrow from the government to keep operating. As soon as it became clear that an institution was dependent on the government for its funding (for example, borrowing heavily for thirty days or more), the government would act. Frankly, I believe few core banks would fail.

However, as will be discussed in Chapter 13, we must move to the core banking concept gradually over time. If we were to operate on this principle immediately, we would precipitate a catastrophic banking crisis because there are a large number of troubled banks (not to mention thrifts) who are liquid today only because they can bid for deposits at rates above Treasuries.

3. *How should we account for banks' assets?* Behind bad lending is a lot of bad accounting. The truth is that banks have been making loans exposed to equity risks and therefore it has been hard to capture the true nature of these risks in current accounting systems.

Some academics argue that we should move to mark-to-market accounting (that is, reflecting the value of all assets at market value), as opposed to historical value accounting (keeping all performing assets at the value established at the time the asset was created) that we currently use. After all, securities firms mark their assets to market.

Market-value accounting could work for all assets and liabilities on a bank's balance sheet that are freely traded in the marketplace like investment in freely traded securities. Although market-value accounting has some appeal in theory, in practice it does not work for most of the important components on a bank's balance sheet. Market-value accounting is difficult to apply to the core deposits of banks and thrifts, which often can have a significantly higher market value than their book value. Similarly, market-value accounting today cannot be applied to a bank's commercial and industrial loans or commercial real estate loans, because most of these are blind pool risks (that is, the value of the loans is not apparent without a loan-by-loan analysis). Either they are not marketable or there are no established markets for them and hence no basis for an accounting measure at current market value.

The biggest problems today are in valuing high-risk loans to developing countries, highly indebted companies, and to commercial real estate projects. Under the core bank model, these assets would not be on the core bank's balance sheet. With these loans removed, I believe it would still be appropriate to use historical value accounting for all performing loans.

Using a combination of market-value accounting for marketable assets and historical accounting for loans will provide a more accurate assessment of capital for regulatory purposes than using only one approach or the historical value approach for all assets and liabilities. I also believe that market-value accounting is appropriate for subsidiaries of the holding company that are principally engaged in the securities business.

4. *Are some banks or other financial institutions too big to fail?*
   If we mean should equity holders be wiped out if an in-

stitution goes economically insolvent the answer is clear: we should be willing to let any institution fail in this case. However, if we define failure as simply closing up shop, we should probably install a more orderly process. With good reason, regulators have not wanted to flirt with risk to the entire banking system and the possible ripple effects to other bank and non-bank customers that could result from the precipitous failure of very large, multibillion-dollar institutions. Moreover, as pointed out earlier in the book, failing a bank causes it to lose its value as an ongoing concern, which dramatically increases the cost to the government of resolution. Later in this book, I will describe an approach the government can use to manage the resolution of failing institutions who are still economically solvent. However, for those institutions that are economically insolvent the least cost will be orderly liquidation. I do believe we need to ensure a process for the orderly resolution of all large, failing financial institutions whether banks or non-banks. The precipitous failure of a large financial institution has excessive social costs. Such procedures were not in place at the time of the Continental Illinois crisis in the early 1980s, but the government now has procedures, personnel, and systems to manage an orderly resolution process. While not a commercial bank, the rapid demise of Drexel Burnham was managed by the government in a way that prevented any sizeable disruption in our financial markets. The Drexel case did require Federal Reserve and SEC intervention, but an orderly liquidating process was observed with creditors defending their claims in bankruptcy court. Most importantly, in this process, the people providing the equity capital took the losses. But Drexel was taken down without causing chaos in the markets.

These four questions, while not exhaustive, represent the kinds of issues now being debated in an effort to reform the deposit insurance system. However, the point remains: *we must do more*. Any solution that only fixes deposit insurance, no matter how clever or air-tight the fix, is no solution at all. It fails because it must address the fundamental flaws in our nation's financial system brought about by years of neglect and misregulation by Washington.

If we merely patch the safety net, we will still have artificial boundaries between the bank and thrift industries (which now perform the same kinds of business) and between commercial banking and investment banking (which also now perform the same kinds of business). We will still be left with artificial geographic boundaries. We will still be protecting uneconomic players from failure. We will not eliminate marginal capacity, and thereby we will continue to destroy the franchise value of institutions. We will, no doubt, continue to interfere with capital flows, over-regulate banks, perhaps overcapitalize banks, and raise deposit insurance premiums needlessly.

What to Do with the FDIC?

In addition to the core bank concept, I believe the most important real reform we could make would be to privatize the FDIC. We are probably years away from being able to do this now for both political and practical reasons. Nevertheless, the concept is sound. The idea would be for the FDIC to charge whatever economic premiums are required to cover the risks it is exposed to. Indeed, under the leadership of Bill Seidman, the chairman of the FDIC, the FDIC has been acting more and more like a private corporation than a government agency, although it still has a long way to go. Conceptually, there is no reason the FDIC could not be a real, private, insurance company. Given the current state of the banking industry, though, there is no source of private capital that would be willing or able to take over the FDIC's current position.

However, if we were to move to a core bank concept and, as a result, were to cure both the credit and deposit anomalies, then we could create a safe enough industry, in time, for the FDIC to be privatized. Under one possible model, the FDIC would be converted into a private, profit-oriented company with 51 percent of the shares in the hands of private owners with shares traded on stock exchanges. The federal government would own 49 percent of the shares and be a reinsurer of the risk. If reserves ever fell below a predetermined "safe" level, which called in question the need to draw on the reinsurance, then the government would be empowered to buy back the 2 percent of the shares needed to regain control and would take whatever actions were required to restore the reserves to "safe" levels.

In the next several years, however, it seems politically unlikely that we will be able to convert the FDIC into a truly private company. In the meantime, we can take some actions that would make the FDIC a bit more like a private insurance company. More private sector input is required in establishing the terms and conditions for extending credit. In the core bank concept outlined earlier in this chapter, one dilemma is how to establish the terms and conditions under which banks would be permitted to extend credit. Regulators, unfortunately, are not close enough to the market to be very good at setting rules. I propose that the FDIC create an independent Credit Advisory Standards Board, composed of the best credit professionals that could be found from industry. They would formally set and enforce reasonable and prudent credit standards for each kind of loan allowed to be placed on a core bank's balance sheet. Private sector input is valuable because practitioners better understand the best (and worst) practices more clearly. They have better understanding of the balance between serving customers' needs and protecting against credit losses. They can be more effective in anticipating how regulations should adjust to changing conditions.

This proposed board would serve as an advisor to the FDIC. Its recommendations would be non-binding; they would be subject to review and approval by the FDIC. However, if the FDIC were ever privatized, then this board would be the instrument that would directly establish the terms and conditions for core banking.

I believe the combination of "core" banking reform, technical reform, and making the FDIC behave more like a private company can ensure that we have a safe banking industry that protects taxpayers from losses from the safety net. However, stopping there is not enough. We must also build a system that works with, not against, the fundamental economic forces that were described in Part II.

12

Liberating Economic Forces

Although reforming the deposit insurance system is essential, it is still only one aspect of a new, healthy banking system. We also need to liberate the economic forces described in the second part of this book. History teaches us that trying to resist these economic forces is both futile and destructive. We need to reform our regulatory system in a way that works with these forces rather than at cross-purposes to them.

In this chapter, we want to concentrate on how to liberate these economic forces without exposing the core bank to risk.

New Holding Company Model

Let's wipe the slate clean and devise an entirely new model for a bank holding company. To do this, we must scrap the Bank Holding Company Acts of 1956 and 1970, described in Chapter 10, and the Glass-Steagall Act, which separates banking from the securities business. Under the new model, a holding company that owned a core bank would have no restrictions on what it might own. This "financial holding company" concept, as this approach is called, is the *quid pro quo* required to make the "core bank" concept workable. It would be the vehicle by which today's current banks could undertake those activities not permitted in the core bank. It would also enable non-banks, such as industrial companies, to own core banks.

Under the financial holding company concept, a holding company could own both federally insured and noninsured subsidiaries. The holding company, and its noninsured subsidiaries, would raise money separately from investors in the marketplace based on the quality of their individual balance sheets. Only the core bank subsidiaries would enjoy any explicit or implicit guarantees from the government. This would be a dramatic shift from the current philosophy of the Federal Reserve, which treats a bank holding company as if it were one integrated entity. It would have to be clear to the markets that the government would not stand behind the non–core bank subsidiaries of a financial holding company.

The objective is to allow the market to limit unwise risk-taking. High risks that could not qualify for FDIC-insured core banks would have to be financed through subsidiaries of the financial holding company or through the holding company itself. Investors would, of course, demand higher rates for their uninsured investments—but the rates banks would get for financing these higher risks would also rise, because uneconomic risk-taking capacity by unskilled insured depositories would be removed from the system. Financial holding companies would have to persuade investors that they could safely underwrite such risks without federal deposit insurance.

This is not to say that the new holding company would be disciplined only by the market. Many subsidiaries would be regulated by function. For example, subsidiaries engaged in securities would be subject to SEC regulation. Subsidiaries engaged in insurance would be subject to insurance regulation. Under this "functional regulation" concept, all players in a given industry would have consistent and identical regulation applied to them. For example, all insured depositories, whether banks, thrifts, or credit unions, would have exactly the same regulation applied to them as core banks. All securities activities, whether formerly affiliated with a commercial bank or a traditional securities firm, would be consistently regulated by the same regulator.

The purpose of functional regulation is to ensure that the market works better. The government *would* be involved to ensure that risks and returns are transparent to investors through adequate accounting disclosure; only competent participants are allowed to practice; contracts are effective; fraud is prevented; and audits verify that assets, liabilities, and exposures are as stated; and so forth. The purpose of functional regulation is to ensure that all participants have a fair opportunity to evaluate the risks and returns. However, participants would not have any ability to rely on the comfort of government insurance to protect them from risk of loss—except in the core banking activities. Government functional regulation would provide oversight, rather than control or subsidy.

Segregating the Core Bank

An obvious requirement for the functional, financial holding company regulation I'm suggesting is protection of the government-insured "core" bank from the risk-taking activities of the holding company or its other subsidiaries. The whole point of the core bank concept is to limit the anomalies caused by government safety nets. Without strict legal separation of the core bank, the new system will not work. In regulatory jargon, these laws are called "firewalls."

In this model, the regulators would have the authority to establish firewalls to prevent either the abusive movement of financial assets out of the core bank or the transfer of risk into the core bank. For example, intercompany transactions such as dividend payments, management contracts, service agreements, and guarantees would be monitored and regulated by the federal authorities. Other types of firewalls, such as restrictions on the cross-marketing of products or the use of common names, have no economic justification and would not be used in the model being proposed. There would be no reason why a core bank could not actively sell and promote money market mutual funds out of their branches provided that the money market mutual fund was functionally regulated by the SEC and that it was made clear through disclosure that the funds were not federally insured.

But this segregation of the core bank cuts both ways. In other words, the holding company's exposure to losses should be limited to its investment in the core bank. Some regulators have argued for cross-guarantees between and among healthy and troubled parts of a banking organization. Some have argued that the assets of a healthy subsidiary should be used to absorb the losses of an affiliated bank facing insolvency. Although such added protection from cross-guarantees sounds attractive at first, it has the effect of making the balance sheet of the bank indistinguishable from the balance sheet of the parent or other affiliates. Moreover, it does little to contain the risks to which a depository is exposed. All too often the FDIC has forced healthy units to pay up, after the fact, to lower its cost of resolution.

It is particularly important to limit cross-guarantees if we hope to convince non-bank organizations to help bail out some of today's troubled banks. Who would be willing to invest in revitalizing a sick, but not yet insolvent bank if it was necessary to expose industrial or other businesses to losses through cross-guarantees?

In fact, as those of you who have read my previous book, Breaking Up the Bank, know, I favor segregating risk wherever possible. It is much more difficult for investors to evaluate commingled risks than disaggregated risks. The more that risks can be unbundled, the easier they are to evaluate.

In describing the core bank in the preceding chapter, I argued that there are two kinds of major risk-taking activities that are now considered to be part of commercial banking, yet which should not be part of the core bank. The first of these are the risks of operating in the money markets and securities businesses. The second are the risks of extending credit on terms and conditions too lax to be allowed on a core bank's balance sheet. I believe these activities should take place in distinctly different, separately regulated subsidiaries. The first of these I'll refer to as a "money market investment bank." The second I'll refer to as a "finance" company or an "uninsured bank."

Money Market Investment Bank

The money market investment bank would serve corporations, institutions, and governments with a broad array of commercial banking and investment banking products. These institutions would operate in the money, foreign exchange, and securities markets. They would buy, sell, underwrite, and distribute both debt and equity securities. This model would eliminate the now obsolete distinctions created by Glass-Steagall and create one kind of wholesale, market-making financial institution with one body of regulation for the money market and securities activities of those institutions that have historically been called either "money center banks" or "investment banks." For example, the main subsidiaries of J.P. Morgan, Bankers Trust, Goldman Sachs, Morgan Stanley, and Salomon would all be within the definition of this "money market investment bank."

These banks would represent our nation in the global capital markets. They would be funded with interbank deposits, uninsured CDs, and other wholesale funds. As a nation, we probably need no more than a handful of these kinds of institutions; however, each one of this handful would need unquestioned strength. As explained in the globalization chapter, the thinness of spreads in the world's global capital markets leaves no room for institutions with any perceived riskiness. Because under the proposed model these institutions would not be insured, their principal source of strength would need to be their earnings strength, the quality of their assets, and their capital base. Moreover, all of these institutions need direct access to the wholesale payment system. Because they would be trading massive volumes every day, they would each have huge amounts of daily settlements. Currently, investment banks have to use money center banks to settle for them. Going forward under this model, there would be no reason why all money market investment banks should not have direct access themselves to settlement.

These institutions would have to be subject to some safety and soundness regulation. A precipitous default by a giant money market investment bank would bring our whole financial system down. Therefore, the costs to our society from a failure of such a bank would exceed the costs to the institution's shareholders. It is in the interests of the nation to protect our financial system from a sudden failure of a giant money market investment bank. However, I believe we could keep these institutions safe without insuring their liabilities and without overly burdensome regulation.

To accomplish this I suggest marking-to-market the vast majority of all assets of a money market investment bank daily. This is equivalent to the way accounting for securities firms is already done. Marking-to-market the assets of a company primarily engaged in the securities and money markets is quite feasible since, by definition, almost all assets on the institution's balance sheet have current market values. With mark-to-market accounting, the safety of the institution is immediately transparent. As long as marketable assets exceed liabilities, the institution can be liquidated without loss to anyone other than shareholders.

Realistically, the money market investment bank would need to have some limited amount of non-marked-to-market assets in order to operate. For example, it would have some investment in its own premises and office equipment. It would also probably need to be able to extend limited amounts of credit in the course of doing business. For these kinds of purposes, it would make sense to allow these banks to have non-mark-to-market assets, provided these assets did not significantly exceed the total of common equity, preferred stock, plus long-term and subordinated debt.

These institutions would also need a liquidity line from the Federal Reserve to protect the institution in a liquidity crisis, like the one that occurred when the stock market crashed in October 1987. At that time, the Federal Reserve provided liquidity to money center banks, which in turn provided credit to securities firms. Because, under this proposal, there would no longer be money center banks (they would be broken up into several separately regulated subsidiaries), it would make great sense to simply provide all money market investment banks with liquidity in times of crisis directly from the central bank. A liquidity line is also required for those banks to compete in the world's global capital markets. Every other major nation should, and does, stand behind its major international banks in times of crisis.

However, this liquidity line should not be used to protect a money market investment bank from failing nor to provide investors with *de facto* insurance. As said earlier, it is important to eradicate the notion that any institution is too big to fail. To accomplish this, the Federal Reserve would automatically take preemptive collateral (for most of these institutions it would probably be Treasury notes and bonds) if the liquidity line was used. If the institution began to live off the liquidity line, the Federal Reserve would simply call its loan and liquidate the institution in an orderly manner. Drexel was taken down by the SEC, with coordination between the Federal Reserve and money center banks, in such a manner in early 1990. As with Drexel, at liquidation, all losses would be borne by the capital holders and unsecured creditors, not the government.

In addition to such safety and soundness regulation, these banks would also need to be functionally regulated to comply with all applicable securities laws. Indeed, except for access to the payment system and the liquidity line from the Federal Reserve, these "money market investment banks" would be regulated in much the same way that large investment banking firms are regulated today.

Finance Companies

If an institution wanted to extend credit that did not qualify for the core bank, it could book that credit in a separately capitalized finance company. Bankers tend to prefer the term "uninsured bank," rather than "finance company," when discussing this concept. Under the model being proposed, this finance company or "uninsured bank" would be completely unregulated other than having to comply, as all public companies have to do, with SEC disclosure requirements. In other words, rating agencies and accounting firms, not regulators, would be responsible for assessing the quality of the uninsured company's assets.

These companies would make most of the large, big ticket, high-risk loans currently made by money center and super regional banks. In addition to highly leveraged transaction and commercial real estate debt, these companies could also make loans that did not qualify for the core bank. For example, large lease transactions that exceeded the lending limit of the core bank would be booked in the finance company. Or, for example, if the core bank was only permitted to lend up to 70 per cent of the value of a house on a home equity loan, the finance company could lend at higher ratios if it wanted to take the risk.

There would be no safety net beneath these companies. They would need to have sufficient equity capital (probably equal to 10 percent to 15 percent of assets or more) to convince the market to provide them with funding. They would need to have sufficient credit skill to stay out of trouble. If they were to get in trouble, they would be allowed to go bankrupt. The sole role of regulators would be to protect any affiliated core bank or money market bank from being brought down by troubles in the finance company. In particular, firewalls would have to prevent the core bank or the money market bank from lending to the finance company or from being drained of capital to shore up the finance company. Moreover, if a run developed at either the core bank or the money market investment bank as a result of the finance company's troubles, which required use of the Federal Reserve liquidity line, the Federal Reserve should have the power to call its loan. If the core bank or money market investment bank was unable to repay, then the Federal Reserve would be empowered to take the core bank or money market investment bank away from the holding company and sell it to the highest qualified bidder.

I believe these finance companies could be quite profitable. Once the credit anomaly is eliminated, the reduction in high-risk lending capacity should cause the prices, terms, and conditions for extending high-risk credit to improve. In other words, it should be possible to make money by taking prudent credit risk again.

Of course, these companies would have to compete against finance companies that were not affiliated with core banks or money market investment banks. In this competition, they would have no real advantages, or disadvantages, of being affiliated with a core bank or money market investment bank that would be any different from GECC (General Electric Capital Corporation) gaining strength from being affiliated with General Electric or GMAC (General Motors Acceptance Corporation) gaining strength from being affiliated with General Motors. Regulation would not provide these companies with competitive advantage or disadvantage.

Changes in Holding Company Law

To effect the changes proposed in this chapter, a number of laws would need to be rewritten. As noted earlier, the Bank Holding Company Acts of 1956 and 1970 and the Glass-Steagall Act would need to be substantially eliminated and replaced with new laws. For example, a new holding company act would need to be written that would specify exactly how the firewalls were to operate.

I personally believe that once we build effective firewalls, we should simply allow core banks and money market investment banks to be owned by any financially strong player including, for example, industrial companies. As already noted, these companies are already massive participants in the financial services industry and are leading providers of services that were once called "banking." Indeed, much of the capital needed to recapitalize the banking industry will need to come from outside the industry itself. However, none of these players will be willing to come in and take over troubled institutions if they are forced to comply with the kinds of restrictions and control by the Federal Reserve inherent in the Bank Holding Company Acts.

In addition to firewall regulation, there are only a couple of other financial holding company regulations required beyond the requirements of any other public company. There probably should be some oversight for the acquisition of core banks or money market investment banks. In other words, drug dealers or financially weak players need not apply. For another, there need to be better rules on how a financial holding company in trouble is liquidated or restructured in an orderly manner. The guiding philosophy is oversight, not control or subsidy. As argued throughout this book, the objective is to regulate to let the market work better, rather than to control it.

Under this type of regulation, any financial holding company should be permitted to own both core banks and money market investment banks and a wide variety of other subsidiaries including those engaged in all types of securities and insurance activities. There would be no distinction between a bank and a non-bank holding company. It would be possible for holding companies owning traditional securities, insurance companies, or even manufacturing companies to own core banks or money market banks and for traditional bank holding companies to own securities firms, insurance companies, or even manufacturing companies.

As described earlier in the chapter, many of the independent subsidiaries of these financial holding companies would, of course, need to be functionally regulated. Functional regulation eliminates industry distinctions and looks directly at the services being offered to the market. In addition to functional regulation of core banks and money market investment banks, retail securities firms, insurance companies, and other subsidiaries would also need to be regulated functionally.

The objective of such functional regulation is, again, to make the market work better. Functional regulation can accomplish this first by providing better accounting and better disclosure of information to the market by preventing fraud. Functional regulation can also ensure that regulation itself does not provide competitive advantage or disadvantage. Under functional regulation, all competitors receive consistent regulation because the same entity regulates everybody.

For example, under functional regulation, the distinction between commercial banks, thrifts, and credit unions would vanish. The core bank components of each would be regulated the same and non–core banking activities would be functionally regulated elsewhere. In many cases, to facilitate effective functional regulation, participants would be required to maintain legally separate and independent subsidiaries.

Move to National Regulation

We need to face the reality that today's financial services business has become interstate commerce and that it no longer makes sense to regulate it as if it was still done within the boundaries of individual states. From a customer's point of view, state lines are meaningless. All banking activities, other than branching, are already essentially being conducted on an interstate basis.

Even in retail banking, the states themselves have permitted some form of interstate banking in all but four states. We now have a crazy quilt of complex regulation and law that, as was described in Chapter 10, is preventing the natural consolidation of the industry. Moreover, these laws add massive unnecessary cost and result in inconsistent regulation.

In banking, the simplest method of curing this problem would be to rewrite the McFadden Act to permit interstate branching. In combination with the removal of the barriers to interstate acquisitions contained in the Bank Holding Company Act of 1956, we would eliminate, overnight, the major regulatory barriers to the economic consolidation of the banking industry. I do not want to minimize how difficult this may be politically; however, it is an essential requirement if we want to restore the health and profitability of the banking industry.

As an aside, we also need to look at reforming the role state regulation plays in the insurance, securities, and finance company industries. Although these industries are outside the primary focus of this book, the regulatory principles that are argued throughout the book equally apply to those industries.

Liberating Market, Competitive, and Economic Forces

By undertaking the reforms described in this and the previous chapter, we would enable the financial services industry to adjust to the natural forces at work in the financial economy. The elimination of the major flaws in the market, that is, the deposit and credit anomalies, combined with the liberation of market, competitive, and economic forces, would enable the healing process to begin in earnest.

The system being proposed would simply allow these forces, not the government, to shape the industry. The market would choose, without the distortion of government subsidy, which financial services to buy. The market would determine the relative size of the core banking system relative to the money market mutual funds industry depending on how many customers preferred the safety, convenience, and services of the core bank to the slightly higher yields available in money market funds. Competition, not regulation, would determine the businesses in which a particular institution could compete. Functional regulation would ensure that all participants in any particular area would play by the same rules. Successful participants would thrive. Unsuccessful participants would disappear, without cost to the general public.

Economic forces would be liberated. The securitization process would proceed up to its natural limits without the distortions caused by Glass-Steagall. Economic disaggregation of banks would be enhanced by the breaking up of the bank into core banks, money market banks, and commercial finance components. Each of these disaggregated industries would develop its own unique economics based on the specific risks, and value added, inherent in each of the businesses.

This breaking up would also enhance consolidation because it is much easier to combine similar enterprises together than to combine dissimilar enterprises. Merging similar enterprises often results in elimination of redundant overhead. Combining dissimilar enterprises increases complexity and increases the costs of control.

Core banks could combine with other core banks. Money market investment banks, either with roots in the traditional commercial banking or in the traditional securities industry, could combine with other money market investment banks. Finance companies, with roots in either the traditional commercial banking industry or in the finance company industry, could combine with other finance companies. Some participants might in fact trade parts of their business with each other. For example, one commercial bank might trade its core banking operations for another's money market investment banking operation.

Indeed, I believe if we reform the system according to the principles outlined in Chapters 11 and 12, we would wind up with a competitive, but safe, financial services industry that meets the needs of the customers and the public at large. In the last chapter of this book, Chapter 14, I'll lay out a scenario of what might happen if these reforms were enacted. At the moment, though, our banking system is headed in a downward spiral. How do we make the transition from today's deeply troubled system to a system based on the principles in Chapters 11 and 12?

In the next chapter, I lay out a plan for such a transition.

13

Transition to a Profitable, Healthy Banking System

We do not have the luxury of making a transition to a new system from a healthy base. Many banks are in deep trouble now, and as we head into a recession their numbers will increase. Further, most banks are tightening their credit standards after years of excess—so we may be facing a prolonged credit crunch that will constrain our economy. As our analysis in Chapter 7 has shown, the Bank Insurance Fund is inadequately funded to resolve all the problem cases, and unless the course of events is changed it seems likely that the Bank Insurance Fund will itself become insolvent. We are in a banking crisis. We need to address the problem directly.

Where do we start?

We need to break the problem into three parts. First, we need to restructure institutions that are now insolvent—that is, those which no longer have enough equity capital to absorb the losses they suffer when their loans are marked down to their economic value. Second, we need to recapitalize weak institutions that will be severely undercapitalized once their loans are marked down to their economic value, but that are still economically viable. In some cases, such recapitalization should probably be undertaken only in concert with government-assisted mergers. Third, we need to allow healthy institutions to make an orderly transition to the new system.

Restructure Insolvent Institutions

If we learn anything from the savings and loan crisis, it should be that it makes little sense to hope that deeply troubled institutions get miraculously better. Once in deep trouble, an institution loses its vitality and stagnates. The point of no return comes when an institution begins to experience a significant negative cash flow from its operations—that is, when the bank has so many nonaccruing loans that its interest income falls below the sum it needs to pay both interest on deposits

251

and operating expenses. At this point, the bank has no recourse but to raise more deposits—not to fund new loans, but rather, to keep on operating. Institutions in this kind of trouble often still show positive net worth even though they are experiencing a cash drain because they have not written down their loans to reflect their real cash value. The problem is that the more they borrow to fund cash losses, the worse the negative cash flow becomes as more and more cash is borrowed. The resulting downward spiral eventually brings such an institution under, even though the rest of its activities—such as its core banking functions—may well be quite sound.

It will be critical for the Bank Insurance Fund (BIF) to restructure insolvent institutions before they enter this death spiral, to preserve the franchise value of the parts of the bank that are not troubled, and to minimize costs to the BIF. In these cases, the Bank Insurance Fund should allow management to be replaced and shareholders to be wiped out, and concentrate on resolution at the lowest possible cost. Large banks often have significant franchise value that can be preserved during restructuring—as the FDIC learned in the late 1980s, particularly in Texas. The franchise value of a bank can be preserved through the use of "bridge bank" and "collecting bank" structures.

This involuntary restructuring would continue essentially as it has been done. For small banks, the FDIC would continue to come in and pay off insured depositors, settle the claims of uninsured depositors and other claimants, and recover as much as it can from the collection and sale of assets. For large banks, the FDIC would continue using "bridge bank" and "collecting bank" structures and other restructuring techniques to lower its cost of resolution. A "bridge bank" structure enables a new investor (usually a well-run bank) to operate the bank while determining which "good" loans it wants to keep and which "bad" loans it wants the FDIC to retain and absorb. These bad loans are then placed in a "collecting" bank. The collecting bank is run under contract to the FDIC by a management team whose sole objective is to recover the maximum possible from the assigned portfolio; usually the manager is the same investor who runs the bridge bank. Often these contracts include incentive clauses. After the "bridge" period is over, the investor winds up owning the new "good" bank.

To reduce its costs, the FDIC always seeks bids from as many well qualified bidders as it can. For example, Citicorp, Wells Fargo, and NCNB were in the final bidding for the First Republic Bank of Texas with NCNB winning at the end of the day. In these bidding situations, what is at stake is exactly how much assistance the FDIC is going to be obligated to provide, not just in new capital but also in loan guarantees or other forms of help. The FDIC is now going through a similar process with the Bank of New England.

There would be two major differences in the FDIC's usual procedures for the involuntary resolution of large banks under the model being proposed. First, there would be more well qualified bidders because non-banks as well as banks would be eligible. This is an important change because there is only a handful of large banks in this country that are big enough to oversee the restructuring of another large bank. A second important change is that instead of the restructuring resulting in a "good" bank, the ultimate restructuring would result in a core bank. Although performing nonqualifying assets would be grandfathered in the core bank, the restructured bank would not be permitted to make new, nonqualifying loans. If the new investor wanted to make such loans, it would have to create an independent finance company to do so.

This restructuring program will require up-front cash, as do the restructuring efforts completed so far. The cash is needed to provide enough equity to plug the hole in the balance sheet created by marking the loans down to their real cash value. Essentially, the FDIC replaces nonperforming loans with earning assets by injecting new equity capital. The institution can then resume profitable operations and generate a positive cash flow.

How much cash is needed?

As stated in Chapter 7, the FDIC finds that in order to resolve a deeply troubled large bank (that is, a bank with over $10 billion in assets), it needs about 9 percent to 12 percent of the bank's assets in cash. For small banks, 16 percent to over 20 percent of assets is required. As a point of comparison, the cash cost of resolution in the savings and loan industry has been as much as 40 percent, or more, of assets because the typical insolvent S&L's assets were worth less and because the franchise value of typical insolvent S&Ls was practically nonexistent. Part of the reason for these large losses at S&Ls is that the government allowed them to remain open—by using the deposit anomaly to fund operating losses—long after they had become hopelessly insolvent.

Although it is hard to tell from available numbers, we believe that commercial and mutual savings banks with $50 to $70 billion in assets have already reached the point where, if you marked their loans down to their economic (cash flow) value, they would be insolvent. We calculate that roughly half of these assets are in banks of under $10 billion and half are in institutions above $10 billion. A fair estimate is that it would cost the FDIC $7.5 billion to $10 billion to restructure and recapitalize these economically insolvent institutions.

The BIF either already has, or is scheduled to collect, more than this much money. It starts with the some $9 billion in existing reserves. As time goes on, it could use premium income as it is collected (the FDIC estimates premiums will bring in $18 billion over the next three years). It also has some investment income. In other words, the FDIC estimates it will have over $27 billion available to it over the next three years to restructure institutions that are currently economically insolvent against a current cash need of some $10 billion without increasing premiums further or borrowing money. That is, the BIF will *not* be made insolvent by its resolution of currently insolvent banks. It will become insolvent if many more banks reach the same stage of decay. To prevent that from happening, the FDIC will need to launch, simultaneously with this effort, the following recapitalization program.

Recapitalize Severely Undercapitalized Institutions

As stated in Chapter 7, we estimate that some $300 billion of assets are in institutions that are approaching economic insolvency—that is, they have enough capital to absorb the marking down of their problem assets to their economic value but then will be trapped without the capital they need to operate. Another $400 billion of assets are in institutions that are not far behind and that face such significant capital losses that they will be barely able to function. Without sufficient capital, these institutions will stagnate. They will continue to constrict credit, thus contributing to the credit crunch. And they will continue to slide toward insolvency. To reverse this trend, we will need to inject over $35 billion in capital into these institutions to ensure that they are safely recapitalized—that is, approximately 5 percent of $700 billion in assets.

Where could this money come from?

One option is for this money to come from the banking industry itself. In January 1991 the FDIC and the banking industry seriously discussed having the FDIC create a special class of preferred stock that would be bought by the banking industry. The money raised by this program would go into a segregated fund earmarked for recapitalizing troubled institutions. These talks broke down partly because well-capitalized institutions were loathe to contribute capital to bail out their more troubled bretheren and partly because they were worried about the prospects for repayment. Moreover, the sense of many was that what the industry needed was new capital from outside the industry. These parties to the debate felt there would be little gained by simply recirculating existing capital from the strong to the weak. A second option would be for this money to come from the government itself through creation of a special corporation, similar to the Reconstruction Finance Corporation, created during the Depression, whose sole purpose would be to assist in the recapitalization and restructuring of troubled but economically solvent banks. I favor the first option, that is, having the FDIC create a special class of preferred stock funded by the banking industry, but I understand why many of my banker friends are opposed to the idea.

Wherever this money comes from, care must be taken that new money is not used to bail out insolvent institutions. Indeed, under this concept, this new capital would *not* be used to absorb economic losses of these banks, and it would especially not be used to absorb the losses of the hopelessly insolvent institutions described in the previous section.

This new money would be used for a voluntary, early intervention, recapitalization and restructuring program* designed to turn around troubled institutions that have not yet gone over the edge. It would be used to preserve the ongoing concern value of solvent, but undercapitalized, institutions—those with prospects bright enough to convince new outside investors to invest on equal terms with the FDIC.

The key to this program is that it would be voluntary. One of the difficulties in other proposed early-intervention programs is that regulators have constraints on their ability to intervene while the institution is still solvent. In troubled institutions existing managers, bond buyers, and shareholders resist regulators' seizing the institution as long as there is any hope at all. The FDIC is often properly reluctant to act while the institution still has any equity left; indeed, because the constitution protects property rights, seizure of an institution is inevitably followed by extended litigation. In the meantime, the value of the institution wastes away. Under this program, the FDIC would have a powerful new carrot (new capital) to go along with the stick of potential involuntary seizure of the institution. This proposed program would provide existing managers and shareholders with both the incentive and the capital needed

---

*If troubled institutions could undertake a private recapitalization by themselves then so much the better. The prospects of a recapitalization and restructuring program overseen by the government will powerfully motivate troubled banks to accomplish private recapitalization programs on their own.

to restructure their institution before insolvency became inevitable.

This recapitalization program would not be a bailout, because the FDIC would invest only if profit-motivated investors can be convinced to put equal amounts of their own capital at risk. We believe that the prospects for profits from the reform of the industry, plus the recovery of troubled loans as the real estate market rebounds from this cycle, should be sufficient to entice outside investors to invest alongside the FDIC.

Under this approach, the money put in by the FDIC, and the new outside investors, would have a first claim on the assets of the institution (that is, existing common stockholders would be subordinated). Our analysis indicates that if the FDIC invested $25 billion and outside investors invested $25 billion more, there would be more than enough capital available to recapitalize all of the troubled, but economically viable, commercial banks of all sizes, provided we do not let the economy slide into a devastating recession. That is, $50 billion is enough money to recapitalize $1 trillion in assets at a "safe" equity ratio of 5 percent of assets.

Our analysis indicates that such an approach can save the insurance fund a minimum of $20 billion, or far more, compared to the more usual and more costly approach of waiting until the institution is economically insolvent and has lost its value as an ongoing concern.

We already have a precedent for such a program. From 1933 onward, the Reconstruction Finance Corporation (RFC) invested directly in preferred stock to supplement the capital of six thousand banks including such New York banks as the Manufacturers Trust, National City Trust, Guaranty Trust, Chase National, and Chemical Bank & Trust, not to mention other large banks such as the Bank of America, and thousands of small banks such as the First National Bank of Amarillo. In fact, Jesse Jones, who headed the RFC, credited the preferred stock program with restoring the confidence of the nation in the banking system in his book, *Fifty Billion Dollars, My 13 Years with the RFC.* As an aside, the last of this preferred stock was retired in the 1950s.

Under the voluntary program being proposed, a troubled institution that was willing to undertake the kind of massive restructuring usually associated with an involuntary FDIC resolution would be eligible for an FDIC equity matching program. Under this program, the troubled institution would move to a good core bank and collecting bank structure involving a large write-down of the problem loans placed in the collecting bank. The FDIC would then recapitalize the core and collecting banks up to safe levels by investing in preferred stock on matching terms with outside investors. (In other words, if an institution needed $2 billion in preferred stock, the FDIC would provide $1 billion and outside investors the other $1 billion.) This would *not* be a bailout. The FDIC's objective would be to make money from its investment. This program could work for small banks, as well, of course. The FDIC could provide amounts as small as $5 to $10 million if a bank could find equal amounts from other investors. For small banks, which are already core banks because of their size, there would be no need to go to a good bank/collecting bank structure, because such structures are too expensive for small banks. The new equity could simply be used to recapitalize the bank.

At the FDIC and outside investors' discretion, the new capital could be invested either directly in the banks or could be in holding company stock that was downstreamed to the subsidiary banks. The latter approach would allow the holding company to retain 100 percent control of its banks and would probably be desirable in many cases. However, in this case the FDIC and the new outside investors would need to take steps to protect their investment in the holding company by such means as taking the holding company's stock in its core bank as collateral. The mechanics of how such a program would work are described, through example, in the next few pages.

Such a program would provide a powerful incentive to the management and existing shareholders of a troubled bank to restructure their institution's businesses and economics to redeem the preferred stock or to force conversion as soon as possible.

The potential returns to new investors and the FDIC from participating in the restoration of troubled banks to a healthy state of profitability is enormous while their downside would be protected by marking assets down to their economic value. This matching program would enable both the new investors putting up the risk capital and the FDIC itself to share in this recovery. The FDIC would, under this approach, never own a majority of the stock of a bank and would be expected to sell the stock in the public market once the institution had recovered—hopefully after realizing a substantial gain.

This type of program would have a number of benefits. The first benefit is that the FDIC would save itself from a number of far more costly involuntary actions by this early-intervention program. The second benefit is that the program would stretch the FDIC's existing capital and premium income to cover the involuntary resolution of hopelessly insolvent institutions. A third benefit is that the potential returns from the recovery of a troubled institution are large enough to reduce the FDIC's need for future premium increases; indeed, the FDIC should be able to redeem the preferred stock whether it was contributed by the industry or by a new RFC. As an aside, the requirement to find matching outside investor money would ensure that this new capital would, for accounting purposes, qualify as a legitimate investment.

The fourth benefit of this plan is that it would enable these troubled institutions to convert to the new core banking model relatively quickly and regain their capacity to serve their communities. Finally, since most troubled institutions are regionally concentrated, this renewal of confidence and strength would help our most troubled regional economies to recover. This, in turn, would help the entire nation to recover—essentially because the banking industry will have pulled itself up by its bootstraps.

In fact, the reason why the whole program works is that we believe the combination of reforms and recapitalization can restore the profitability and soundness of the core banking business of these troubled banks. Part of this soundness comes simply from eliminating the ability of the core bank to be involved in high-risk activities. Our analysis indicates that a core bank would need less equity capital because its assets would be safer, and the cost of equity capital would decline because its earnings would be more stable. In addition, there would be further profit opportunities for significant cost reduction through consolidation of core banking activities through the proposed reforms of the McFadden Act and the Bank Holding Company Act. Most importantly, the elimination of the credit and deposit anomalies will directly boost the profitability of core banking functions. In particular, the restriction of deposit prices to Treasury rates should add a half percent, or more, to the returns earned from price-sensitive deposits although some of this will be offset through loss of deposit volume.

Having the FDIC as an investing partner has further benefits in terms of attracting outside investment capital. Rather than having to fear that the FDIC will come in and wipe out their investors, new investors will be partners with the FDIC. First, they will have the benefits of the FDIC pushing to mark assets down to their realistic economic value; this is something outside investors are in a poor position to do. Moreover, the FDIC will be intent on ensuring that enough total capital is raised to ensure that the institution is truly adequately capitalized. Finally, the investors will be able to participate in the FDIC's powers to protect its own investments.

Recapitalization and restructuring would also permit investors to speculate on the prospects for recovery of real estate loan values. Presently the high likelihood that the FDIC will come in and restructure the bank, in the short term, before the real estate markets have a chance to recover, makes it very risky for investors to speculate on the long-term recovery of real estate values. Moreover, the commingling of troubled real estate assets with the rest of the bank makes it difficult for investors to assess what those assets are really worth today. On the other hand, after the segregation of the assets and markdown of those assets to their economic value, investors can speculate on their future value without fear that an FDIC restructuring will jeopardize their ability to participate in the long-term recovery of real estate from their current depressed values. If the commercial real state markets begin to recover in a few years, and history says they always do, then it will be possible to sell off these troubled assets to investors at their long-term economic value rather than at today's distressed values. In other words, this approach reduces the economic loss from the bad assets both to the FDIC and to the troubled institution.

The reason why such a program can have these benefits is that it helps weak, troubled banks become economically vital once again. Let's use an example to explore how this might work. Assume, for the moment, that there is a hypothetical Bank Holding Company, let's call it BHC, with one large bank subsidiary, the Aggressive National Bank. To make this simple, let's assume that BHC has no other significant subsidiaries. Let's assume that the Aggressive National Bank has $50 billion in assets and has $10 billion in high-risk loans (principally commercial real estate). Further, assume that after making a one-time $2.5-billion loan loss provision, it was left with only $1 billion of common equity (that is, 2 percent of assets). The remainder of the bank's business is fundamentally solid, but the severity of its troubles have begun to erode its value as an ongoing concern.

In such a situation, the equity markets begin to fear the worst. That is, investors start fearing that the FDIC will come in and force an involuntary restructuring, wiping out the equity of the holding company. In this case, this may make the market value of the equity as little as 35 percent of the book value of the company or, in this example, only $350 million, even though, if this bank were performing well, it could be earning as much as $500 million a year (1 percent of assets) with a market value of $5 billion.

BHC cannot restructure itself because equity capital becomes more difficult and expensive to raise the more risky are the expected returns. In other words, we saw in Chapter 7 that the cost of equity increases as risk increases. In a deeply troubled bank, the risk of loss to equity is so great that it becomes impossible to raise new equity under any conditions. In other words, the cost of raising new equity rises to infinity—even though, as in this case, the core banking activities of the bank may not be risky at all.

On the other hand, suppose that BHC applies to the FDIC for a voluntary investment in callable, convertible preferred stock of $1 billion and can find $1 billion of matching convertible preferred stock from outside investors. This $2 billion would be invested on the conditions that Aggressive National is broken into a good core bank and a high-risk collecting bank, and that all of the preferred stock is downstreamed as common equity, to the good core bank and to the collecting bank. Assume further that the FDIC and the new outside investors take as collateral for their preferred stock investment the common stock in both the new core bank and the collecting bank. In other words, unless the preferred stock is either converted into common equity or is redeemed, at a predetermined future time, the ownership of the core bank and the collecting bank reverts to the FDIC and the new outside investors.

Let's look at how BHC and Aggressive have now been restructured. BHC now has a safe core bank with $40 billion in assets supported by $1.6 billion in equity (that is, 4 percent of assets, which should be sufficient for its level of risk, as described below). It also has a collecting bank with $10 billion in marked-to-economic value assets (that is, formerly valued at $12.5 billion) with $1.4 billion of common equity (14 percent of assets). In other words, the $1.0 billion of BHC's remaining equity has been combined with $2 billion of newly invested equity and divided among the two newly created subsidiaries.

In addition, the collecting bank would be assigned some $2.5 billion of Aggressive National's loan loss reserve giving it a total of $3.9 billion in reserves and equity to absorb the costs of nonaccruals and charge-offs from loan collection. Of course, the expectation is that the full $2.5 billion of reserves will be needed to absorb losses—that is, what it means to mark the loan portfolio to economic value.

What is critically important, from the point of view of the FDIC, is that the ongoing concern value of the sound parts of BHC has been preserved. Thus, employee morale can be restored and key employees can be kept, and BHC preserves the considerable tax loss carryforwards a troubled institution always has. Moreover, BHC's borrower/lender relationships are preserved. If such relationships are lost, through an involuntary restructuring, borrowers often lose much of their moral obligation to repay. In real estate projects, this is quite important because the worst thing that can happen to a project, in economic terms, is for its developer to walk away (assuming the developer is honest and competent). If the original developer leaves a project, it is very difficult to find any other developer who will put the same energy into the project, without some massive concessions from the lender, to make the project economic. Moreover, borrowers often sue if they feel mistreated and can often tie up assets, preventing them from being either sold or restructured. In other words, destroying a borrower/lender relationship can increase the economic losses to everyone.

Now, following recapitalization and restructuring, how would the FDIC and the outside investors get repaid if everything worked well?

The key, of course, is improving the profitability of the total enterprise. The core bank's profitability would first improve by having a lower cost of funds; the combination of more capital and the Treasury ceiling on deposits would widen deposit margins. Moreover, the shrinkage of the core bank's balance sheet would make it a far less aggressive bidder for deposits.

Credit risk-taking would also be more profitable as the credit anomaly was eliminated. In addition, the new investors might well push for major cost restructuring and better pricing. In our experience, focused cost redesign programs can reduce an institution's cost base by 15 percent or more and a focused repricing program can have a dramatic impact on profitability. Moreover, it is highly likely that, given time, real estate values will recover especially since new construction is beginning now to grind to a complete halt. The point is that once the institution had been recapitalized, once new investors were in place to push for change, and once the system has been reformed, it should be possible to make dramatic improvements in profits of the enterprise. If not, and if the institution failed to repay the new preferred stock on schedule, the FDIC and its outside investment partners would have the right to take the stock of the core bank and the collecting bank and sell them to the highest bidders.

However, assuming profits recovered, BHC's core bank would produce dividends that would be first used to cover the preferred stock dividends to the FDIC and to the outside investors. The common stockholders would probably get few dividends in the early years. Then, over time, the collecting bank's assets would decline as loans were repaid but no new loans were being made. This would allow some of the capital of the collecting bank to be freed up; it could also be used to redeem the FDIC's investment. This approach envisions allowing the FDIC and the outside investors to have an option either to have the stock redeemed or to convert the preferred stock into common at the stock price of the common as of the date of the recapitalization. Then, over time, as the collecting bank continues to shrink, more and more capital would be released until the preferred stock was completely redeemed or converted. Hopefully, the collecting bank would not just recover the markdown value of the high-risk loans but some portion of what had been written off earlier as well. As more and more of the preferred stock was redeemed, the dividends from the core bank could also be freed up to resume common dividends to the holding company's common stockholders and to redeem even more preferred stock. Once dividends to common stockholders resume, it will be possible at some point for the holding company to go to the public equity markets to accelerate the redemption of the FDIC and outside investor's preferred stock.

This kind of approach has substantial managerial advantages. First of all, it would give a troubled institution powerful motivation to restructure itself, by providing the means, in terms of capital and breathing space, to pull it off. Second, it would make the managerial task easier. It is quite difficult to work off problem loans and to grow businesses under the same management structure. Forced separation enables some groups of managers to place full attention on serving customers and growing the core bank, while an entirely different group of managers can focus on loan recovery.

Assisted Mergers

One of the chief arguments against the "bootstrap" recapitalization program just described is that it will slow down the economic consolidation of the industry. Although, as will be explained in the next chapter, this is not necessarily so, it is true that in many cases recapitalization is not the complete answer. In situations that involve banks operating in the same market, with significant redundant capacity, the only long-term economic answer may be in-market mergers of the weakest banks with the strongest. One sure sign that this is the only answer will be if outside investors cannot be attracted into recapitalizing a bank even if the government is willing to provide matching money.

It may therefore be appropriate for the government to have an alternative "assisted merger" program to complement the "bootstrap" recapitalization program. Under an assisted merger program, the government would use its regulatory powers to encourage a "shotgun marriage" between a weak institution and a stronger one. Under such a program, the burden of raising the capital needed to recapitalize the troubled bank falls on the stronger bank. In order to assist the stronger bank in its effort, the FDIC could offer to guarantee 80 percent of any losses beyond the economic markdown of the troubled institution's bad assets that are placed in the "collecting" bank. Without such guarantees, it may be very difficult to convince a strong bank to take the risks of assuming a troubled bank's loan portfolio even after the assets are marked down. Moreover, the last thing the government would want to accomplish through such a program would be to weaken the strong bank.

A further means of encouraging such a merger would be again to have the government provide matching capital on the same terms and conditions as those accepted by outside investors. In the case of a strong bank, this could be nothing more than common equity (as compared to the convertible preferred stock suggested for the bootstrap program).

The key to making this program work is having one strong bank operating within the troubled bank's market. A fallback would be to bring in a strong bank from another market. In either case, what is needed is not just capital, but also consolidation and management skills. In particular, the strong banks must have the capacity to take over most of the activities of the weaker bank—that is where the economic savings will come from. In some cases the stronger bank may want to break apart and sell off those parts of the weaker bank it does not want.

I do not believe, however, that it makes any sense to offer such an assisted merger program to two troubled banks. Merging weak players is likely just to create a bigger mess. For one thing, in such a situation it will be difficult to raise the needed outside capital since neither bank will have the confidence of investors. Also, neither institution is likely to have the skills needed to make the merged entity a success. In the short run, a merger complicates the management challenge;

it is unlikely that two institutions that have had difficulty operating separately will suddenly develop the skills needed to manage the larger, more complex enterprise that would result from the merger.

The decision on whether it is best to follow a "bootstrap recapitalization" or an "assisted merger" approach will depend on the particular circumstances of individual banks.

Transition for Healthy Institutions

Of course, all of the healthy institutions with some $2 trillion in assets also will have to make the transition to the core banking structure under the proposal advocated by this book. The magnitude of the reform package being proposed argues that commercial banks be given time, perhaps three to five years, to make the full transition to the core banking model. Moreover, there are a number of other steps that can be taken to ease the transition. Detailing all of the day-to-day steps involved in transforming to the new model is beyond the scope of this report. There are, however, several key guidelines that could be followed.

The most important of these would be to allow all existing performing loans in well-capitalized institutions to be grandfathered and to remain in the bank until they were repaid. Essentially, the risk has already been taken on these loans so there is no reason why the bank should not be permitted to earn the return as it gradually converts itself into a core bank. However, all nonperforming, nonqualifying loans would have to be marked-to-economic value within a transition period, probably some twenty-four months, and taken out of the core bank. After passage of the law, all future nonqualifying loans would have to be booked outside of the core bank in a separately capitalized subsidiary.

Money market investment banking activities would also have to be taken out of the core bank. This would be a wrenching change for some of the money center banks. It would probably be appropriate to give banks at least thirty-six months or more to make the transition. Similarly, limitations on pegging deposit rates to Treasuries would need to be phased in, because such regulation would be impracticable until many of the troubled institutions had been restructured and recapitalized.

It would also take time to put in place all of the firewall regulation. Not only will it take a considerable period of time to write the detailed regulations, it will take existing holding companies substantial time to unwind some of the intercompany transactions (such as intercompany lending) that are already in place. Also, time will be required to raise the capital to fund the new nonbank subsidiaries such as finance companies. Again, a twenty-four-month or more transition period would appear to be appropriate. Similarly, it will take time to convert qualifying S&Ls and credit unions into core banks for regulatory purposes. Moreover, it would take some time to write the detailed regulations governing how holding companies would be regulated going forward. In addition, some grace period is probably appropriate before non-banks should be allowed to acquire healthy core banks, because many healthy banks' stocks are selling at depressed levels owing to overall industry conditions.

All in all, the transition period could last several years or more after passage of the reform legislation.

The quicker we act to recapitalize troubled banks and to reform the system, the better off we will be. The program being proposed is designed to prevent the vast bulk of the some $750 billion of assets in the hands of troubled commercial and mutual savings banks from sliding into economic insolvency. Moreover, we need to recapitalize troubled banks in order to restore confidence in the banking system so we can shorten the recession we have now entered. Otherwise, loan losses may rise to the point where there is no alternative to a massive taxpayer bailout. The choice is ours to make.

14

Building a Better Banking System

As this book is being published, the nation is engaged in a debate over how we are going to restore the health and profitability of our banking system. The great danger is that each of us will look to our own narrow self-interest and fail to back a program of reform that is in the interest of the common good.

The banking industry itself is divided. Small banks have different interests than big banks. Banks in the economically troubled Northeast have different interests than banks in the solid Midwest. Strong, well-capitalized banks have different interests than undercapitalized banks facing massive loan losses. Bank holding company shareholders have different interests than bond holders.

Within the financial services industry, the securities and insurance industries have their own particular interests. Industrial companies, with great stakes in the financial industry and in the health of the overall economy, have different interests still.

In the federal government, regulators themselves have different interests. One senior government official related to me a remark by another senior official that characterizes the turf-protection problems within the regulatory structure: "Yes, I understand that what is being proposed is good for the banking industry, but it's bad for my agency."

Congress, of course, has different interests from the Administration's. For that matter, the House of Representatives and the Senate have very different perspectives on many important issues. And, of course, Democrats and Republicans in both houses have fundamentally different viewpoints on many of the basic issues.

Even individuals have different interests. Depositors have different interests than borrowers. People in the distressed Northeast have different interests than people in the relatively healthy Midwest. In fact, individuals themselves have conflicting interests. For example, as depositors many people have become "interest rate" junkies, dependent upon the deposit anomaly for high yields on insured deposits. However, those same people as taxpayers have a great stake in avoiding another S&L-size taxpayer bailout of the banking industry.

Yet, as a nation, we have only one banking system and one economy. Unless we fix it, it will completely break down and our economy will suffer, as will our competitiveness as a nation. If we try to muddle through this mess, we will suffer collectively.

What this book has attempted to do is to help the nation understand its self-interest in this crisis and to build the case for fundamental reform of the banking system. In the remainder of this chapter, I will lay out a scenario for what I believe would happen, to both the economy and the industry, if the proposals contained in this book were actually to be implemented.

Impact on the Economy

I believe that the program outlined in this book, if implemented, would have little impact on the economy this year. Even a best case for passage of a fundamental reform bill makes passage before summer or fall unlikely. Moreover, given logistics and the time it would take to negotiate the transactions, it is unlikely that we would be able to begin the recapitalization or assisted mergers of economically solvent but undercapitalized banks until the end of 1991 or early 1992.

In other words, whatever unwinding in the economy that is going to take place in 1991 due to the weakness of the banking system is locked into place. Moreover, the embedded economic losses of having overbuilt commercial real estate and having overleveraged many companies will have to be realized. Let's all hope that accommodative monetary policy takes the edge off the weakness in the banking system.

The trick is to prevent 1992 from being worse than 1991, and 1993 from being worse than 1992. I believe that if by the end of 1991 we are well on our way to recapitalizing the industry and are implementing a program of fundamental reform, we can lay a solid foundation for sustained economic growth. In other words, a massive reform of the banking system can help both to arrest the downward spiral in the economy and to prime economic growth over the next several years. Once the troubled banks are recapitalized, in conjunction with accommodative (but noninflationary) monetary policy, we can create an environment in which banks will be willing to lend again. Once lending resumes, we will be able to get the economy moving again. Such a development happened in Texas once the FDIC stepped in and restructured the major Texas banks that had failed. If the Texas experience is any guide, the New England and Mid-Atlantic recessions now underway should bottom out in 1992, and the Southeastern and West Coast downturns now started should be significantly shorter and less severe than they otherwise would have been.

Part of the reason for economic recovery would simply come from restoring the nation's confidence in its banks. Instead of daily headlines detailing the latest massive bank loss or bank failure, we should see, instead, stories about recovery and renewal. Massive injections of capital and fundamental reform should restore the confidence of both the public and the bankers in the safety of the banking system. Since *psychology* is such an important element in business and consumer spending, such a recovery of confidence should begin to lead directly to economic activity.

Indeed, we should be able to convert the vicious path we were headed down into a recovery cycle of stronger banks lending to economic borrowers, who grow the economy, which in turn begins to help marginal borrowers service their debt and to fill up empty buildings. As banks get stronger and their confidence increases, more and more credit will flow to creditworthy borrowers.

It may take years, however, for real estate values to recover. Stopping new construction will help, but in the short term, newly completed buildings are going to continue coming onto the market in 1991 and even into 1992. Moreover, the recession itself is reducing demand for real estate as companies shed employees and businesses fail. However, as the buildings currently being constructed are completed, and as no new buildings are started, the supply of real estate should stabilize. With the resumption of economic growth, space will again be absorbed and real rents should stabilize. Finally, as absorption of space continues to exceed new construction, we should begin to see recovery of rents and the values of real estate. A rough rule of thumb is that the bust should last roughly as long as the boom. In this case, the real estate boom lasted from 1982 through 1989. Therefore, it may well be 1994 or 1995 before we see a serious recovery in commercial real estate values.

Over the longer term, there should be significant economic benefits from fixing the credit and deposit anomalies and from taking the other steps to make the financial markets work better. By making the financial markets more "perfect," we will get far better allocation of credit and capital in the economy.

Specifically, eliminating the credit and deposit anomalies would affect the prices for a wide variety of financial instruments. For example, if the deposit anomaly is eliminated and insured depositories pay less for funds, funds would flow away from these depositories into other instruments such as Treasury notes or money market mutual funds. In turn, finance companies underwriting high-risk loans that had migrated off the balance sheets of insured depositories would bid for funds in the money markets without government subsidy. Eventually, as the distortions of the credit and deposit anomalies are eliminated, and as prices, terms, and conditions change, new pricing equilibriums in the financial markets would be reached.

My guess is the net result will be that insured depositories would lose some trillion dollars of funds (over what they would have otherwise been) over a period of several years. Most of these funds would be rechanneled into money market mutual funds, money market investment banks, and finance companies. However, since uneconomic lending (e.g., unneeded commercial real estate projects) would also be eliminated, some funding would simply disappear.

Since most core banks would have more core deposits than attractive, qualifying loans, those borrowers that did qualify for core bank financing would probably get rates similar to what they have earned historically because core banks would be competing aggressively on price for their business. Banks would earn more, however, because eliminating the credit anomaly would cut loan losses. On the other hand, depositors would earn less for their deposits because banks would no longer be overbidding for their deposits.

Customers forced to borrow from finance companies would have to pay more, and with more restrictive terms and conditions than they were able to get in the 1980s through commercial banks. Indeed, many of these borrowers would have to use a far higher mix of equity in their financing.

Large corporate borrowers still dependent on banks for financing, such as large private companies, either would have to spread their business among more core banks or would have to go to finance companies, money market investment banks, or foreign banks to overcome the smaller legal limits at core banks. To some extent, this need would be offset by the probable emergence of very large core banks as the McFadden Act and other barriers to consolidation are eliminated. For example, a $200 billion core bank, with $8 billion in capital, would be able to lend up to $400 million (5 percent of $8 billion) to a single corporation of AA credit standing under the rules discussed in the core banking chapter.

Overall, as the credit anomaly is eliminated, the proposed reforms would probably lead to a gradual reduction of debt finance relative to the national income and an increase in equity finance. To the extent that debt finance has been financing risks that should have been borne by equity, this process should be entirely healthy.

Over time, as the interactions between funds seekers, funds users, and intermediaries become more and more "perfect"—by eliminating the distortions of government safety nets and policy—capital would be allocated by Adam Smith's "invisible hand" to its best use in the economy. Unlike today, when increased efficiency simply means that the market becomes more adept at exploiting government-created anomalies, increased efficiency in financial markets in such a future world would be a public good.

As a final note on the economy, the proposed reforms would, as will be described next, make the financial marketplace far more efficient and productive. In particular, they would facilitate the economic securitization of assets and encourage the economic consolidation and disaggregation of the financial services industry. Increasing the efficiency and productivity of the financial services industry would have a direct impact on the nation's real economy. Over the last forty years, as the nation's economy has converted to more of a service economy, productivity has lagged. Since the financial services industry is an important part of that service economy (representing something over 10 percent of total GNP), improving its productivity can have a direct benefit on the productivity of the entire nation.

Impact on the Financial Services Industry

The combination of reforms outlined in this book should lead to a far healthier, more profitable, more effective commercial banking system and a vastly reshaped financial services industry. I believe that the proposed reforms would accelerate the economic consolidation and disaggregation of the industry.

Obviously, elimination of the McFadden and Bank Holding Company Acts, by themselves, would greatly help. However, over the intermediate term, one of the greatest barriers to economic consolidation is the portfolio of bad credits on the balance sheet of troubled banks, which serves as a "poison pill" to protect them from takeover. Another constraint is the lack of a sufficient number of well-capitalized banks to lead the consolidation process.

On the surface, the proposed recapitalization of economically solvent but undercapitalized banks would seem to slow

consolidation of the banking industry by propping up institutions that would otherwise have failed. I believe, though,
that this would not be true. Clearly, the assisted merger program discussed in Chapter 13 will help accelerate consolidation. However, I believe that the recapitalizing of institutions,
even if there is no immediate merger, would actually help
accelerate consolidation. First of all, splitting off the bad assets into a collecting bank would create a "clean" bank, one
that would be very attractive to a potential acquirer. Should
the recapitalized bank fail to recover sufficiently to redeem
the preferred stock invested by the FDIC and the outside investors, the clean bank would be sold to the highest bidder,
and this would most likely be the player best positioned to
consolidate the clean bank (that is, the player with the greatest economic benefits from consolidation). Secondly, the outside investors coming in with the FDIC would most likely be
investors with an interest in eventually gaining control of the
troubled institution. The convertible preferred stock being proposed provides a prospective acquirer with a low-cost stake
out. In fact, many troubled institutions would likely seek a
"white knight" potential acquirer as an investor. Again, the
outside investors most interested would likely be players who
had the greatest interest in the economic consolidation of core
banks.

Indeed, I believe if the reforms being proposed are passed,
we will see a frenzy of restructuring, recapitalizing, and economic mergers over the next five years not just among troubled
banks but throughout the industry. My guess is that the combination of the expanded number of interested parties, the profit
potential for winners, and the threat of a painful, involuntary
restructuring by the FDIC for losers who fail to find a partner
will produce a massive, rapid consolidation of the core banking
business. Indeed, I believe we will see the emergence of ten to
twenty very large core banks, each with $50 billion to $200 billion or more of assets, with earnings of over 1 percent of assets
or more. Most of these banks will be formed by consolidating
the largest 125 bank holding companies, which already account

for two-thirds of the banking industry's assets. I believe the cost of equity of these banks will be less than 14 percent and the returns in equity could well be 18 percent or higher. This level of profitability would come from two sources. First, the elimination of the costs of running separate banks, by eliminating the McFadden Act and enabling more scale-effective banks to be put together, should enable as much as 15 percent of the costs to be removed from the core banking industry; cost savings could run from $10 to $15 billion a year or more. Second, putting a ceiling on deposit pricing at the Treasury rate should reduce the costs of deposits of core banks by at least 0.5 percent by eliminating overbidding. As an aside, very well run super-regional banks, which are close to core banks today, are earning close to 18 percent on their equity without benefit of the reforms being proposed.

But, as described earlier, there will remain thousands of small independent "core" banks that will continue to prosper by serving their local communities very well. Most of these institutions have carved out for themselves secure niches in the marketplace; they have already been competing against much larger institutions for a long time. Indeed, the reason small banks will be able to prosper against bigger banks is that they will be safe, secure depositories that maintain public confidence because of the FDIC's insurance.

There will, however, be few small players in either the money market investment banking or finance company business. Players in these industries will need unquestioned strength to be able to raise money cost-effectively without a federal safety net behind them. I believe all successful players in these industries will be at least AA credits, and this in turn will cause them to be not only conservatively capitalized, but also big. Because of the need for size, I expect that most of the owners of these money market investment banks and finance companies would also either own big core banks or have another independent source of strength (such as a profitable, well-capitalized industrial company).

There will also likely be a large number of specialized players as well as those financial services businesses that require little capital. For example, good independent investment managers and small, well-run, independent service bureaus providing disaggregated computer and operating services will always be able to prosper.

In short, I believe the economic forces described in Part II will take over. Financial service businesses naturally requiring large amounts of capital will be undertaken by large firms. Niche businesses naturally requiring great skill, flexibility, and quick response will be undertaken by small firms. Economics, not regulation, will drive the industry's structure. Well-run financial services businesses will prosper, whereas poorly run financial services businesses would disappear—without cost to the government.

It is possible to contemplate the creation of a wide variety of different kinds of financial services companies in the next few years. In addition to the creation of massive multiregional core banks, it is possible to contemplate the combination of major banks with major insurance companies or major securities firms. In other words, you could see Aetna or Prudential in the banking business, or you could see combinations of banks with Merrill Lynch or Morgan Stanley. Moreover, you may see such companies as AT&T, General Electric, IBM, Ford, or General Motors owning major core banks.

Although this is a scary thought to many, I believe even the very largest of these would be only a small player in global terms. In other words, even a $200 billion bank holds less than a 1 percent share of the world's deposits. Indeed, as described in Chapter 9, we *need* institutions of such size and unquestioned strength to be competitive as a nation. The central thesis of this book is that we need such reforms to enable us to create the kinds of financial institutions we need as a nation to compete in the world's financial markets. We are a great nation, and we need world-class financial institutions.

Treasury Proposal

Of course, it would be naive to believe that the proposals being advocated by this book will be adopted in their entirety. In fact, the agenda for the debate over the future of the banking system was set by the release of the Treasury reform package in early February of 1991. This book represents only one of many proposals hoping to amend the Treasury reform package before it becomes law.

Many of the proposals advocated by this book are consistent with the program advocated by the Treasury. Indeed, the Treasury's proposals for the reform of the McFadden Act, the Glass-Steagall Act, and Bank Holding Company Acts, and the use of "firewalls" to segregate the insured bank from noninsured subsidiaries, are virtually identical to the reforms advocated in Chapter 12 of this book.

There are, however, some differences worth highlighting.

One important difference is that under the Treasury proposal, insured depositories would be regulated by two functional regulators: a newly created Federal Banking Agency that would regulate national banks and their holding companies, and the Federal Reserve, which would regulate state banks and their holding companies. As readers will remember from Chapter 12, I believe there should only be one functional regulator for all insured depositories. The approach being advocated by Treasury would have some benefits in that banks would wind up with one primary regulator versus the three or more most now have. However, the potential for destructive competition between regulators would remain. Different institutions would have different advantages and disadvantages depending upon who their regulator was. The only way to have a truly "level playing field" is to have a single regulator who applies regulation identically to all the institutions it regulates.

By far my greatest disagreement with the Treasury proposals, though, is over the Treasury's proposed reform of the deposit insurance system. More accurately, I believe the Treasury proposal does not go far enough in reforming the deposit insurance system. In essence, other than a proposal for a risk-based insurance system and some further modest limits on deposit insurance, the Treasury proposal for reform largely relies on more capital and more supervision to make banks safe. As you know from reading the first part of this book, I believe that this is an insufficient response to reforming the deposit and credit anomalies. In essence, this approach could lead to regulators' making loan-by-loan judgments on which loans should be made. Indeed, in troubled banks that are regulated by the OCC, these judgments are already being made by individual examiners. This puts individual institutions at either a competitive advantage, or disadvantage, depending upon the personality, skills, and judgment of the particular person assigned to supervise the institution by the regulatory agency. Frankly, I believe that such judgments should be left to the marketplace. As stated in the first chapter of this book, I believe that most of the problems with our existing system result from the government's influence on risk/reward judgments that should be made solely by the market. I believe this problem is particularly acute in determining and evaluating the risk in complex, wholesale loans such as large commercial real estate loans and highly leveraged transactions. Regulatory supervision works fine in portfolios of small, relatively simple loans to individuals, small businesses, and mid-sized companies, but it is inadequate for complicated and risky transactions. I fear that institutions would still have incentive to book risky loans in the insured bank (because of the subsidy created by the safety net) and that regulators would always be one step behind. I believe that moving to a core banking concept, as advocated in Chapter 11, is a far better approach to reforming the credit anomaly.

In addition, I believe that the Treasury proposal does not adequately address reforming the deposit anomaly. Although brokered deposits would be eliminated, individual institutions would still be able to bid whatever they wanted for deposits. For this reason, I fear that institutions with earnings pressures would still have incentive to overbid for deposits. I believe that since the Treasury proposals do not go far enough in eliminating the deposit and credit anomalies, strong institutions will have to continue paying more for deposits and will be earning less for extending credit than they should. In other words, I believe that the Treasury proposals do not go far enough in restoring the long-term health and profitability of the banking system.

Finally, the Treasury has been silent to date on the issues raised in Chapter 13 relating to the recapitalization of the FDIC and the recapitalization and restructuring of troubled banks. Perhaps by the time this book is published, the Treasury will have made specific proposals on these issues. Apparently the Administration is hoping that loosening monetary policy and urging banks to lend will ease the credit crunch and get the economy restarted. In other words, apparently the hope is that conditions are not as bad as my analysis in Chapter 7 would indicate them to be.

One feature of the Treasury proposal that is quite creative is the proposed regulation of capital. In essence, the Treasury creates incentives for institutions to be highly capitalized by allowing institutions with more capital to have more freedom. Institutions with high risks, relative to their capital, would be more tightly supervised. Only institutions with very strong capital positions would be allowed to take advantage of the freedoms provided by a financial holding company concept. This approach thus gives bank regulators very strong bargaining chips in dealing with insured depositories and their holding companies. Undercapitalized institutions would be so disadvantaged under this approach that they would have strong incentive to recapitalize either by finding capital directly or by merging with a stronger institution. Non-banks that wanted to own a bank would first have to recapitalize any insured bank being acquired up to target levels before being allowed to acquire the bank. My problem, of course, with this proposal is that it would be up to regulators, not the market, to determine adequate capital levels. Again, I have no problem with regulators' determining minimum capital standards, consistent with BIS guidelines, for relatively simple portfolios of loans to individuals, small businesses, and mid-sized companies. However, I have no hope that regulators can accurately evaluate how much capital is needed for large, complex portfolios of wholesale loans.

Despite these specific disagreements, I must congratulate the Treasury's overall effort. When I started this book in August 1990, I was highly skeptical over the prospects for a true reform proposal emerging from Treasury. The Treasury proposals are quite bold and courageous, given political realities and given that they had to be introduced at a time when the country, and its president, were properly focused on the war in the Persian Gulf.

I believe we should consider the Treasury proposals as the minimum acceptable reforms of the system. Indeed, I hope that as a nation we can muster the courage to go further.

Leadership and Statesmanship

In the coming months, we will need leadership and statesmanship. As this book goes to press, we are beginning to see leaders emerge as the gravity of the banking crisis has become evident. In the private sector, people such as Thomas "Lud" Ashley and John Rippey of the Association of Bank Holding Companies, Tony Cluff of the Association of Reserve City Bankers, and Don Ogilvie and Robert Dugger of the American Bankers Association are all playing active roles in Washington, trying to bring the various groups of bankers together in a common effort. In addition, many individual leaders of different financial institutions are playing significant roles.

Although private sector leadership is important, including the individual leadership of key bankers across the country, the greatest need for leadership and statesmanship is in the U.S. government. Fortunately, we are beginning to see such leadership emerge. Led by President Bush and U.S. Treasury Secretary Nicholas Brady, the Administration has put together a comprehensive plan, much of which is consistent with the principles and thinking contained in this book. Key participants in developing the Administration's plan include such people as Under Secretary for Domestic Finance Robert Glauber, Assistant Secretary Jerome Powell, and Deputy Assistant Secretary John Dugan, all from the Treasury Department, who did the actual drafting of the Administration's guiding principles and plan. Bill Seidman, Chairman of the FDIC; Bob Clarke, Comptroller of the Currency; Richard Breeden, Chairman of the Securities and Exchange Commission; Larry Lindsey, Special Assistant to the President; Richard Darman, Director of the Office of Management and Budget; Allan Greenspan, Chairman of the Federal Reserve; David Mullins, Vice Chairman of the Federal Reserve Board of Governors; and Bill Taylor, Director of Bank Supervision at the Federal Reserve, all played critical roles in the development of the Administration's plan.

By the time this book is on the shelves of bookstores, however, the need for leadership and statesmanship will have passed to the Congress as well. In the House of Representatives, we will need to see leadership from the Committee on Banking, Finance and Urban Affairs. In particular, Chairman Henry Gonzalez of Texas, Ranking Member Chalmers Wylie of Ohio, and others such as Frank Annunzio of Illinois, Jim Leach of Iowa, Charles Schumer of New York, John LaFalce of New York, Doug Barnard of Georgia, Tom Carper of Delaware, Tom Ridge of Pennsylvania, and Steve Neal of North Carolina will have pivotal roles. Moreover, John Dingell of Michigan, Chairman of the Energy and Commerce Committee, which oversees the securities industry, will be a key player. And, of course, Speaker of the House Tom Foley and his counterpart, Republican Leader Bob Michel, will play a critical part in the reform process.

In the U.S. Senate, the leadership roles will fall to key members of the Senate Banking Committee, including Chairman

Don Riegle of Michigan, Ranking Member Jake Garn of Utah, and Senators Chris Dodd of Connecticut, Alphonse D'Amato of New York, Alan Dixon of Illinois, Phil Gramm of Texas, and Terry Sanford of North Carolina. Other thoughtful senators (not on the committee) who understand the workings of our economy and our financial system, such as Bill Bradley of New Jersey, will have a critical part to play as well. Moreover, we will need leadership from such people as Senate Minority Leader George Mitchell of Maine and Minority Leader Bob Dole of Kansas as the legislative process unfolds this year.

Actually, as I finish this book, I am beginning to become modestly optimistic that the combination of the magnitude of the banking crisis, the increasing volume and quality of press coverage of the issues, and the leadership emerging from the private sector, the Administration, and Congress is going to be sufficient to finally get the nation to address the fundamental reforms that are needed. I hope so. We can either hang together, or we can hang separately.

Glossary

arbitrage profiting from differences in prices between two or more markets

bank an institution that (1) serves funds providers by giving a provider a claim on the institution's balance sheet and (2) serves funds users by extending credit from the institution's own funds

Bank Holding Company Act Amendment of 1970 the amendment to the Bank Holding Company Act of 1956 that restricted the ownership of one-bank holding companies by commercial concerns to activities permitted by the Federal Reserve

Bank Holding Company Act of 1956 the federal statute that regulates the ownership, product offerings, and geographic scope of bank holding companies in the United States

Bank Insurance Fund (BIF) the accounting designation for those funds within the FDIC that are used to insure depositors in commercial banks

bank panic the collapse of a bank or banks due to a loss of confidence of all depositors simultaneously in the safety of their money

basis point 0.01 percent (i.e., one hundredth of one percent)

"blind pool risk" the risk associated with assets, such as CRE and HLTs, on the books of banks that are impossible for outside investors to assess accurately

bridge bank a temporary bank chartered by the Comptroller of the Currency to assume all the assets and liabilities of a large failed bank until a new bank can be chartered through a merger or acquisition

brokered deposit a deposit that is sold to investors as if it were a security because of the investors' confidence in the government's safety net

capital permanent financing needed for the normal operation of a business; requirements for depository institutions are set by federal bank regulators

capital markets markets where debt and equity investments are traded

cartel the domination of a particular market or commodity by a few participants, who exhibit strong influences over prices

charge-off a loan that is uncollectible and must be written off against the loan loss reserves of a financial institution; if the reserves are inadequate to cover charge-offs, new reserves must be created by charging earnings or, if necessary, equity capital

289

collecting bank   a separate bank (or asset pool) designed to segregate nonperforming and other troubled banks from the performing part of a bank's loan portfolio; designed to allow for an orderly and segregated workout process of the impaired loans

commercial paper   short-term promissory notes issued by corporations as a means of borrowing in the securities markets rather than borrowing from commercial banks

competitive forces   changes in the ways financial institutions serve customers due to the pursuit of profits

Comptroller of the Currency   the primary federal regulator of national banks; a bureau of the U.S. Treasury Department, the Office of the Comptroller of the Currency (OCC) is under the direction of the Comptroller

consolidation   one of several forces at work in the banking industry, resulting in a fewer number of banks and, as a result, larger banks; economic consolidation occurs whenever the long-term profit of the resulting merged institution is greater than the profit of the institutions as separate entities

core bank   an institution that adds value to customer groups who are unable or unwilling to use the securities markets

CRE   commercial real estate

credit anomaly   the ability to make (risky) loans based on the ability to gather funds with a government guarantee (see deposit anomaly); characterized by prices, terms, or conditions out of line with the risks incurred

credit enhancement   a guarantee provided by a government agency or private company (for a fee and/or interest) of the cash flows that underlie the issuance of a new security based on an original credit

deposit   a claim on a bank (usually assumed by the funds provider to be risk-free)

deposit anomaly   the ability of depository institutions insured by the FDIC to use the protection of deposit insurance to gather limitless funds at whatever rate is necessary to attract the funds; enables depositors to obtain interest rates too high for the risks they are assuming

depository institution   a financial institution that accepts deposits; in the United States all are insured by the Federal Deposit Insurance Corporation, in the case of banks and thrifts, or by the

National Credit Union Share Insurance Fund, in the case of credit unions

destructive regulation   regulation of the financial marketplace that creates market anomalies

disaggregation   one of several forces at work today in the banking industry, wherein complex organizations such as banks are being converted into numerous, simpler businesses; a natural response to intense competition and overcapacity

discount-to-book value   when the accounting value of a company's common stock exceeds its market value, usually characterized by lower returns

disintermediation   the shift in the flow of funds from banks to the securities markets; typically thought of when depositors' funds flowed out of regulated accounts in the 1980s into higher-yielding securities such as money market mutual funds, thus encouraging securitization

double leverage   allowing bank holding companies to raise debt at the parent level and invest it in subsidiary funds as equity capital

economic forces   changes in the financial marketplace due to the interaction among funds suppliers, funds users, and competitive suppliers operating out of their natural self-interest

economic regulation   regulation of the financial marketplace that makes it more "perfect"

economic returns   the financial results that are due to each participant in a "perfect" market

equity   funds extended in return for a share of a company's long-term cash flows in exchange for sharing in the risks of failure (also applies to sharing in a project such as the construction of a building)

equity capital   permanent financing that is provided by investors (stockholders) in a company

exchange rate system   the system that exists to allow currencies to be traded by corporations and individuals across national borders

Federal Deposit Insurance Corporation (FDIC)   the government agency that insures deposit funds up to $100,000 and resolves failing commercial banks and thrift institutions

Federal Home Loan Bank Board (FHLBB)   the primary federal regulator of savings and loan associations from 1934 to 1989

Federal Reserve System   the central bank of the United States and the primary federal regulator of bank holding companies and state-chartered banks that have joined the Federal Reserve System

Federal Savings and Loan Insurance Corporation (FSLIC) the insurance fund that insured deposits in savings and loan associations from 1934 to 1989

finance company an institution that raises money in the securities markets without relying on safety nets and which extends credit to customers who lack direct access to the securities markets; also called an "uninsured bank" by some commentators

financial claim the cash returns due a participant in the financial marketplace as a result of a transaction

financial economy changes in the prices of financial claims and the flow of funds resulting from the operation of the financial marketplace

financial institutions suppliers that help in the intermediation between funds providers and funds users

Financial Institutions Reform, Recovery, and Enforcement Act of 1989 the federal statute that, among other things, restructured the savings and loan industry, required higher capital standards for S&Ls, created the Office of Thrift Supervision, and abolished the FSLIC

financial marketplace the interaction among funds suppliers, funds users, and financial institutions that results in the exchange of financial claims at given prices

firewalls barriers executed between an insured bank and any subsidiary or affiliate to ensure that risks in the subsidiary or affiliate will not be transferred to the insured bank

flow of funds the movement of funds from suppliers to users

functional regulation all participants in a given industry are consistently and identically regulated, regardless of the corporate ownership structure

Garn–St Germain Depository Institutions Act of 1982 the federal statute enacted to further restructure the thrift industry in response to its financial problems in the early 1980s, accelerate the removal of deposit rate ceilings through the creation of a Money Market Deposit Account, and deregulate S&L investments

Generally Accepted Accounting Principles (GAAP) the accounting conventions used in the preparation of a company's financial report to the public

Glass-Steagall Act   that portion of the Banking Act of 1933 that attempted to separate commercial banking from investment banking

globalization   the integration of national capital markets into worldwide capital markets

global money market bank   a commercial or investment bank that intermediates in the global capital markets

"good bank/bad bank"   a term referring to a structure wherein a bank's loan portfolio is effectively split in two, with performing loans retained in the "good bank" and all nonperforming and troubled loans segregated into a "bad," or collecting, bank

goodwill   an intangible asset that is created when the going concern value (because of the deposit franchise, business name, or brand recognition, for example) exceeds the value of a company's assets

"haircuts"   taking some proportional loss on an investment that has failed; sometimes applied to uninsured depositors in a failed depository institution

highly leveraged transactions (HLTs)   the funding of leveraged buyouts, recapitalizations and restructurings, mergers and acquisitions, by substituting massive debt for equity in the financial structure of a company

historical value accounting   accounting principle that requires all financial statements to be based on the original cost or acquisition cost

investment   a claim by a funds provider that provides a cash return in exchange for the time value of money and the risks taken

junk bonds   the popular name used for high-yield debt of non–investment grade corporations

LDC   less-developed country

leverage   the means of enhancing an investor's return or value without increasing the equity investment; in this context insured depository institutions (because of the government's safety net) can operate with more assets relative to capital than can other financial institutions

LIBOR   London inter-bank borrowing rate (used for inter-bank loans in the London market)

loan   credit extended in return for a claim on the borrower's cash flows or assets, which should ordinarily protect the lender from losses due to defaults

market anomaly   a flaw in the marketplace that provides a funds provider with too high cash returns for the risks taken, enables a funds user to raise money at too low a cost relative to the claims on cash flows given up, or provides a financial institution with uneconomic returns for serving as an intermediary

market forces   changes in the way funds suppliers and funds users behave due to the pursuit of their natural financial self-interest

marking-to-market   valuing assets of a financial institution at current, observable market prices, in contrast to what may be their ongoing economic value or their historic accounting value

McFadden Act   the 1927 federal statute that prohibits banks from establishing branches across state lines without the permission of the host state

moral hazard   the net result of the deposit and credit anomalies that encourage managers of depository institutions to take greater and greater risks with insured deposits as the institution approaches insolvency because they are betting the government's money rather than their own

natural financial self-interest   (1) the desire of funds providers to seek higher cash returns for the risks they are willing to take in a transaction; (2) the desire of funds users to seek lower cash costs for the risks they are asking funds providers to take in a transaction; (3) the desire of financial institutions to seek profits by serving funds providers and funds users

net interest margin   interest income minus interest expense, usually expressed as a percentage of average assets

noneconomic forces   changes in the financial marketplace for any reason other than funds' suppliers, funds' providers, or financial institutions seeking their natural self-interest

non-interest expense   operating expenses (such as salaries and rent) not associated with interest expense

Office of Thrift Supervision   since 1989, the primary federal regulator of savings and loan associations (successor to the FHLBB); a bureau of the U.S. Treasury Department

oligopoly   a market dominated by several strong participants who are able to effectively control prices

overcapacity   a situation where there are too many producers (e.g., banks) serving a given number of customers (e.g., depositors and borrowers)

payments system   that part of the financial system through which financial transactions for individuals and corporations are executed

"perfect" financial market   a financial marketplace in which funds flow from funds users to funds providers based on prices that are set entirely through the informed natural self-interest of all participants in the marketplace

playing the yield curve   a practice used by financial institutions of borrowing funds short-term, at usually lower rates, and in turn lending the funds longer-term, usually at higher rates

preferred stock   the class of common stock that pays dividends at a specified rate and has preference over common stock in the payment of dividends and the liquidation of assets; convertible preferred stock is exchangeable over a certain time period for a given number of shares of common stock

premium-to-book value   when the market value of a company's common stock exceeds its accounting value, usually characterized by high returns

primary market   the market for newly issued funds

prime rate   the base interest rate used by a bank for pricing many of its loans

"real" economy   the distribution of goods and services at prices based on the market interactions of customers and their suppliers

Real Estate Investment Trusts (REITs)   a fund (much like a mutual fund) used to pool money for investment in real estate assets; in the 1970s many REITs were active construction and development leaders

Reconstruction Finance Corporation (RFC)   the government agency created in the 1930s to recapitalize basic industries, including the banking industry, particularly through the issuance of preferred stock to the troubled company or bank

Regulation Q   the federal regulation that was used by the Federal Reserve to control interest rates paid to insured depositors from the mid 1960s to the early 1980s; part of this regulation (the differential) also allowed savings and loan associations to pay 0.25 percent more for deposits than commercial banks because of the S&Ls' housing mission

return on equity (ROE)   the profits earned on a company's common stock investment in a single year, usually expressed as a percentage

safety net   regulation designed to protect the financial marketplace from sudden losses that are so severe that they can destroy the ability of the financial marketplace to operate

secondary market   the market for trading funds after they have been issued

Securities and Exchange Commission (SEC)   the federal agency established in 1933 to ensure the prompt and accurate financial reporting of all companies publicly listed on the stock exchange

securities firm   an institution that serves funds providers and funds users by selling and exchanging financial claims through the securities marketplace

securities markets   the marketplace for the exchange of tradable financial claims

securitization   the process of transforming loans into securities, thus encouraging disintermediation

security   a tradable financial claim

super-regionals   regional bank holding companies that have spread throughout a region by acquisition and *de novo* growth, usually with over $20 billion in assets

time value of money   the risk-free return on an investment (usually thought to be the return from long-term claims on the government, such as the 30-year Treasury bond rate)

"too big to fail"   the ad hoc informal government practice that will not allow the failure of a large bank; results in subsequent payoff of all depositors (insured or not) because of the fear of a systemic failure of the financial system

uneconomic regulation   regulation of the financial marketplace that makes it less "perfect," for example, regulation of the financial marketplace to restrict competition between competent participants

uneconomic returns   financial results that are higher or lower than would result in a "perfect" financial market due either to suppression of competition or to a market anomaly

References

American Bankers Association. *International Banking Competitiveness: Why It Matters.* Washington, DC: American Bankers Association, 1990.

Bryan, Lowell L. *Breaking Up The Bank: Rethinking an Industry Under Siege.* Homewood, IL: Dow Jones-Irwin, 1988.

Chernow, Ron. *House of Morgan: An American Banking Dynasty and The Rise of the Modern Financial World.* Boston: Atlantic Monthly, 1990.

Committee on Banking, Finance, and Urban Affairs, U.S. House of Representatives. Report on the Banking Industry in Turmoil: A Report on the Condition of the U.S. Banking Industry and the Bank Insurance Fund. Washington, DC, December 1990, 101st Congress, 2nd Session.

Committee on Banking, Housing, and Urban Affairs, U.S. Senate. Hearings on Changes in Our Financial System: Globalization of Capital Markets and Securitization of Capital Markets and Securitization of Credit. Washington, DC, October 1987, 100th Congress, 1st Session.

Committee on Banking, Housing, and Urban Affairs, U.S. Senate. Hearings on Deposit Insurance Reform and Financial Modernization. Washington, DC, April 1990, Volumes I–II, 101st Congress, 2nd Session.

Corrigan, E. Gerald. *Financial Market Structure: A Longer View.* Federal Reserve Bank of New York, 1987.

FDIC. *Annual Report, 1989.* Washington, DC, 29 October 1990.

FDIC. *The Federal Deposit Insurance Corporation: The First 50 Years.* Washington, DC, 1984.

FDIC. *Mandate for Change: Restructuring the Banking Industry.* Washington, DC, 1987.

Fischer, Gerald C. *The Modern Bank Holding Company: Development, Regulation, and Performance.* Philadelphia: Temple University Press, 1986.

Golembe, Carter, and Holland, David S. *Federal Regulation of Banking, 1983–1984.* Washington DC: Golembe Associates, Inc., 1983.

Green, Edwin. *Banking: An Illustrated History.* New York: Rizzoli International Publications, 1989.

Jones, Jesse H. *Fifty Billion Dollars: My Thirteen Years with the RFC (1932–1945).* Macmillan, 1951.

Kindleberger, Charles P. *Manias, Panics, and Crashes.* New York: Basic Books, 1978.

T.A. Myers & Co. *Real Estate Problem Loans: Workout Strategies and Procedures.* Homewood, IL: Dow Jones-Irwin, 1990.

Smith, Adam. *Wealth of Nations.* New York: Random House, 1977 edition (originally published 1776).

Trescott, Paul B. *Financing American Enterprises: The Story of Commercial Banking.* New York: Harper and Row, 1963.

U.S. Treasury Department. *Modernizing the Financial System: Recommendations for Safer, More Competitive Banks.* Washington, DC: GPO, 1991.

Upham, Cyril B., and Lamke, Edwin. *Closed and Distressed Banks: A Study in Public Administration.* Washington, DC: The Brookings Institution, 1934.

Name Index

301

Subject Index

303

About the Author

LOWELL L. BRYAN is a director of McKinsey & Co., an international management consulting firm. Since joining McKinsey in 1975, Mr. Bryan has advised the top management of banks and financial institutions in the United States, Europe, and Japan; he now leads the firm's North American Banking & Securities practice. He is among the premier authorities on banking in the country, and has been an outspoken critic of our financial system since the early 1980s. Mr. Bryan is the author of two previous books: *Unbundling Full-Service Banking* and *Breaking Up the Bank: Rethinking an Industry Under Seige.*

Prior to joining McKinsey, Mr. Bryan worked for the State Street Bank & Trust Co. in Boston. Born and raised in Oklahoma, he also served in the army in Vietnam. He majored in history at Davidson College and graduated from the Harvard Business School with distinction in 1970. He lives in New Canaan, Connecticut, with his wife, Debbie, and his three children, Russell, Amanda, and Than.